Contents

Chapter 1	Introduction	5
Chapter 2	Fuel Injection and Carburetors	10
Chapter 3	Options and Costs	27
Chapter 4	Computers and PROMs	33
Chapter 5	Sensors	44
Chapter 6	Actuators	50
Chapter 7	Hot Rodding Your Fuel Injection	61
Chapter 8	GM Tuned Port Injection	78
Chapter 9	Installation Do's, Don'ts, and Maybes	87
Chapter 10	Setup and Tuning	102
Chapter 11	Troubleshooting	111
Chapter 12	Project Car–1970 Dodge Challenger 383	119
Chapter 13	Project Car–L-Jetronic XKE Jaguar with Rajay Turbo	128
Chapter 14	Project Vehicle–Cadillac 500ci-Powered GMC Motorhome	133
Chapter 15	Injecting the Chevrolet Small-Block V-8	137
Chapter 16	Project Car–Turbo Lotus Europa with DFI Injection and Nitrous Power	140
Chapter 17	Project Car–Triple-Turbo Jag XKE with Staged Injection and Nitrous Power	148 / 154
Chapter 18	Project Vehicle—The 460 Eddie Bauer Bronco	158
	Appendices	160
	Index	

Chapter 1

Introduction

Why would someone consider fuel injecting their hot rod–whether a private enthusiast with a classic '55 Chevy two-door, or a General Motors engineering team working to introduce a new 280 horsepower (hp) twin-turbo V-6 truck?

Emotional and marketing justifications aside, there are solid technical reasons why the automotive companies stampeded toward fuel injection in the 1980s, and why automotive enthusiasts and hot rodders have been willing to pay good money in the last few years to at least half a dozen aftermarket suppliers of add-on electronic fuel injection in order to "fix something that ain't broke."

Car Companies and Fuel Injection

In the case of the car companies, electronic fuel injection (EFI) is a tool that allowed engineers to fight the horsepower wars of the 1980s while complying with federal legislation which mandated increasingly stiff standards for fuel economy and exhaust emissions. The ability to intelligently control engine air-fuel mixtures within extremely tight tolerances has become a potent tool enabling car companies to carve out a precarious existence between the Environmental Protection Agency (EPA), the gas-guzzler tax, and the performance-conscious consumers who still fondly remember the acceleration of a 1970 vintage muscle car (or have at least *heard* the legends).

Back in the 1950s, engine designers had concentrated on one thing—getting the maximum power from an engine within certain cost constraints. This was the era of the first 1hp per cubic inch motors. By the early sixties, air pollution in southern California was getting out of control, and engine designers had new worries. They were worried about making *clean* power, mainly because the Clean Air Acts of 1966 and 1971 forced them to worry, setting increasingly strict state and federal standards for exhaust and evaporative emissions. Engine designers gave it their best shot, which mainly involved add-on emissions control devices like exhaust gas recirculation (EGR) valves, air pumps, inlet air heaters, vacuum retard distributor canisters–and modifications to the carburetor.

The resulting cars of the 1970s ran cleaner, but horsepower was way down and driveability sometimes suffered—as did fuel economy—just in time for the oil crises of late 1973 and 1979. Government response to the energy crises was to pass laws mandating better fuel economy. By the late 1970s the car companies were caught between a rock and a hard place, desperately seeking some

The Tull Systems' twin turbo EFI Chevrolet small-block engine uses cross-ram induction and Haltech programmable fuel management control. Tull calls EFI turbo systems the "Last, Best Speed Secret."

new magic that would solve their problems.

The first electronic fuel injection had been invented in the 1950s by Bendix Corporation, in America. The Bendix Electrojector system is the basis of nearly all modern electronic fuel injection systems. The system used modern solenoid-type electronic injectors with an electronic control unit (ECU) based on vacuum-tube technology (which was kind of like inventing the jet engine, and strapping it on a 1915 vintage Sopwith Camel biplane). The Electrojector system took forty seconds to warm up before you could start the engine. Sometimes it wigged out when you drove under high-tension power lines. In addition to the problems of vacuum-tube technology, Bendix didn't have access to modern engine sensors. Solid-state circuitry was in its infancy, and although automotive engineers recognized the potential of electronic fuel injection to do amazing things based on its extreme precision of fuel delivery, the electronics technology to make EFI practical just didn't exist yet. Bendix eventually gave up on the Electrojector, secured worldwide patents, licensed the technology to the Robert Bosch Corporation, and went back to less esoteric pursuits.

Mechanical fuel injection had been around in various forms since before 1900. Mechanical injection had always been a toy used on race cars, effete foreign cars like the Mercedes, and a handful of very high performance cars in America—like the Corvette. Mechanical fuel injection avoided certain performance disadvantages of the carburetor, but was expensive and finicky, and not particularly accurate.

In the meantime, America entered the transistor age of the 1960s. Suddenly, electronic devices came alive instantly with no warmup. Solid-state circuitry was fast and consumed minuscule amounts of power compared to the tube. By the end of the decade, engineers had invented the microprocessor, which combined dozens, hundreds, then thousands of transistors on a piece of silicon smaller than your fingernail (each transistor was similar in functionality to a vacuum tube bigger than your entire finger).

Volkswagen introduced the first Bosch electronic fuel injection systems in 1968. There was a trickle of other cars using electronic fuel injection by the mid-seventies. By the eighties, that trickle had become a torrent.

In the early eighties, the turbocharger also stood out as a powerful tool in the hands of automotive engineers as they pursued high performance, good fuel economy, and low emissions. Turbochargers, which made small engines feel like big engines, could teach the driver in the next lane with a V-8 a good lesson about humility, both at the gas pump and at the stoplight drags. Unfortunately, the carburetor met its Waterloo in a major way when it came up against the turbo; having been tweaked and modified for nearly a century and a half to reach its current state of "perfection," the carb was implicated in a series of stunning failures when teamed up with the turbocharger. The fact that there is not currently a single forced-induction vehicle being manufactured with a factory carb is no coincidence. The

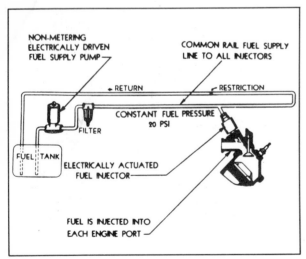

The Bendix Electrojector system was the first electronic fuel injection invented in America. Ahead of its time, it was not practical for production use until the transistor came along. The system used timed fuel injection directly into the intake ports via solenoid-type electronic injectors attached to a 20psi fuel rail, controlled by a vacu-

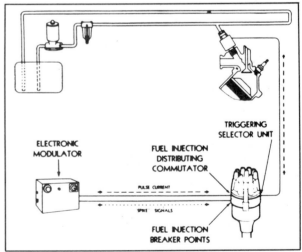

um-tube electronic control module. A triggering selector unit on the distributor sent timing pulses to the injectors with timing duration controlled by the control module. Electromechanical sensors produced cold-starting enrichment, idle enrichment, and mixture compensation for altitude. Jan P. Norbye

ones that *were* manufactured—the early Mustang 2.3liter turbo, the early Buick 3.8 turbo, the early Maserati BiTurbo, the Turbo Trans Am, and others dating all the way back to the early 1960s *Corvair* turbo—are infamous. If one wanted a turbocharged "hot rod" to run efficiently and cleanly—and more important, to behave and stay alive—the car companies discovered the hard way that fuel injection is the One True Path.

Therefore, in the case of the car companies, the cost disadvantages of fuel injection have been more than outweighed by avoiding the potential penalties resulting from noncompliance with emissions and corporate average fuel economy (CAFE) standards. They also avoid losing sales to competitors by offering superior or at least competitive horsepower and driveability.

Hot Rodders and Fuel Injection

This brings us to the motivations of the enthusiast who may be contemplating fuel injecting his or her hot rod.

Back in the 1950s, the hot rodder or racer's choices for fuel systems were carburetion or mechanical fuel injection. Carbs were cheap out of the box, but getting air and fuel distribution and jetting exactly right took a wizard—a wizard with a *lot* of time. By the time you developed a

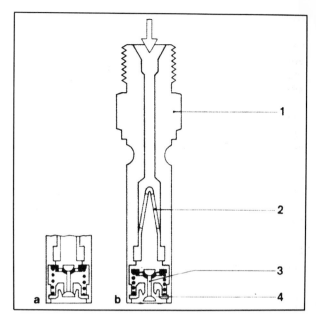

K-Jetronic injectors contain a spring-loaded valve which is continuously forced open by fuel pressure when the engine is running (to a threshold of 50psi). It varies fuel delivery by pressure variations rather than opening and closing like electronic injectors. In illustration "a," the injector nozzle is closed. It is open in "b," with these parts labeled: 1. holder, 2. filter, 3. needle, and 4. valve seat. Jan P. Norbye

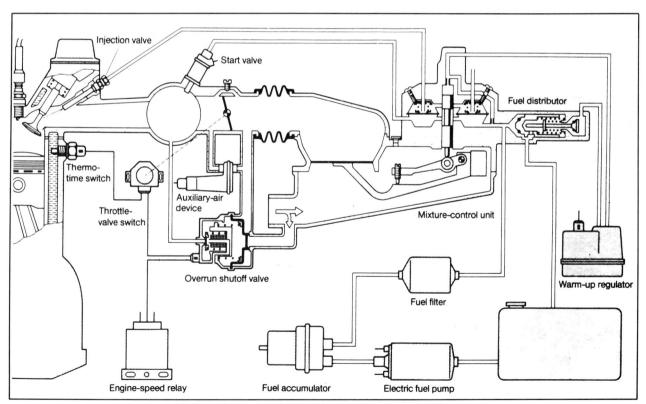

Volkswagen mass-produced the K-Jetronic constant flow mechanical fuel injection system for the seventies *Rabbit, Scirocco, and Dasher. Eventually it received computer control in the KE-Jetronic. Jan P. Norbye*

great set of carbs and manifold, it might cost more than mechanical injection, which achieved equal air and fuel distribution with identical individual stack-type runners to every cylinder and identical fuel nozzles in every runner. Assuming the nozzles matched, fuel distribution *had* to be good.

Mechanical fuel injection had been around in various forms going back to the turn of the century. It *could* squirt a lot of fuel into an engine without restricting airflow, and it was not affected by lateral G-forces and the up-and-down pounding of, say, a high-performance boat in really rough water (which causes fuel to bounce around in the carburetor's float chamber). Racers used Hilborn mechanical injection on virtually every postwar Indy race car until 1970. The trouble is, mechanical injection relies on crude mechanical means for mixture correction at various engine speeds, loads, and temperatures. This type of system was not accurate enough to provide the precise mixtures required for a *really* high output engine that was also usable on the street. Chevrolet tried constant-flow mechanical injection in the 1950s and early 1960s, but it was expensive and finicky. (Bosch later refined a good constant mechanical injection called K-Jetronic, but it quickly evolved into a hybrid system using electronic controls.)

By the late 1970s carburetors had been engineered to a high state of refinement, but there were inescapable problems intrinsic to the concept. In addition to distribution and accuracy problems, carbs require restrictive venturis which force tradeoffs between top-end and low-speed performance. Their inability to automatically correct for changes in altitude and ambient temperature was not a problem if the goal was simply decent power at sea level. But distribution and accuracy problems were deadly if you cared about emissions or economy, or if you wanted to turbocharge.

Throughout the 1970s, hot rodders and tuners applied turbochargers to engines to achieve large gains in horsepower. Mainly, of course, rodders had to work with carburetors for fueling, and unfortunately, they discovered most carbs were problematic when applied to forced induction. It was possible to make a lot of power, but there always seemed to be a sacrifice of driveability. Carbs were a problem, but what could be done?

In the meantime, the auto makers began switching over to EFI, which gave tuners who wanted to modify late-model cars a whole new set of headaches.

The problem was, users had no easy means by which to reprogram the proprietary software data that controlled the EFI systems that came in new cars; it was locked away internally in a Programmable Read-Only Memory (PROM) chip. In many of these electronic control units (ECU), changing this data literally required installing a new ECU. Even where the data was located on a removable PROM chip, the equipment and expertise needed to "blow" new PROMs was not accessible to most hot rodders. You might have been able to buy a new PROM, but it was still not practical to tune your fuel injection. And if you made further modifications to the engine, the new PROM would likely be out of tune. It was not until the late 1980s and early 1990s, as user programmable ECUs became available, that many hot rodders and racers began to take a hard look at the advantages of EFI.

It's been said you can't be too rich or too thin. Hot rodders might paraphrase that statement this way: You can't have too much horsepower. Modern rodders would probably admit that clean air is nice and low fuel consumption is good. These days, hot rodders also expect good driveability. Throw in a few concerns about dollar signs, and that about sums up the hot rodder's goals.

Knowledgeable racers and hot rodders have discovered that modern programmable EFI systems produce higher horsepower and torque than a carburetor (staggering gains in power are sometimes possible on nearly identical engines, especially where the engine is supercharged or turbocharged), combined with good driveability, cleaner exhaust, and lower fuel consumption.

Here's the injection-equipped engine of a snowmobile drag racer. Kinsler mechanical injection enables snowmobile engines to make tremendous power with virtually no VE loss to inlet restrictions. Kinsler

There are solid technical reasons behind the superiority of fuel injection.

Advantages of EFI

Electronic fuel injection provides the rodder with several advantages. One is the greater flexibility of "dry" intake manifold designs to achieve higher inlet airflow rates and consistent cylinder-to-cylinder distribution of the air-fuel mixture. Higher and more efficient engine compression ratios are also possible with electronic injection. A third benefit is that the extremely accurate fuel delivery (at any rpm and load) lets every cylinder receive air-fuel mixtures that fall within the tiny window of accuracy required to produce superior horsepower. This has been called the "last, best speed secret."

Computer-controlled air-fuel mixture accuracy enables all-out engines to operate safely much closer to the "hairy edge." In addition, personal computer (PC) programmable EFI can easily be adapted to future engine modifications as a vehicle evolves (perhaps in competition) much more easily than original equipment (OE) PROM changes. When adjustments and changes are required to match new performance upgrades made to your engine, it's as simple as hitting a few keys on a PC.

Of course, as the car makers discovered, if you're simultaneously converting to forced induction, in the long run there's not a whole lot of choice. Electronic fuel injection is fully compatible with forced induction, resisting detonation with programmable enrichment, and often providing huge power increases by providing the correct air-fuel mixture at every cylinder.

An additional advantage of EFI is that it is not susceptible to failure or performance degradation due to sudden and shifting gravitational and acceleration forces; these forces can upset the usual behavior of fuel in a carburetor. Also, injection automatically corrects for changes in altitude and ambient temperature.

And finally, solid-state electronics are not susceptible to the mechanical failures possible with carburetors. Tuning parameters stay as you set them, with no need for readjustment to compensate for wearing parts or passages.

Disadvantages of EFI

Unlike car companies, enthusiasts face no government regulations pressuring them to fuel inject a hot rod. Ironically, given the potential superiority of fuel injection to achieve clean exhaust, there are government regulations that discourage or even prohibit fuel injection systems under certain circumstances (more on this later).

Let's summarize a hot rodder's possible objections to going the fuel injection route.

The Circus Circus offshore race boat uses Haltech-injected Chevrolet big-block-style engines for record-setting performance. EFI has a tremendous advantage in choppy water since there are no float chambers as in a carbureted engine. Haltech

Quite simply, in addition to legal issues, some hot rodders may have negative views about EFI. First, because it's "high tech," it may appear complex, finicky, difficult, incomprehensible, mysterious, impossible to install and debug. And it uses computers. People assume it's difficult or impossible to modify, too expensive, and that racing rules sometimes prohibit its use.

And last of all, regarding the carburetor, "It ain't broke, so why fix it?" Which brings us to the objective of this book.

Purpose of This Book

This book is designed to remove the mystery about fuel injecting a vehicle, and give you the information you'll need to do the job—from theory to practical installation details. It is designed to supply enough information about fuel injection control unit innards to remove the mystery about them, and enable you to feel confident about tuning aftermarket fuel injection systems by computer.

Fuel injection *can* be modified, and this book tells you how.

The book also provides information on what it costs to fuel inject a hot rod using various technologies, including original equipment manufacturer (OEM) injection systems such as General Motors' tuned port injection (TPI).

This book will also help you decide whether your hot rodding plans violate government regulations.

Overall, the book is designed to provide enough information about the pluses and minuses of injection and carburetors, so that you'll be able to determine whether the existing carburetor on your hot rod is "broken" after all, and in need of an electronic fuel injection system.

Chapter 2

Fuel Injection and Carburetors

Anyone who's ever stared at the guts of a real carburetor knows nothing is ever as simple as it might appear to be, right?

Actually, if an engine always worked at one speed, the job of a carburetor would be relatively simple, and a simple venturi-based model would do the trick. But in order to handle cold starting, transient enrichment, idling, correction for differential flow characteristics of air and fuel, full-throttle enrichment, and emissions concerns, real carburetors contain myriad add-on systems. These include choke valves, fast-idle cams, accelerator pumps, two-stage power valves, air corrector jets, emulsion tubes, idle jets, booster ven-

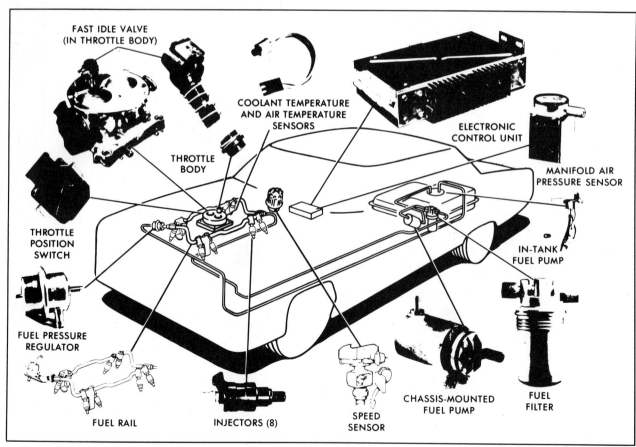

FAST IDLE VALVE
(IN THROTTLE BODY)

COOLANT TEMPERATURE
AND AIR TEMPERATURE
SENSORS

ELECTRONIC
CONTROL UNIT

THROTTLE
BODY

MANIFOLD AIR
PRESSURE SENSOR

THROTTLE
POSITION
SWITCH

IN-TANK
FUEL PUMP

FUEL PRESSURE
REGULATOR

FUEL RAIL   INJECTORS (8)   SPEED
SENSOR

CHASSIS-MOUNTED
FUEL PUMP

FUEL
FILTER

Cadillac Speed-Density injection system, vintage 1975 and later. Cadillac has used speed-density injection on virtually all engines since 1975. Cadillac

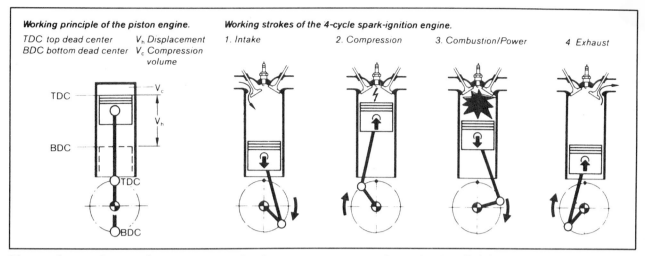

Working principle of the piston engine.

TDC top dead center V_h Displacement
BDC bottom dead center V_c Compression volume

TDC
BDC
TDC
BDC

Working strokes of the 4-cycle spark-ignition engine.

1. Intake   2. Compression   3. Combustion/Power   4 Exhaust

Most modern engines produce one power pulse for every two revolutions of the crankshaft. Because there are four up-and-down events or strokes necessary to produce *power, the engine is called four stroke or four cycle.* Jan P. Norbye

turis, and air bleed screws, not to mention fast solenoids that pulse open and closed under computer control to variably restrict fuel flow through the main jet of an electronic feedback carb.

And this list doesn't even include add-on emissions control devices like charcoal evaporation canisters, and so on.

Perhaps you suspect the same is true of fuel injection?

Read on.

What Is Fuel Injection?

The first thing to keep in mind about fuel injection is that it is not one thing; rather, it is a class of systems designed to get fuel into an engine by blowing fuel into inlet air under pressure. Experts frequently begin their explanations of fuel injection by starting with the carburetor, and moving from this (presumably) known ground to the uncharted territory of fuel injection. This book does the opposite. It starts with the simple facts—and that doesn't mean the carburetor.

Carburetion is an ancient technology, refined by more than 150 years of engineering and tinkering. Carburetion is an esoteric, delicate system of countless moving parts and fluids, overlapping air-fuel metering systems, and complex interactions between all of the aforementioned, in which a given problem usually has a long list of possible causes that may include everything from the weather to a speck of dirt in a tiny passage to a wrongly sized part or a design flaw.

To truly *master* carburetion requires a thorough knowledge of fluid mechanics, engine design, and air-fuel theory, along with a great deal of experience. Fortunately (or unfortunate-

CARBURETOR TROUBLESHOOTING / POSSIBLE CAUSE	PROBLEM	Stalling	Rough Idle	Flooding	Hot Start	Economy	Hesitation	Acceleration	Surge	Back Fire (cold)	Power	Stalling (cold)
Idle Adjustment		X	X		X	X	X		X	X		X
Idle Needles (Damaged)		X	X									X
Idle Vent Adjustment		X	X		X							X
Fast Idle Adjustment		X										X
Idle Passages (Dirty, Plugged)		X	X				X		X	X		X
Auto. Choke Adjustment										X		X
Choke Diaphragm Adjustment										X		X
Choke Rod Adjustment										X		X
Choke Unloader Adjustment										X		
Metering Jets (Loose, Plugged)					X	X	X	X	X	X		
Power Valve (Loose, Sticking					X		X		X	X		
Fuel Inlet Needle & Seat (Loose, Leaking)		X	X	X	X	X	X			X		
Float (Leaking, Rubbing, Wrong Setting)		X	X	X	X	X	X		X	X		
Gaskets (Brittle, Improper Seal)		X	X		X	X		X				
Pump Discharge Holes (Dirty, Plugged)					X	X		X				
Pump Diaphragm (Worn, Cut)					X	X		X				
Pump Ball Checks (Dirty, Sticking)					X	X		X				
Choke Diaphragm Adjustment (Vacuum Leak)									X			X
Choke Valve & Linkage (Dirty, Sticking, Damaged)									X			X
Secondary Carb. Linkage Adj.						X	X		X	X		
Secondary Lockout Adjustment						X			X			X
Throttle Valves (Loose, Damaged, Sticking)		X	X			X		X				X
Venturi Cluster (Dirty, Loose)		X			X	X	X	X	X	X	X	X

Chart specifies carburetor problems only. It's assumed engine is in good mechanical condition and in tune. Many ignition and carburetor problems have same symptoms. Don't assume fault is with carburetor.

Carburetor troubleshooting is complex. Notice that the Holley chart on carb troubleshooting documents many possible causes for each symptom, due to the physical complexity of the carb. Holley

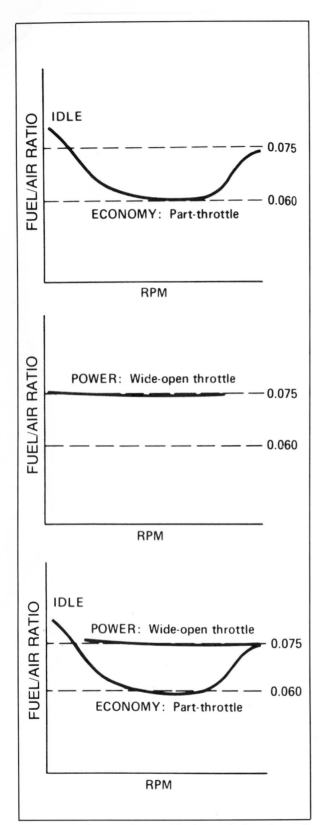

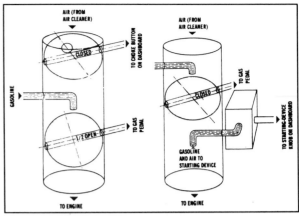

When an engine is cold, only the heavier fractions of fuel tend to remain in droplets rather than atomizing into a gas vapor, meaning massive fuel enrichment is necessary to get the engine running. Both carburetion systems and fuel injection require cold starting enrichment. The diagram shows two types of cold starting devices used by carb systems—the choke, which blocks off air, and a choke with starting device to add extra fuel downstream of the throttle. Injection systems simply inject more fuel by longer energization of the injector, or may also use an extra injector when the engine is very cold. Jan P. Norbye

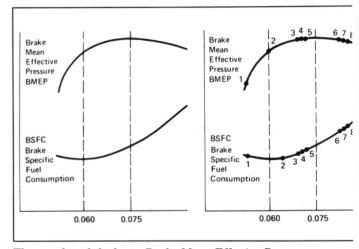

The graph at left charts Brake Mean Effective Pressure (BMEP) of an engine operating with perfect distribution showing relationship of fuel-air ratio. For maximum power, a fuel-air ratio of 0.075-0.080 produces the lowest fuel consumption. For best economy, a fuel-air ratio of 0.060 is optimal, although producing less horsepower. The graph at right charts the fact that most carburetion systems produce poor fuel distribution. Cylinders 6, 7, and 8 are too rich, producing less power and wasting fuel. Cylinders 3, 4, and 5 produce best power and consume the least fuel for that output. Cylinders 1 and 2 are lean. To prevent detonation in 1 and 2, all would have to be enriched to bring 1 and 2 to the flat part of the curve, meaning only 1 and 2 would produce peak power with minimum fuel consumption for that output. Holley

Ideal air-fuel ratios vary with the engine's volumetric efficiency and the necessity in modern automotive engines to produce maximum power at full throttle, maximum economy at part throttle and idle, and low emissions and good driveability at all ranges. Holley

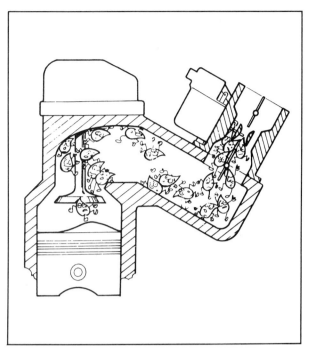

Carburetor systems—which depend on manifold vacuum to suck in fuel droplets to mix with incoming air—run a big risk of wetting the manifold walls with fuel droplets, which upsets the balance of the mixture. Jan P. Norbye

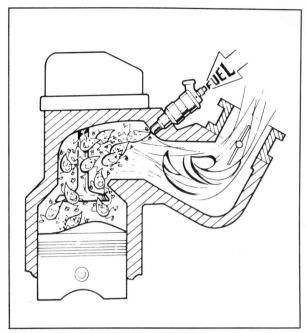

Port Fuel Injection systems squirt fuel droplets into swirling air near the intake valve, leaving little possibility of wetting the manifold walls. All fuel enters the combustion chamber without delay, allowing very precise control of the air-fuel ratio in all cylinders. Jan P. Norbye

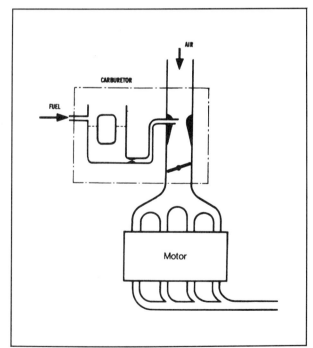

Carburetors: Most street engines use one carburetor which utilizes the pressure drop through a venturi to suck fuel from a float chamber into the incoming air stream. A jet (restrictor) in the fuel supply tube meters fuel, but neither fuel or air is actually measured. Jan P. Norbye

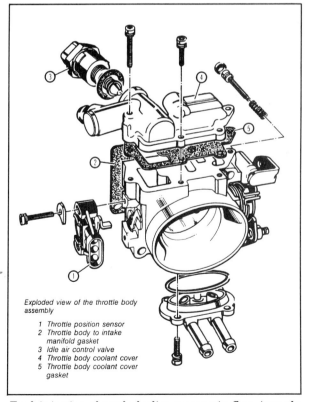

Fuel injection throttle bodies meter air flow into the engine.

ly), it's easy to get carbs running badly. But have you ever wondered how much better your engine might run if the carb were running *really* right?

In contrast, a modern electronic fuel injection system is marvelously simple and easy to understand because, in the end, it does only one basic thing: it turns on and off the fuel injectors. Need more fuel this engine cycle? Open the injectors a little longer. Less fuel? Open the injectors a shorter time. Pure and simple. Virtually everything else going on in electronic fuel injection has to do with reading the condition of the engine at a

---

Four Cycles of an Engine

In the first cycle of a four-stroke engine, *intake,* the piston is moving down, drawing in air and fuel through the open intake valve. Somewhere near the bottom of the stroke, the intake valve closes. The intake valve actually closes after the piston has passed bottom dead center (BDC), which allows incoming air-fuel mixture to continue filling the cylinder due to the inertia of the mixture at high inlet velocities.

Particularly in engines designed to operate at high speeds, the valve stays open a long time (called *duration*) in order to make more power as explained. However, at low speeds, this late closing can allow some of the intake mixture to be *pumped back into* the intake manifold, particularly at small throttle openings where high vacuum exists in the intake manifold. This pump-back phenomenon means that engines with "longer" cams have higher manifold pressure (lower vacuum) at lower rpm ranges, although airflow through the engine is no greater.

It is important to understand that a computer sensing engine speed and manifold pressure has no way of distinguishing between a shorter cammed engine at a heavier load and a longer cammed engine at a lighter load. Yet, very different fueling is required for best power and economy in these two situations.

In the second cycle, *compression,* the piston moves upward, compressing the mixture. The spark plug fires as the piston moves upward near the top of the stroke, timed in such a way that the maximum cylinder pressure produced by combustion peaks at about 15 degrees after top dead center (ATDC)—in order to produce the best torque. It is necessary to fire the plug while the piston is moving up because the flame that starts when the plug fires initially exists as a tiny kernel that is expanding relatively slowly. (This lead time is called spark advance.)

Combustion is a chain reaction of sorts; once a very small percentage of the compressed mixture is burning, the rest of the combustion process proceeds quickly. Depending on various considerations, spark advance can be anywhere from 5 to more than 50 degrees of crankshaft rotation before top dead center (BTDC). Normally, engine designers strive to correlate spark advance so that for all combinations of speed and loading, the engine produces minimum best torque (MBT). If the engine begins to knock before MBT is achieved, it is considered knock limited.

In the third cycle, *power,* the piston is pushed down by pressure produced in the cylinder by combustion, typically over 600 pounds per square inch (psi).

In the final stroke, *exhaust,* the exhaust valve opens near bottom dead center, and as the piston rises, exhaust gases are pushed out past the open exhaust valve. On high-speed engines, there is usually a certain amount of valve overlap—the exhaust valve stays open after top dead center, the intake opens before top center. This produces greater volumetric efficiencies at high rpm. At low rpm, particularly with high manifold vacuum (low pressure), there is reverse flow—mainly exhaust gases flowing back from the higher pressure exhaust into the low pressure intake.

At lower rpm, a cam with more duration and overlap results in higher manifold pressures, but lower air flow through the engine.

Cams have a great effect on ideal spark advance and fuel mixture requirements. Other factors are compression ratio, fuel octane rating, and engine operating conditions (speed, temperature, and loading). Spark advance requirements tend to increase with speed—up to a point. Advance requirements decrease with loading, since dense mixtures produced by the high volumetric efficiencies of wide-open throttle (WOT) tend to burn more quickly. With a big cam, the advance at full throttle can be aggressive and quick; low volumetric efficiency (VE) at low rpm results in slow combustion, and exhaust dilution lowers combustion temperatures and the tendency to knock.

Part-throttle advance on big-cam engines can also be aggressive due to these same flame speed reductions resulting from exhaust dilution of the inlet charge due to valve overlap.

Before computer-controlled spark advance, mechanical rotating weights advanced spark with engine speed by exerting centrifugal force against a cam-actuated advance controlled by the force of mechanical springs. Engine loading and increased manifold pressure decreased vacuum against a spring-loaded diaphragm and retarded timing. Limitations of mechanical complexity meant that the spark advance curve might be less than optimum at some areas in order to prevent knock at other points. If the engine had a big cam, low-idle manifold pressure meant there was no good way to achieve required advance at low speeds without overadvancing at mid- and high-rpm ranges.

The chemically idle air-fuel mixture, by weight, in which all air and gasoline are consumed, occurs with 14.6 parts air and 1 part fuel. This is called stoi-

given moment, and then doing a little math to compute injection pulse width—*before* firing those injectors.

So, let's start by looking at the easy stuff, an actual modern electronic fuel injection system.

Designing an Injection System

Unlike the carburetor, air and fuel metering in EFI are separate functions. As a designer you can generate any air-fuel relationship you want, based on the status of the engine—or anything

chiometric. Mixtures with a greater percentage of air are called lean mixtures and occur as higher numbers (for example, 14.7 and up). Richer mixtures, in which there is an excess of fuel, are represented by smaller numbers. The rich burn limit for an engine at normal operating temperature is 6.0; the lean burn limit for an EFI engine is above 22.0. The following table, courtesy of Edelbrock Corporation in Torrance, California, indicates characteristics of various mixtures.

Air-Fuel Mixtures and Characteristics

Mixture rating	Comment
6.0	Rich burn limit (fully warm engine)
9.0	Black smoke, low power
11.5	Approximate rich best torque at wide-open throttle
12.2	Safe best power at wide-open throttle
13.3	Approximate lean best torque
14.6	Stoichiometric air-fuel ratio (chemically ideal)
15.5	Lean cruise
16.5	Usual best economy
18.0	Carbureted lean burn limit
22+	EEC and EFI lean burn limit

Note: These figures do not indicate anything about the effect of various mixtures on exhaust emission.

Air-fuel mixture requirements are mainly a function of engine operating mode: temperature, rpm, and loading. Cold engines require enrichment to counteract the fact that only the smallest fractions of fuel will vaporize at colder temperatures, while the remaining fuel exists as globules or droplets which do not mix well with air. Consequently, most of the fuel will be wasted. At temperatures below zero, the air-fuel mixture may be as low as 4.0:1, and at cranking as rich as 1.5:1!

Big cams result in gross dilution of air-fuel mixture at idle which then burns slowly and requires a lot of advance and a mixture as rich as 11.5:1 to counteract the lumpy, uneven idle resulting from partial burning in some cycles. Short-cam engines may run at stoichiometric mixtures at idle for cleanest exhaust emissions.

Coming off idle, a big-cam engine may require mixtures nearly as rich as at idle to eliminate surging, starting at 12.5-13.0 and leaning out with speed or loading. Mild cams will permit 14.0-15.0 mixtures in off-idle and slow cruise.

With medium speeds and loading, the bad effects of big cams diminish, resulting in less charge

dilution and allowing the engine to happily burn mixture ratios of 14.0 to 15.0 and higher. At the leaner end, additional spark advance is required to counteract slow burning of lean mixtures.

At high loading and partial throttle, richer mixtures give better power by making sure that all air molecules have fuel present to burn. Typical mixtures giving best driveability are in the range of 13.0 to 14.5, depending on speed and loading.

At wide-open throttle, where the objective is maximum power, all four-cycle gasoline engines require mixtures that fall between lean and rich best torque, in the 11.5 to 13.3 range. Since this best torque mixture spread narrows at higher speeds, a good goal for naturally aspirated engines is 12.0 to 12.5, perhaps richer if fuel is being used for cooling in a turbocharged or supercharged engine.

The main difference between computer-controlled engines and earlier modes of control is that every point of speed and loading (and other engine parameters) can generate spark advance and fueling that are completely independent of each other—something that is unrealistic with mechanical control systems. Computer-controlled engines eliminate compromises in fueling and spark control. Multi-port injection eliminates problems of handling wet mixtures in the intake manifold that are associated with carburetors. The result of this multi-port injection is improved cold running, improved throttle response under all conditions, and improved fuel economy without driveability problems.

Equivalent Ratio Table

A/F (air/fuel)	F/A (fuel/air)
22:1	0.0455
21:1	0.0476
20:1	0.0500
19:1	0.0526
18:1	0.0556
17:1	0.0588
16:1	0.0625
15:1	0.0667
14:1	0.0714
13:1	0.0769
12:1	0.0833
11:1	0.0909
10:1	0.1000
9:1	0.1111
8:1	0.1250
7:1	0.1429
6:1	0.1667
5:1	0.2000

An individual runner EFI manifold uses one injector and one throttle per runner. Note the balance tubes con-

necting runner vacuum to MAF sensor for reliable manifold pressure. Tull Systems

else in the world. The only relationship between air and fuel in EFI is defined electronically in a computer and is, therefore, completely *flexible*. If you wanted to, you could change the way your system injected fuel based on what day of the week it was!

So, since anything is possible with EFI, once we've had a chance to see what an EFI system looks like, we'll take a quick look at some alternate design choices before getting down to the business of relating specific fuel injection components to fuel, ignition, and engine theory. In the end, it should be clear what kind of fuel delivery is ideal under various circumstances, and how injection systems go about providing it.

Building a Sample Injection System, and Understanding the Process

If we're going to design a fuel injection system, where's a good place to start? How about at the beginning, the fuel tank?

Step 1: Getting Fuel to the Engine

The fuel is resting in a tank, ready to make miracles, probably at the opposite end of the vehicle from the engine. Unless we want to put the fuel tank on the roof, we need a pump to move fuel to the engine. Let's put the fuel pump right *in* the fuel tank (which will also help keep it cool).

We will drive our roller-vane centrifugal pump with an electric motor so it's not tied to the speed of the engine. Therefore we'll have available plenty of fuel pressure, anytime—let's say at

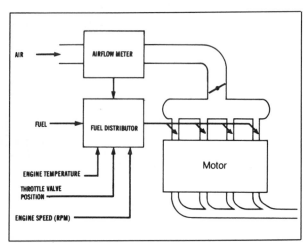

Port Fuel injection systems deliver fuel in uniform quantities to individual cylinders in relation to engine conditions as determined by mass air flow, engine speed, throttle position, engine temperature and other factors. Jan P. Norbye

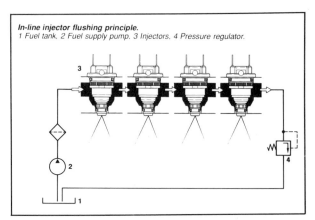

This Bosch illustration documents port injection fueling principles using EV 8 injectors. Fuel is delivered from the fuel tank to the injectors by the fuel pump. A pressure regulator on the back end (at the fuel return line) monitors fuel pressure in the system. Bosch

16

least 50psi. The pump should be sized to continuously move enough fuel to satisfy the engine at its highest consumption—at maximum horsepower—under full load. We'll run a steel fuel line from the pump to the engine, and route a second fuel line from the engine area back to the fuel tank. When the engine isn't using all the fuel we're pumping, it'll allow the excess fuel to flow back into the fuel tank. That way we don't ever have to turn the pump off when the motor is running, or wear out the pump quickly by forcing it to pump against a deadhead of pressure during low fuel consumption, such as at idle.

OK, let's move to the other end of the car.

There's the engine. Metal plumbing already connects each exhaust port to a common collector pipe (the exhaust manifold header) that is connected to the muffler. A tailpipe dumps the muffled exhaust gases out the back of the car.

The exhaust is taken care of, but what about the intake? Currently, the intake ports are naked holes—no intake manifold installed. Time for some fabrication.

Step 2: Building an Intake Manifold and Throttle

We begin by attaching a pipe (a runner) to each intake port, sized with the same internal

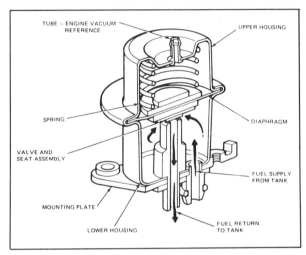

The pressure regulator maintains a constant relationship between fuel pressure at the injectors and manifold pressure such that the only variable in fuel delivery is injector open time.

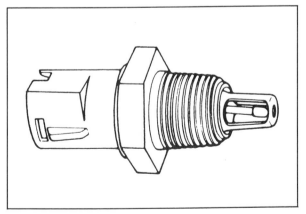

The air temperature sensor in the intake manifold or air cleaner system allows an electronic control unit to trim the mixture in relation to density changes in air related to temperature. Air and coolant temperature sensors enable fuel enrichment or enleanments based on engine and air temperature.

Characteristic curves.
DFR (dynamic flow range): Variation ratio between minimum and maximum injected fuel quantity at maximum 5% deviation from the linearized flow function. Periodic time T = 10 ms.

Bosch EV 1.3 A injector, injector schematic, and injector flow characteristics. Bosch

diameter as the port itself. We collect the runners in an air chamber (plenum) that has a single circular intake throat bolted to the plenum. Airflow is regulated into the plenum chamber (and subsequently into the engine) using a throttle plate (a

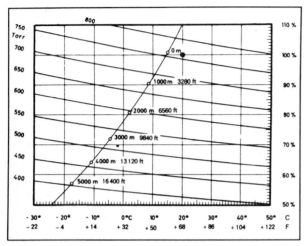

Air density varies with temperature and altitude. The EFI system must adjust fuel to air density. The attached chart for aviation use shows why engine performance drops off with altitude as the air gets "thinner." Less oxygen by weight being drawn into the engine means less is available to support combustion. Aircraft operating at high elevation airports must have a method for computing the loss of power as shown in this chart in order to compute takeoff roll distance and rate of climb once airborne. Jan P. Norbye

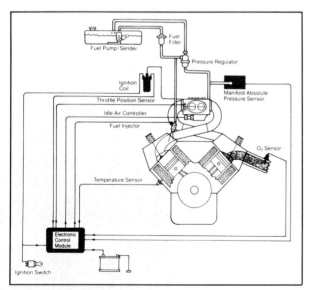

This injection block diagram shows how a fuel injection control unit makes use of sensors and actuators to control an engine. Information gathered at the sensors is analyzed by the computer, which orders the actuators to undertake certain operations. DFI

flat, circular plate completely blocking the circular air intake throat). This spring-loaded throttle plate is designed to pivot on a shaft and allow more or less air into the motor. The chamber containing the throttle plate is called a throttle body. Now, we'll run a cable from the throttle plate shaft to the accelerator pedal. Pushing down opens the throttle. This will control the speed of the engine and the power output by regulating how much *air* enters each cylinder in the intake stroke.

Great. Now we can regulate air into the engine, but still don't have fuel.

Step 3: Figuring Out a Way to Meter Fuel

Metering fuel? No problem.

We drill a hole in each intake runner near the intake port, and install a miniature fuel valve in each hole, aimed straight at the intake valve where air is moving fast and swirling as the engine sucks in air. These little valves are called electronic fuel injectors. Each will actually contain a small electromagnetic coil. When we energize this coil with direct electrical current from the battery of the car, the energized electromagnet will overcome the force of a tiny spring in the injector that holds closed a miniature check valve—thereby snapping open and allowing fuel to spray a fine mist through a tiny orifice at high pressure.

At high engine speed, this injector must be able to open and close like a frantically buzzing

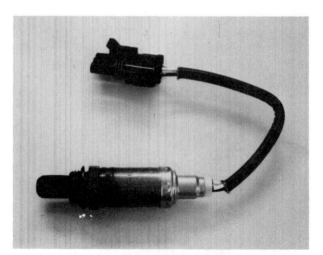

The Exhaust Gas Oxygen (EGO) sensor (also called O_2 sensor, or Lambda sensor by Europeans) allows an injection system to tune itself based on oxygen content in the exhaust which is correlated to air-fuel mixture. The sensor can be thought of as an "air battery" which changes voltage flow based on O_2 around its components, something like how a lead-acid battery changes voltage with the content of the acid mixture surrounding the components.

bee at up to 400 times a second! When the injector is open, fuel always flows from it at the same rate per unit of time as long as the fuel supply pressure to the injector remains constant. Therefore, we must meter the amount of fuel going into the engine based on how *long* we leave the injector open per engine cycle.

Clearly, we must carefully select our injectors so that the flow rate matches engine requirements, keeping in mind the following: Any injector's high-flow threshold occurs when it is *constantly open,* providing an absolute maximum fuel flow. Providing *more* fuel than this maximum would require either increased fuel pressure, injectors with a larger orifice, or additional injectors.

On the other hand, when the engine is idling, the *same* injectors must be able to open and then close quickly enough to inject the tiny amount of fuel required. In fact, most injectors cannot provide accurate flow below a threshold of 1.3 milliseconds' open time. To get *less* fuel requires changing to smaller injectors or decreasing the fuel pressure (it is common practice to lower fuel pressure at idle). In any case, correct injectors are sized to supply both idle and wide-open throttle requirements

Pushing ahead, our next step is to plumb the fuel supply line to each injector, being careful in our fuel rail design so that each injector receives equal fuel supply pressure. Then we plumb in the fuel return line via an inline pressure regulator designed to maintain an exact fuel pressure in the fuel rail (loop) in relation to manifold pressure. This kind of regulator, usually referenced to intake manifold pressure by an air hose, is designed to choke off fuel going back to the tank until fuel pressure builds up at the injectors to a predetermined pressure. At this point the regulator begins allowing excess fuel to return to the fuel tank, maintaining fuel pressure. Idle vacuum piped to the regulator fights the force of the regulator's spring against the fuel diaphragm, lowering fuel pressure at idle when manifold vacuum is high. As manifold pressure rises with increasing engine loads, vacuum at the regulator drops, and the full force of the regulator spring comes to bear on the diaphragm, raising fuel pressure. The injectors, therefore, always inject against manifold pressure that is *fixed* in relation to fuel pressure.

At this point, we have a system ready to handle the physics of air and fuel delivery into the engine: a throttle body and intake manifold to deliver and measure air, and a fuel pump and regulator supplying high pressure fuel to a set of injectors ready to precisely spray fuel into the inlet ports in exactly the correct amount as a function of how long each is opened.

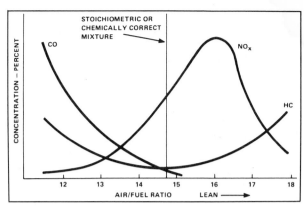

Closed Loop mixture control reduces emissions by searching for the stoichiometric (14.7-1) air-fuel mixture, computed by the fuel injection Electronic Control Unit (ECU) based on exhaust gas oxygen content. Reducing emissions is a delicate balancing act due to the fact that CO, HC, and NOₓ emissions are not minimized at the same mixture, which is also not the optimal mixture for fuel economy, which is not the best mixture for best power (lean best torque). Holley

Everything from here on is related to reading and evaluating certain engine vital signs, and translating this information into actual engine fuel requirements which can then be used to compute injector open times (pulse width).

Step 4: Turning On (and Off!) the Injectors

At 10,000rpm, a fuel injector must turn on and off at least 167 times a second (and possibly 333 times a second). The on-time must be computed accurately to less than a thousandth of a second to get the air-fuel mixture just right.

This is a job for a microcomputer. A modern digital microcomputer can perform millions of instructions per second. Its speed is so much faster than what is happening mechanically in an engine, that the microcomputer can treat the engine, at any given moment, as if it is *standing still.*

A microcomputer is able to continuously read the current status of an engine via electro-mechanical sensors. Supplied with this information, it quickly looks up preconfigured tables of numbers in memory that provide information about injection pulse width modifications at various engine speeds and loading. A fast microcomputer, which maintains a highly precise internal clock, has the ability to combine engine sensor and internal data table look-up information with arithmetic computations to schedule injector start or stop times—all before the engine has virtually moved.

Certain vital engine events (such as the crankshaft arriving at a particular position) can be made to automatically interrupt the microcomputer for action. As engine conditions change, the computer is able to reschedule injector start and stop times on the fly.

OK, now we have a computer. What sensors do we need to install so the computer can understand what is happening in the engine?

Step 5: Telling the Computer What's Going On in the Engine

What does the computer need to know about the engine?

Let's start with cam position, speed, engine loading, and so forth.

First, we'll need to install an optical triggering device near the camshaft or distributor, designed to count teeth on a gear that is missing one or two teeth as a reference point. The cam sensor and gear are set up to send a special electrical signal to the computer each time the crankshaft passes through top dead center compression stroke on number one cylinder. In between, the cam sensor counts gear teeth, passing electrical signals to the microcomputer as it does, enabling the computer to know the exact position of the crankshaft. The computer uses the toothless reference point (and offsets from it in numbers of teeth) to sequentially schedule timed fuel injection events for each cylinder correlated to each intake valve opening. The cam trigger also enables the computer to calculate engine speed (movement per time).

Beyond knowing camshaft and crankshaft position and speed, in order to time a sequence of fuel delivery opening and closing events for all the injectors, the microcomputer must know the

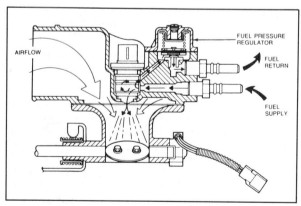

Throttle body injection (TBI) uses one or more large solenoid-type injectors similar to port injectors— although larger—to squirt fuel into the air stream near the carburetor-like throttle body (usually upstream of the throttle plate[s]). Throttle body injection allows precise computer control of engine fueling, but still has certain disadvantages of a carburetor since the wet intake manifolding may have integral problems with mixture distribution and fluctuation.

number of injectors and cylinders and displacement, and the injector flow rates. The microcomputer combines these factors into a single number which has no meaning in and of itself, but simply is a scaling constant representing the combined impact of all these factors on injection pulse width. This number is called the *fuel injection constant*. The computer plugs it into a mathematical formula to compute pulse width.

But most important of all, the microcomputer must know how much *air* is entering the engine at a given moment so it can compute the basic fuel requirement in weight (which is roughly 1/14.7 of the air mass). The microcomputer then determines special modifications to this mixture at the current engine speed and loading, and begins scheduling injector opening and closing times needed to achieve the correct pulse width (hence, the correct mixture).

To measure air entering the engine, our system utilizes a tiny heated wire located in the inlet air stream just upstream of the throttle body. This wire measures the cooling effect of incoming air—exactly proportional to the number of air molecules entering the engine at a given moment. This is called *air mass*. This mass airflow (MAF) sensor's output voltage is constantly converted electronically to digital values available to the microcomputer to use in its fuel computations.

Step 6: Gentlemen, Start Your Engines

Let's fire it up, see how it runs! We twist the key and...the engine sputters and coughs a little, but *it won't start!* After cranking for a long time and nearly running down the battery, we resort to a long shot of starting fluid straight in the throttle body while cranking. The engine struggles to life, coughing and backfiring through the intake manifold and running badly. After a few minutes of warmup, it runs great.

After considering the problem, we install another sensor—a coolant temperature sensor designed to give the microcomputer information about engine temperature so it can tell when there's a cold-start situation. We instruct the computer to run the injectors extra rich (wider injection pulse width) when the engine and air are cold. It's a known fact that gasoline doesn't mix well with *cold* air, that only the smallest fractions of gasoline will vaporize in the cold. In addition, a normal but cold air-fuel mixture will not burn well in a cold engine since much of the injected gasoline has not vaporized or atomized well; it exists as liquid droplets or threads of fuel suspended in the air and coating the cold cylinder or manifold walls as "dew."

Plain liquid fuel doesn't burn; motor fuel must be well mixed with air to burn properly. Once the engine is running, much of the fuel

20

vaporizes in the hot cylinders, but during cold cranking, the cylinder walls are stone cold too, and the necessary cold-start air-fuel ratio may be in the 1.5 to 4.0 range in cold weather!

With a coolant temperature sensor installed, when the engine and air are cold, the microcomputer knows to inject plenty of extra fuel so that at least *some* will vaporize properly. The microcomputer gradually diminishes this enrichment as the engine warms up.

The next time the engine is cold, we turn the key and it starts beautifully, warms up great. So we back out the driveway.

After a few tanks of gas, during which time we noticed the car stumbled on sudden acceleration, got poorer fuel economy than we expected, and had less power than we expected at wide-open throttle, we're back in the garage installing one final sensor. It's a throttle position sensor (TPS), and once it's installed we reprogram the computer one final time.

On rapid-throttle opening, manifold air pressure rises, but airflow metering systems may have difficulty keeping up with the rapid changes. With its new TPS, the computer detects when we are opening the throttle. Now the microcomputer adds transient enrichment to ordinary injection pulse width on throttle opening. The stumble goes away. We also program the computer to affect a richer mixture than normal when the throttle is more wide open, and to cut the pulse width a little to lean the mixture when we're running with the throttle only partly open.

Presto! The fuel economy improves, and maximum power snaps our neck back. We're happy.

Step 7: Naming the System and Making It Smart

We decide to name the system we've built sequential port injection of fuel (SPIF), and give it one more interesting capability: We make it *smart*.

A sensor located in the exhaust system enables SPIF to deduce the actual air-fuel ratio of pre-combustion mixture in the cylinders based on the amount of exhaust gas oxygen present after combustion—and to make adjustments to injection times to achieve a target air-fuel mixture. This mode of operation, in which the microcomputer is able to evaluate its own performance and make corrections on the fly, is called *closed-loop* programming.

Step 8: How Did We Do?

We still haven't tried to get the beast to pass emissions testing, but so far, so good: We've built an electronic fuel injection system that gets the job done, and our SPIF system is, in fact, very similar to some injection systems you can get on new cars from Detroit, Europe, and Japan.

We design the operating firmware on our SPIF microcomputer so that we can adjust the behavior of SPIF ("reprogram" it) something like a video game—using a joy stick or a few keystrokes to change the height of graphs on the video screen of a personal computer connected by cable to our SPIF microcomputer.

Now we can tune SPIF on the fly, almost like

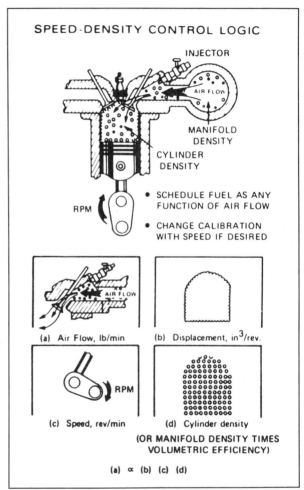

Speed-density injection control comes in two varieties: Those that compute air flow based on engine speed and manifold pressure, and those that simply use speed and manifold pressure as indexes to a computer data table of injection pulsewidth times for engine speed and manifold pressure, using linear interpolations for speed-density points that fall between values in the table. For any given engine configuration, airflow is proportional to the product of cylinder air density (volumetric efficiency) and engine speed. Volumetric efficiency (how well the cylinder fills with air while the engine compared to atmospheric pressure in the same volume) depends on engine design, RPM, and manifold pressure—which, in turn, depends on manifold design, RPM, throttle opening, altitude, air temperature, and whether the engine is turbo/supercharged. Jan P. Norbye

drawing pictures. (This capability is currently available on some programmable aftermarket fuel injection systems you can buy off the shelf.)

We will discover that if we were planning to go into business selling SPIF systems in the real world, we might want to make some modifications to our design for certain marketing and technical reasons, depending on the type of use anticipated. Our current version of SPIF may not be *quite* ready for the real world. But it's very close.

But consider this: SPIF delivers fuel to a set of injectors aimed at the intake ports of an engine. There is a certain amount of programming logic going on behind the scenes to compute pulse width under various circumstances, and to make corrections according to exhaust gas feedback. But as noted before, SPIF really only does one thing to fuel the engine: it opens and closes injectors, sometimes faster, sometimes slower, sometimes longer or shorter, but *that's all*. At idle, at part throttle or full throttle during sudden acceleration, or even during warmup, the microcomputer makes its calculations and the injectors buzz along, opening and closing. That's it. Pure

and simple.

This, unfortunately, is not true of carburetors—as we'll see.

Step 9: Reconsidering the Situation

OK, we seem to have gotten our SPIF engine running pretty nicely. But before we take it to the races or to the emissions lab, before we install a supercharger or nitrous oxide injection or other wild stuff (which is perfectly compatible with EFI, as we'll see), it might be valuable to reexamine the engineering decisions we made in designing SPIF, and to consider other approaches we could have taken in our fuel injection system design.

Alternate Injection Points

SPIF injects fuel into each intake port, directly at the inlet valve, in time with the intake stroke. As an alternative, we could have injected fuel directly *into* each cylinder—like a diesel engine—or, taking a different approach, we could have injected fuel for all cylinders farther upstream in the intake manifold at a single point near the throttle body.

Injecting fuel directly into a cylinder requires a pump with extremely high operating pressure capabilities since it is injecting against full cylinder pressure near top center compression stroke, and must get the fuel into the cylinder *very quickly*. Such a pump is noisy and robs horsepower. Injection timing is critical, since fuel must be injected during the compression stroke and given time to atomize—in a very short period of time on high-speed engines operating near redline (a few thousandths of a second)! However, such a system was used for many years on gasoline-engine Mercedes cars until the 1970s.

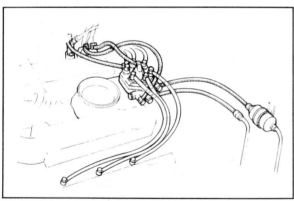

Volkswagen used Bosch K-Jetronic constant injection on millions of cars in the seventies and eighties. Unlike Bosch L-Jetronic timed port injection, K-Jetronic is not under electronic control. Instead, it is a mechanical system in which air flow, as measured by a spring-loaded air door (the round opening to the left of the fuel distributor), is used to alter fuel pressure to continuously-flowing port injectors. A fuel distributor (to the right of the airflow sensor) delivers fuel to all injectors, which are spring loaded to cut off all fuel flow when fuel pressure drops below about 50 psi, preventing fuel dripping when the engine is shut down. The K-Jetronic system was relatively inexpensive to produce, although less precise than EFI. Since injection occurred even when the intake valves were closed, efficiency was slightly reduced compared to sequential EFI. Bosch later added electronic control to trim fuel delivery, which electromechanical actuators under computer control based on engine sensors similar to those used in timed fuel injection.

What is Standard?

Not all engines are run at the same air temperature and altitude, of course, and not all test labs share a common temperature and altitude. So to ensure proper design work and testing, engineers adjust all airflow and engine power readings to determine what they would be at a standard temperature and air pressure.

Readings are adjusted to reflect airflow and output at a standard temperature of 59 degrees F (Fahrenheit) and an air pressure of 14.7psi, which is air pressure at sea level.

In working on carburetors, engineers often measure air pressure in inches of mercury rather than psi. Their standard pressure in inches of mercury is 29.92, with 1in Hg approximately equal to 0.5psi.

It turns out that in port fuel injection, timing is not necessarily critical. Bosch L-Jetronic systems inject half the required fuel from all injectors *simultaneously,* twice per complete engine cycle. There are some fairly minor fuel consumption, power, and emissions advantages to timed sequential port injection like SPIF, but many EFI systems *batch* it—and perform very well.

Batch injection would have enabled us to dispense with the crank sensor, since the microcomputer could easily determine engine speed by counting sparks at the ignition coil (and timing would be irrelevant).

Throttle-body injection need not be timed either, although it must use an injection strategy that provides for equal distribution to cylinders. With any such "single point" injection there is plenty of time on the way to the cylinder for the fuel to atomize. However, as in a single-carburetor fueling system, all single-point injection systems must deal with the opposite problem: Fuel can *separate* from air on the long (and usually unequal-length) path to the cylinders. In such a case it can wet the surface of some sections of the intake manifold, resulting in uneven and unpredictable mixtures in various cylinders at any given moment.

Single-point systems such as this can suffer from difficulties in achieving equal air-fuel mixtures in individual cylinders. This is particularly true since getting equal amounts of *air* to all the cylinders does not always equate to getting equal amounts of *air and fuel* to each one. (Fluid mechanics of air and fuel are not the same.) Heavier fuel is more likely to gravitate to the outside of a manifold bend, for example, compared to air.

Alternate Air Measurement

Another alternate injection design would have us eliminate the hot-wire MAF sensor measuring the amount of air entering the engine. Instead, the microcomputer could have done a good job setting pulse width by using data from an airflow meter that measured the *velocity* of air entering the engine. The velocity reading would be based on air pressure against a spring-loaded flapper valve suspended like a door in the air stream and linked to a linear potentiometer (something like a volume control).

Air velocity is not necessarily the same as air mass, but can be corrected for ambient temperature of intake air and altitude (two additional easy-to-install electronic sensors) to equal air mass. Bosch L-Jetronic systems use velocity air metering.

In fact, an alternate version of SPIF could throw out the entire concept of metering air, and deduce how much air is entering the engine based on manifold pressure and engine speed, correcting for air temperature—which is then the same as air mass flow. Although engines always displace the same *volume* of air in the cylinders, at various throttle positions, speeds, and loading (and with various camshafts, manifolds, and so on), an engine varies in *efficiency* at pulling in total *mass* of air. An engine operating at high vacuum (with the throttle nearly closed), for example, is unable to pull in as much air as the same engine operating at wide-open throttle (with higher manifold pressure). The engine is also less efficient on a hot day or at the top of a mountain when the air is thinner. So-called speed-density injection systems sense engine speed and manifold pressure, plus ambient air temperature, to deduce the air mass entering the engine—or look it up in a table. This is the same figure supplied by SPIF's MAF sensor, arrived at using a different method.

One advantage of *speed-density* systems is that they do not restrict inlet airflow like velocity air meters (with the pressure drop that exists at the air metering door) or MAF sensors. Speed-density systems also compensate automatically for any air losses or leaks in the engine's inlet system; this is not true of MAF sensors. Speed-density injection systems, without MAF sensors, may allow greater flexibility of inlet air plumbing to the throttle body, particularly on turbocharged engines.

On the other hand, speed-density systems can have problems at idle if engine vacuum fluctuates and wanders (as it might on engines with high-lift, high-overlap cams). Cadillac offered one of

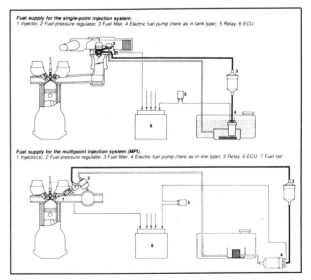

These diagrams display fuel supply for both single-point injection (top) and for multipoint injection (MPI). Bosch

the first speed-density EFI systems as an option on its 1976 500 cubic inch (ci) engines. Early 1980s Ford 5.0 liter V-8s, GM throttle-body injection for 1990 and later TBI engines, and many aftermarket systems use manifold absolute pressure-sensing speed-density methods to deduce mass airflow into the engine.

Some aftermarket speed-density systems available include the: E6 and E8 from Emtech (Haltech, Australia); the F3 from Haltech Incorporated in Garland, Texas; the TEC injection system from Electromotive Incorporated in Chantilly, Virginia; Edelbrock's Pro-Flo; Accel's DFI Calmap System, Farmington Hills, Michigan; the Competition/Race EFI systems from Nitrous Oxide Systems (NOS) in Cypress, California; and systems from EFI Technology in Torrence, California, and Zytek from England.

Alternate Injectors

It may already have occurred to you that adjusting the *on-time* of injectors is only one way to regulate how much fuel ends up in the engine's cylinders. Instead of using injectors that always

---

Theory of Electronic Engine Control

The computer controls four basic functions in an engine: (1) accumulates data in the ECU from engine sensors; (2) computes engine status from sensors that provide data on engine temperature, engine speed, loading, air temperature, and other important factors; (3) determines and schedules the next events to control spark advance and/or engine fueling; and (4) translates computer output signals into electrical signals that directly control actuators (injectors, coil driver, idle air by-pass control, fuel pump, and so on).

The microprocessor handling this process executes a program that can be divided into the logical *strategy* that understands sensor input and computes what to do next, and the *calibration* logic which determines exactly how to execute the event to achieve precise results.

EFI control systems can be divided into several types, all of which break down fuel and spark event scheduling based on engine speed, but which use different methods to estimate engine loading. Three types are: throttle position or Alpha-N systems which use throttle angle and engine speed to estimate engine loading; mass airflow systems which directly estimate loading by sensing speed and measuring air entering the intake manifold; and speed-density systems, which estimate loading based on rpm and manifold pressure.

Naturally aspirated race cars use throttle position and speed to estimate loading. These systems are not bothered by lack of or fluctuating manifold pressure on engines with wild cams. There is no airflow restriction on the inlet. However, tiny changes in throttle angle can result in huge changes in engine loading, particularly on engines with very large throttle area (such as one butterfly per cylinder). This means that the Alpha-N may have resolution problems at small throttle angles.

MAF systems are used by the car companies and measure air mass entering the engine based, for example, on the cooling effect of the air on a hot wire held electronically at a fixed temperature.

These systems are sometimes restrictive to inlet air. Designers may find it difficult to locate the meter such that it is unaffected by reversion pulses in tuned inlet systems. MAF meters tend to be slow to respond to very rapid changes in load (sudden wide-open throttle) and therefore require supplemental means of control to handle rapidly changing conditions. Advantages of MAF control include the ability to compensate for changes in volumetric efficiency (VE) as the engine wears over time, and the ability to compensate for modest user modifications that affect VE, such as camshaft changes. MAF systems automatically correct for altitude and air density changes.

Velocity airflow metering uses a spring-actuated door that is forced open by the action of air rushing into the intake through the air meter. A linear potentiometer measures the opening of the door, and therefore air velocity into the engine. This must be converted to air mass by considering charge air temperature and altitude. This system is similar to MAF metering, with the additional disadvantages of further inlet flow restriction from the air door, and the limitation that the meter has no sensitivity to increased airflow beyond the point where the air door is fully open.

Speed-density systems have also been used by car companies for engine control. They may directly deduce mass airflow into the engine by considering engine speed and manifold pressure, correcting for air temperature and barometric pressure. Or they may use these same parameters as an index into a look-up table of fueling values (and, in some cases, spark advance values) at the various operating points, performing calculations to interpolate fueling and spark for operating points that occur between points on the look-up table grid.

Look-up speed-density systems, in particular, are not able to compensate for modifications to the base engine configuration or changes in VE caused by wear over time. Speed-density control systems respond quickly to changes in load, offer good resolution at low loading, and do not restrict inlet airflow as do air metering systems.

flow the same amount of fuel (like SPIF), and regulating how long the microcomputer turns them on (pulse width), we could turn on a set of injectors *continuously while* varying how *much* fuel is forced through the injectors via fuel pressure changes in order to match engine requirements.

Such injectors would be purely mechanical devices, using a spring-loaded check valve to stop fuel from dripping or spraying out of the injector until a threshold pressure forced the injector open.

Bosch KE-Jetronic fuel injection uses a microcomputer and a set of sensors—including an air meter—to vary fuel flow through a set of continuous-flow injectors (called continuous fuel injection). Based on computed air-fuel requirements, the computer controls a valve that regulates fuel pressure exerted against the slits of a metering valve on the way to continuous port fuel injectors. More fuel through the slits means more fuel out of the injectors on a continual basis.

Mechanical Injection

If we were using a continuous injection scheme instead of SPIF, we could have eliminated the computer entirely—as Bosch did in the original K-Jetronic. Fuel was regulated to the injectors by entirely mechanical means. A carefully designed velocity air metering flapper valve suspended in the inlet air stream *mechanically* actuated a fuel control plunger contained in a vertical fuel "barrel" (something like a piston in a cylinder). Vertical slit openings in the sides of the fuel barrel were progressively uncovered as the control plunger moved upward, allowing more fuel to flow through the greater unblocked area of the slits and on to the injectors.

For a given amount of air entering the engine at any given moment, the fuel metering plunger in K-Jetronic reached equilibrium at a point

where the force of air entering the engine—as transmitted mechanically to the plunger—exactly balanced the fuel pressure, tending to force the plunger the opposite direction.

Single-Point Injection

But why inject fuel at the ports at all? A single large-capacity injector, pointing straight down at the throttle body, could provide fuel for *all* the cylinders. This injector could operate continuously, and could operate at reasonably low pressures since there would be no need to force fuel through a multi-injector fuel rail at high pressure to ensure accurate fuel delivery and pressure at multiple injector locations.

In fact, we might even decide to operate our single injector at *atmospheric pressure*. To do this, we would pump fuel into a reservoir near the throttle body, utilizing a float-operated check valve to keep the fuel pump from overfilling the reservoir. The fuel in the reservoir would exist at ambient atmospheric pressure. Cleverly utilizing Bernoulli's principle, we could then narrow the inlet *air* passage slightly above the throttle plate, just above the height of the fuel reservoir; this would create a minor restriction in airflow. Air headed into the engine would speed up as it passed through the restriction, and slow down again on the other side.

Bernoulli's principle states that when air speeds up as it flows past a solid surface, it exerts decreased pressure. Presto! We've created a small place that always has lower pressure than atmos-

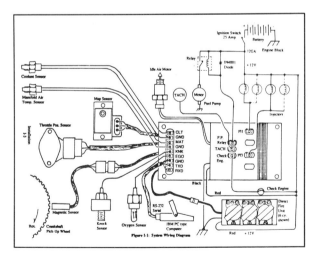

This Electromotive TEC wiring diagram offers a detailed view of all connections. The combined fuel injector load should be roughly 1.2ohm per output. The fuel pump relay should be 160 MA max, 90ohm coil. The Direct Fire chassis must be grounded. Plus 12volts and ground wires should be 12 GA. RS-232 connectors—black is GRD, red is RXD, white is TXD. Electromotive

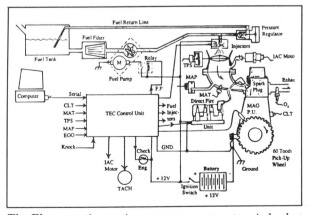

The Electromotive engine management system is broken down in this schematic. Note the crank trigger and direct-fire ignition coils. Electromotive

pheric when the engine is running, and in proportion to the amount of air flowing through it. (The more air entering the engine, the faster the air will rush through the restriction and the greater the pressure drop in the restriction compared to atmospheric.)

We'll put a tiny injector in the restriction, and run a fuel line to the reservoir. No check valve is needed in the injector; since the injector is located just above the fuel level in the reservoir, fuel flow will cease the instant pressure rises to atmospheric in the restriction (known as a venturi)

when the engine stops. We could tune the flow rate of the passage connecting the injector and reservoir in order to get the correct air-fuel mixture.

Oh, no! We just invented the carburetor! But does it suck or does it blow?

It is, in fact, the higher pressure of the earth's atmosphere that forces fuel out of the float chamber and into the low-pressure area of the venturi. So I guess we can conclusively say that the carb blows.

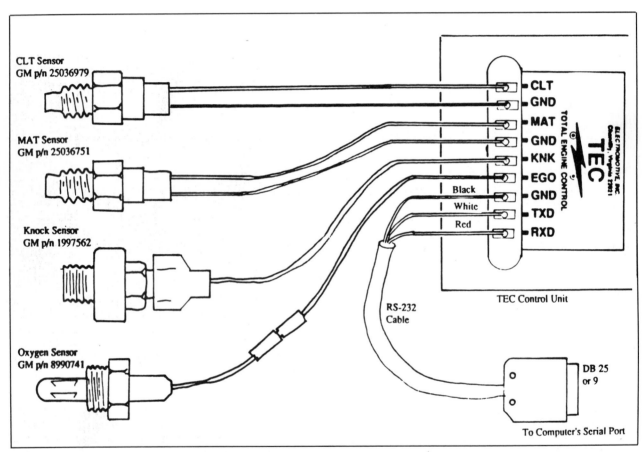

The Electromotive system sensor installations are clarified with this closeup view. Electromotive

Chapter 3

Options and Costs

This book examines several options for fuel injecting your hot rod, including: 1) a complete EFI engine swap; 2) an original equipment EFI component swap; 3) a Holley Pro-Jection kit; 4) a combination of options (one or two with an aftermarket ECU); 5) a complete add-on EFI kit; and 6) a "roll-your-own" kit.

Complete EFI Engine Swap

One option is to swap in a complete fuel-injected engine and supporting equipment (such as the high-pressure fuel pump) with or without the late-model overdrive transmission. Many existing transmissions currently mated to carbureted engines will mate to a fuel-injected engine, which may be almost identical except for the addition of electronic fuel injection.

Common examples are the 5.0 and 5.8 liter Ford port EFI V-8s which Ford began to install in many of its vehicles after 1985, and the Chevrolet/GM 305/350 tuned port injection V-8s fitted to GM cars of the 1980s and 1990s.

These V-8s will bolt up to transmissions that, in the case of GM models, date as far back as the 1950s, and in the case of Ford, date as far back as the 1960s. Ford's 260ci V-8 came out in about 1964, and GM's 265ci V-8 was introduced in the mid 1950s. These engine blocks are externally very similar to the modern EFI V-8s of the same family.

You may be able to find a complete junkyard EFI V-8 in good shape for a few hundred dollars, but more likely in the $500 range. The job then will be to adapt the EFI engine to your car. (Companies like Howell, Street and Performance, and others sell simplified wiring harnesses designed for engine and injection swapping.) Generally it is legal to swap a later model engine, complete with all emissions control devices, into an older vehicle. (In California, however, you will need to have the vehicle and engine inspected at a referee station.)

Street and Performance specializes in adapting EFI engines to new environments, including swapping hardware ranging from specialty wiring harnesses to accessory mounting hardware.

Several examples of EFI engine swapping are covered later in this book: an injected 530ci Cadillac into a GMC motorhome, first using Cadillac electronic controls and later Haltech injection, and a hemi-head Renault turbo EFI motor into a Lotus Europa, replacing the stock wedge Renault engine, controlled by DFI electronic injection and ignition controls. GM TPI/TBI engine swapping is specifically covered in a separate chapter.

Original Equipment EFI Component Swap

It is frequently possible to adapt port EFI manifolds, fuel rails, throttle bodies, and so on from an equivalent EFI engine to your existing engine using the principles already discussed. This would be particularly attractive if your existing engine is in very strong condition, yet similar

27

or identical to a factory EFI engine in camming, porting, and displacement.

The danger is that engine variables that affect breathing and volumetric efficiency, particularly cam changes, could mean that the OEM EFI electronic controls will no longer provide correct air-fuel ratios on *your* engine. This may still be a good choice, even with a heavily modified engine, as long as you hot rod the factory EFI to provide the additional fuel enrichment required for your engine—perhaps only under heavy loading, or possibly under all conditions.

PROM changes, fuel pressure changes, add-on black boxes that change injector pulse width, larger injectors, extra injectors, and other hot rodding techniques are available to do this; they're probably even turn-key, in the case of a common engine with common modifications.

Naturally, enrichment costs money. The OEM EFI parts will be available used for a few hundred dollars and up in a salvage yard. Fuel enrichment will cost from a hundred or two (PROM replacement or increased fuel pressure via special regulator) on up into the $500 to $1,000 range for more complex systems.

Tuned port injection and other manifolds and parts can be polished for an excellent look on a custom car. GM and other car companies sell packages to retrofit TPI to older engines. Incidentally, many European car companies adapted EFI to carbureted engines in the seventies and eighties. Later in this book you'll see an OEM Bosch L-Jetronic EFI swapped onto a Jaguar XKE 4.2 liter engine, and you'll learn what's involved in swapping GM TPI equipment for the Chevy engine.

Holley Pro-Jection Kit

Another option is to bolt on a Holley Pro-Jection system. These two- and four-butterfly throttle-body injection systems are relatively inexpensive ($500-$1,000), easy to install (since the throttle body with integral injectors and fuel pressure

Electromotive Total Engine Control (TEC) controller is rugged enough to live in the harsh environment of the engine compartment as show in this naturally-aspirated Dodge-Maxwell Jaguar V-12.

Swapping in a complete EFI motor may be a cost-effective way to fuel-inject your vehicle. After some modifications, a turbo Renault Fuego motor fit nicely in the author's Lotus Europa in place of the stock Lotus-Renault wedge non-turbo engine. The swap increased power from 70-80 to 200hp (with EFI/Turbo mods and nitrous oxide injection).

Accel/Digital fuel injection offers high-flow small-block Chevy TPI runners, Chevrolet large- and small-block Super Ram large port/plenum EFI manifolds, plus a large variety of EFI parts.

regulator bolts onto a four-barrel manifold exactly like a carburetor), and they're true electronic fuel injection systems with *many* of EFI's advantages—but not all! As a so-called single-point injection system (all fuel is injected near the throttle plate or plates), the intake manifold must handle a wet mixture like a carbureted system. The Pro-Jection 2, a two-butterfly two-injector system that flows roughly 675 cubic feet per minute (cfm), comes complete with fuel pump, wiring harness, computer, and almost everything else you'll need to do the installation. It costs roughly $600, while the Pro-Jection 4 (with four injectors and four butterflies, good for 950cfm), costs $900.

You'll also need some additional parts that are relatively inexpensive, such as the materials to construct a second fuel line to return unused fuel from the throttle body back to the tank (all electronic injection systems require this). This book later illustrates Pro-Jection 2 installation on a 1970 Dodge Challenger 383.

EFI Engine or Components Swap and Aftermarket ECU

A fourth alternative is to combine options number 1 or 2 with an aftermarket programmable ECU (electronic control unit) and associated parts; that is, to use factory air metering equipment (EFI manifold, throttle body, and so on), factory fuel metering equipment (injectors, fuel rail, and other components), with aftermarket computer, wiring, and usually engine sensors.

These aftermarket systems cost from roughly $700 for the four-cylinder throttle position sensing Haltech F7A, on up to the Full Race System from EFI Technology Incorporated in Torrance, California, which costs around $8,000. The EFI Tech system has the ability to handle over fifteen engine sensors and actuators, including direct-fire ignition, wastegate position, and proportional

Edelbrock's Pro-Flo injection kit supplies everything you need to port-inject a small-block Chevy, from the camshaft on up. The system includes an interface module and does not require a personal computer to tune.

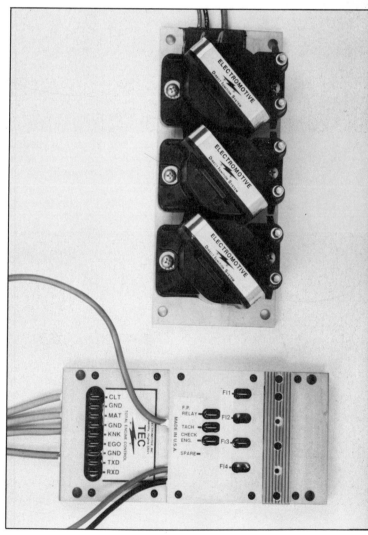

Electromotive EFI systems offer optional automated air-fuel mixture programming.

Holley's Pro-Jection 2 and Pro-Jection 4 supply a relatively inexpensive way to inject a vehicle via a kit that converts to two- or four-injector throttle body injection.

29

UK-based Zytek sells racing EFI systems. Motorsport Design near Phoenix, Arizona, has used the system on radical street cars like its twin-turbo Porsche.

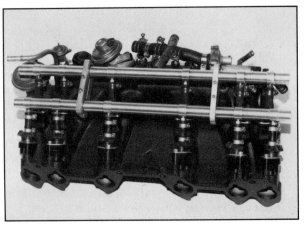

Cartech's inline 6-cylinder manifold uses two injectors per runner for excellent idle with six injectors operating, and it provides high horsepower levels on 12 injectors. This type of manifold is excellent for inline BMW or older Z-car type engines. Cartech

nitrous oxide injection!

Later on in this book you'll read about the installation of aftermarket EFI controls onto the stock EFI of a Cadillac-powered motorhome, and a Lotus Europa.

Complete EFI Add-On Kit

If you opt to purchase a complete EFI kit for your car, you will have everything you'll need to do the job. Such a system may even have an emissions exemption, making it legal on certain or all late-model vehicles. The Edelbrock-Weber system for small-block Chevys controls all engine management functions including ignition and injection. The kit for the '55 Chevy (or other non-emissions engines), manufactured by Tull Systems in San Antonio, Texas, costs between $3,000 and $4,500, and includes a Haltech control unit. (Installation is covered in a later chapter.)

Roll-Your-Own Kit

With a complete "roll-your-own" add-on fuel injection system, you might modify a carburetor intake manifold to hold port injector bosses (or buy an aftermarket EFI manifold), construct a fuel rail and mountings to hold injectors and provide fuel, select and install a fuel regulator, filter, supply and return lines, and injectors, build (if you're a machinist!) or buy a throttle body (available from TWM in Santa Barbara, California, Cutler Inductions and others), and purchase an aftermarket controller, sensors, and wiring loom.

Costs might include $1,300 for a Haltech F3 speed-density ECU and sensors, $150 for a fuel pump, $20-$150 each for injectors, a regulator at $50-100, single-plane manifold plus mods for $200 and up, throttle bodies at $150 each, for a total cost of over $2,000. We will explore this option later in a nitrous-injected, triple turbo Jag XKE project, a Chevy 350ci twin-turbo, a big-block Mopar 383, and a 460 Ford in a late-model Bronco.

Major Players

Without exception, the major auto makers have designed their own proprietary EFI electronic control units. GM units, at least through 1992, store data in a replaceable PROM (Programmable Read-Only Memory), making it relatively easy for knowledgeable aftermarket entrepreneurs who have somehow obtained access to GM ECU documentation, or who have reverse-engineered the data structure of the PROM, to blow new PROMs with altered data that changes the operation of the ECU. The Ford EEC-IV does not have an easily replaceable PROM; aftermarket suppliers have been able to "reprogram" it by adding plug-in circuitry that connects via the diagnostic port, or in-line between the computer and the stock wiring harness.

As of this writing, major players in the EFI replacement ECU aftermarket include Haltech, Electromotive, Emtech (Haltech of Australia), DFI, NOS, EFI Technology, Zytek, and Edelbrock, who recently introduced a complete system for small-block Chevrolets. Most other suppliers resell electronic controls from GM or one of the above control unit suppliers. Crane Cams, HKS, and others market black boxes designed to enhance, but not replace, the stock ECU.

The following chart compares features of some aftermarket multi-port EFI systems.

ECU Comparison

Function	Emtech	Haltech	Electrom.	DFI	NOS/ EFI Tech	Edelbrock
Cost 8-cyl w/sensors & harness (approx.)	$1592	$1400	$1400	$1200	$3-4K	NA
Battery backup required to retain memory	no	no	no	no	no	no
Battery voltage correction	yes	yes	yes	yes	yes	yes
Fuel map can be altered w/engine running	yes	yes	yes	yes	yes	yes
Number of injector drivers	8	8	4	4	3/4/8	NA
Minimum impedance allowed/driver (ohms)	2	2	1.2	1.2	1.2	NA
Injector drivers can be staged (aux. inj.)	no	yes	no	yes	yes	no
No. of ignition events per injector squirt	adj.	4	adj.	4	NA	NA?
Sequential Fuel Injection	no	no	no	avail.	yes	NA
Individual cylinder fueling adjustment	no	no	no	no	yes	no
Idle control	IAC	none	IAC	IAC	yes	yes
OEM harness connectors available	no	no	no	GM, Ford	GM	NA
Can be mounted under hood	no	no	yes	no	yes	no
Data Logging	yes	yes	yes	yes	yes	NA
Limp home mode	yes	yes	yes	yes	yes	NA
Programmable limp home	no	no	yes	no	yes	NA
Check Engine light w/diagnostics	no	no	yes	no	no	keypad
Number of fuel map ranges (by RPMs)	16	8	8	16	16	NA
Ranges matchable to engine RPM range?	no	no	yes	yes	yes	no
No. programmable points in each range	64	64	8	8	adj.	NA
Total prog. points in base fuel map	1024	512	64	256	256	NA
Separate engine warmup fuel map	yes	yes	yes	yes	yes	yes
Separate engine cold cranking map	prime	no	no	yes	yes	NA
Prog. TPS temporary enrichment percent	dual	yes	yes	yes	yes	NA
Prog. TPS rate of return to base map	yes	yes	yes	yes	yes	NA
Separate TPS fuel map (power valve sim.)	NA	no	no	yes	no	NA
Three-dimensional fuel map display	no	no	yes	yes	yes	no

OEM Ignition Compatibility

Function	Emtech	Haltech	Electrom.	DFI	NOS/ EFI Tech	Edelbrock
Closed loop feedback with EGO sensor	yes	no	yes	yes	yes	yes
Closed loop startable by temperature sensor	yes	yes	yes	yes	yes	yes
Closed loop can be ended by RPM	yes	NA	yes	yes	yes	yes
Closed loop can be ended by TPS	yes	NA	yes	yes	yes	NA
Ignition Control	yes	no	yes	yes	yes	yes
Rev limiter	yes	NA	yes	yes	yes	NA
No. programmable points on ign. map	1024	512	64	128	NA	NA
Programmable boost retard	yes	NA	yes	yes	yes	NA
Detonation sensor	no	NA	yes	yes	no	NA
Prog. detonation sensor retard rate, sens.	NA	yes	yes	NA	NA	NA
Compatible w/Hall Effect, magn., points	yes	NA	yes	yes	yes	NA
Extra ignition amplifier required	no	NA	no	yes	yes	no
Waste spark type coil pack included (DIS)	no	NA	yes	no	no	no
NOS triggering	yes	no	yes	yes	yes	NA
Injector enrichment during NOS operation	yes	NA	yes	yes	yes	NA
Proportional NOS control	prog out	NA	yes	no	yes	NA
Multi-stage NOS operation	no	NA	no	yes	no	NA
Separate NOS ignition timing map	no	NA	no	yes	no	NA
Fuel pump relay control	yes	yes	yes	yes	no	yes
Wastegate or EGR control	prog out	no	yes	yes	no	NA
Electric fan control	prog out	no	no	yes	no	NA
Torque convertor lockup control	prog out	no	no	yes	no	NA

Source: Sutton Engineering of Evanston, Illinois.

As you can see from the chart, the Haltech F3 speed-density system is designed to control only fuel injection (not ignition or any other engine management function beyond firing fuel injectors). Injection pulse width is computed to very fine granularity based on engine speed, manifold absolute pressure, barometric pressure, engine temperature, and inlet air temperature. Haltech has been around longer than anyone except Air Sensors, and probably has the greatest installed base. Most installers think they are exceptionally easy to program, particularly compared to some other aftermarket ECUs (but not easier than the Holley Pro-Jection throttle-body injection).

Beside these Haltech-type capabilities, the DFI system adds the ability to read an oxygen (O_2) sensor, enabling closed-loop on-the-fly tuning of air-fuel ratio by computer at idle and cruise conditions. To be on the safe side, a user might set the base fueling map slightly rich and allow the ECU to tune it lean in closed-loop mode. The DFI unit also has an additional cold-cranking fuel enrichment map, additional throttle position switch maps that simulate a power valve, and the ability to read and react to a detonation sensor. A two-stage nitrous map is available for providing fuel enrichment during nitrous injection. The DFI unit's ignition control correlates injection and ignition events to engine sensors. (Correlating spark advance to engine conditions is critical for achieving mean best torque).

Nitrous Oxide System's (NOS) Competition ECU is a downscale version of the full-race ECU built in partnership with EFI Technology for all-out, cost-is-no-object racing. Clearly, NOS and EFI Technology are trying to segment their market according to the price inelasticity of racers and relative price sensitivity of street users. The race units come standard with incredibly rugged mil-spec wiring harnesses; all circuitry is burned in and sealed in place with a coating of liquid plastic poured over the circuitry and allowed to harden. The competition unit is less rugged and has less memory.

Given NOS' dominant position among nitrous injection suppliers, it is not surprising that their injection system has the ability to pulse nitrous solenoids similarly to electronic injectors in order to continuously vary the amount of nitrous injected, exactly coordinating additional fueling enrichment from the injectors. It is one thing to bring on ungodly power gradually in a drag race engine using this strategy; however, it is not clear how well NOS solenoids would hold up to this type of abuse under street conditions.

The Electromotive TEC II (for total engine control) unit includes new advanced features enabling the unit to evaluate air-fuel mixtures under all conditions (even full throttle!) via a standard oxygen sensor. This means the ECU can configure its base fuel map on the basis of user input regarding what air-fuel mixture ratios are required at various engine loading, rather than specifying injection pulse width.

In *Turbo* magazine testing, a TEC II unit programmed itself better than an expert tuner could achieve in engine dynamometer testing. The goal, according to Electromotive, is to tune the system so that the raw fuel maps and the modifying VE maps produce such accurate fueling that air-fuel ratio mixture modification is unnecessary. The new unit has wastegate control, NOS control, and rev-limiting capabilities. This unit and the older TEC I unit are the only systems that enable direct-fire ignition as part of the basic package. The TEC I accomplished this with a separate electronic module for ignition; the TEC II includes integral direct-fire capabilities.

Later in the book, we will discuss project vehicles featuring Holley, Haltech, NOS, and DFI aftermarket ECUs: a 1970 big-block Challenger 383 using Holley injection; a twin-turbo small-block Chevy and a 530ci stroker Cadillac 500-powered motorhome using Haltech injection; a NOS-equipped turbo Lotus using DFI injection; a turbo 460 Ford-equipped full-size Bronco using Ford and Emtech engine management; and a triple-turbo NOS-equipped Jaguar XKE using NOS fuel injection. In addition, we will cover vehicles that have been injected or hot rodded using Bosch L-Jetronic/Lucas fuel injection, Ford EEC-IV injection, and GM tuned port injection.

Sovereign Motors' four-cam Jaguar V-12 engine uses custom-tuned port runners and a large plenum with twelve injectors under an Electromotive speed-density control to make 640 naturally aspirated horsepower in a 400ci stroked version of the Jag V-12 with twin 4.0liter twin-cam heads grafted onto the V-12 block.

Chapter 4

Computers and PROMs

It's time to take a harder look at the demands of real engines and how the logic of an electronic fuel injection system works to satisfy that.

Let's see how a sample fuel injection computer operates.

How a Computer Works

A digital microprocessor is essentially an array of tiny switches and circuits, each of which has the ability to do a few simple things—like switch on one wire if equal voltage is present in two other wires. From this extremely basic "decision-making" ability comes all functionality of modern computers, from the simplest arithmetic to complex algorithms that actually simulate human thought. In the same sense that electrons, protons, and neutrons can be combined to make atoms—and atoms combine to make molecules— the basic electronic switching abilities of a digital computer can be combined to perform more complex functions. Arithmetic and logical operations can be synthesized to create a series of steps to solve a problem, like setting the pulse width of an intermittent fuel injection event.

Microcomputers use a quartz crystal that resonates at a particular frequency to coordinate internal operations. Some microcomputers with very fast crystals and circuitry perform millions or even billions of instructions per second. Using amplification circuitry, a digital microcomputer has the capability to activate or deactivate *external* circuits—for example, to send a strong voltage to a fuel injector, or stop such a voltage—as well as to read the status of an external circuit, store it in internal memory, and use this value in additional mathematical calculations.

Random Access Memory (RAM) is vital to the operation of a digital computer. Memory once consisted of tiny magnetic "cores" that could be written on (magnetized) with electrical currents in the same way that a cassette or tape recorder writes the electrical "music" signals on a magnet

tape. Today, memory is contained in semiconductors, or silicon chips, containing hundreds of thousands or even millions of locations that are either on or off, electrically speaking.

RAM is extremely fast, and can be written to, and read from. Data in RAM is lost when electric power is turned off (unless there is a battery backup), so other means are required to store data while the computer is turned off. Computers use RAM as a scratch pad to store data used or generated by a computer program, as well as the *instructions themselves* which tell the computer how to manipulate the data—collectively referred to as a program or software (sometimes also firmware).

A simple program might fetch a few data values (numbers), add them, output a signal of a certain duration, and then start repeating over and over again—which is the basic function of a fuel

ECUs like this one from NOS meet mil-spec standards for extreme ruggedness of design so they can withstand harsh conditions and environments and continue to perform.

33

injection computer! Different results can be obtained from the same computer circuitry by using a different program and/or data.

Programmable Read-Only Memory (PROM) retains its data when power is turned off, but it can only be read from, not written to. PROM is ideal for storing programs and data that never change. PROMs are written or "blown" in a special machine that uses ultraviolet light as the writing medium, and may contain numbers that actually represent commands to the microcomputer, and numbers that are simply numbers (data). The microcomputer transfers these instructions and data into RAM at power-up time.

Electrically Erasable PROM (EEPROM) is slow and cannot hold much data, but it can be read from *and* written to, and it retains data when the power is off. Double-E PROM is ideal for storing a limited number of data values that must occasionally be changed by a computer user or program. (For example, the volumetric efficiency specifications could be altered on an EFI engine if a user made a cam change.)

The arithmetic-logic unit (ALU) of a computer, as you'd expect, performs arithmetic and logical operations based on instructions from a program, and generates the condition codes (status bits) that notify the program whether the operation was successful. The ALU performs its operations using its own special high-speed memory called registers. Typically, the ALU instructs the computer as to which data to store in its registers, what simple operation to perform on the registers (such as "Arithmetic Shift Left," or "Logical OR"), and where to store the result of the operation—plus a data bit to indicate the status (success) of the operation. The ALU is a subset of the central processing unit (CPU). The CPU controls computer operations, and is usually located in a microprocessor on a single silicon chip.

The input/output (I/O) system controls the movement of data between the computer and the outside devices with which it communicates in order to have an effect on the external world. A fuel injection computer receives data from *sensors* via the I/O system, which give it information about the engine and vehicle status. The computer also controls *actuators*—such as fuel injectors—which enable it to make things happen via the I/O system. The EFI computer must read data from engine sensors, perform internal processing on this data, and then send the data via the I/O system to an injector driver which will active a solenoid-type injector (actuator) for a precise amount of time or affect other engine/vehicle operations.

Analog-to-digital (A-D) circuitry onboard the microprocessor converts analog voltages from sensors to digital numbers that are meaningful to the computer and useful in computations. Digital computer output is similarly converted back to analog voltages and amplified to become powerful enough to actuate a physical device such as an injector or an idle air control (IAC) motor. The input and output devices, RAM, PROM, A-D circuitry, and the CPU are connected together using a data/address *bus* which enforces a strict protocol defining when a device on the bus may move data to another device so that the bus can be shared by all.

A typical EFI computer contains programs and data enabling it to compute raw fueling parameters correlated to engine volumetric efficiencies, and to modify these with additional enrichments or enleanments for cold or hot cranking, after-start operation, warmup operation, and acceleration. Software routines additionally regulate closed-loop idle and cruise air-fuel calibration. ECUs designed to control ignition events also compute engine speed and loading-based spark advance and knock sensor-controlled ignition retard. An ECU may also contain programming for wastegate control, control of emissions devices such as EGR, and activation of nitrous oxide injection and fuel enrichment.

Computers and Fuel Injection

Sutton Engineering likes to compare high-performance aftermarket EFI systems to the Hilborn injection system used for decades on all postwar winning Indy cars until about 1970. These systems are still used in racing because they're relatively inexpensive, at roughly $3,000, and easy to install. An Indy car EFI system costs roughly $15,000.

A critical thing to understand about fueling an engine is that peak torque occurs at the rpm at which an engine is achieving its best volumetric

Electromotive offers direct fire injection via coil-modules mounted on the ECU in the TEC II system. The TEC system is built rugged enough to withstand mounting in the engine compartment; clearly high voltage radio energy in close proximity doesn't bother its operation.

efficiency (cylinder air-filling). Engines may make more horsepower at speeds exceeding this, but only because they are making more power pulses per unit of time; the cylinders are not filling as well, and therefore, the fuel flow as a function of rpm no longer increases as steeply (the "elbow" in the curve occurs at peak VE).

The problem with constant-flow mechanical injection systems is that the mechanical fuel pump, driven by the engine, increases in speed with the engine. Assuming there's a linear increase in fuel pumped with pump speed, that is, the amount of fuel pumped doubles as pump speed doubles, the engine will begin to run rich as rpm increases beyond peak torque and fuel flow continues to increase at a constant rate while air-flow into the engine increases more slowly as VE decreases.

Hilborn systems used multiple fuel by-pass systems to alter the shape of the fuel curve by returning excess fuel to the fuel tank. The main by-pass contained a restrictor (a jet—sometimes also referred to as a "pill"). A secondary by-pass returned fuel based on throttle position, through a barrel valve, which served to send varying amounts of fuel to the injectors based on slits or orifices progressively uncovered in the barrel valve as throttle position changed. A high-speed by-pass used an adjustable-diaphragm regulator to prevent excessive richness at higher rpm when fuel requirements began to level off. It is easy to understand how changing jets and adjusting regulators would mechanically alter fuel delivered by a mechanical injection system.

Altering the look-up tables, which affect a computer software's functionality in a programmable aftermarket EFI system, requires at the very least the ability to understand the basic principles of fueling and of operating the graphical interface on a PC or interface module connected to the ECU.

To reprogram the operation of many OEM ECUs—specifically designed to discourage tampering and to protect proprietary logic from easily falling into the hands of competitors—requires enormous skills. Among them is the ability to use complex electronic debugging tools like a microprocessor emulator which connects into the ECU circuitry. Also required are the skills to *deduce* how undocumented proprietary data structures might be organized, and how they affect computer operations in controlling fueling and everything else in a late-model car from ignition advance to emissions control devices, turbo wastegates, cooling fans, torque converter lockups, and other factors affecting engine power, economy, and exhaust emissions.

This sort of reverse engineering is complex and requires bright, experienced electrical engineers and microprogrammers. Once the existing OE ECU operation is understood, the engineer has to determine the impact of making changes to the internal data tables, based on theory and, ultimately, trial and error. This is the sort of thing an aftermarket performance chip designer may have to go through. Of course, it is easier if you can hire a former employee of the OEM, or somehow obtain access to the OEM ECU documentation (this is called industrial espionage).

The builder of an aftermarket ECU has a task that is at once simpler and more complex than reverse engineering and reprogramming an OE ECU. He or she doesn't have the hassle of reverse engineering an existing ECU, but must design a complex system from scratch. The amount of fuel squirting out of an actuator (electronic injector) is determined by the opening time, which is determined by the length of time (referred to as injection pulse width) electricity is supplied to the actuator's solenoid electromagnet under control of the computer.

Under unusual circumstances, fuel delivered by the injector is affected by the fuel pressure supplied to the injector, but this is usually held *constant* in relation to the air pressure of the manifold into which the fuel is being injected. The computer must vary pulse width in response to engine status—speed, temperature, and loading, throttle position, air density and temperature,

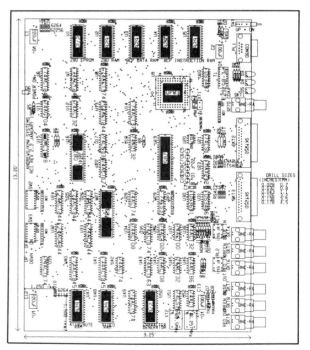

Computers and PROMs. This is a printed circuit board plot from JRL Systems. Modern ECUs usually contain one PC board containing a microprocessor and a selection of memory and logic "chips."

and exhaust gas oxygen content—which it determines in a fraction of a second via sensors.

Modern sensors use mechanical force or energy to change the resistance of some media to a flow of electricity. Therefore, the electrical output or flow through the sensor varies continuously in response to some physical phenomena, such as air pressure. Analog-to-digital circuitry (these days, usually embedded in tiny microprocessors) converts this voltage to discrete binary numbers that a computer can use in calculations. The computer is programmed to understand the characteristics of a particular sensor.

Fuel injection computers execute logical routines over and over in an endless loop when the engine is operating. The computer is: sampling engine sensors (input and status calculation),

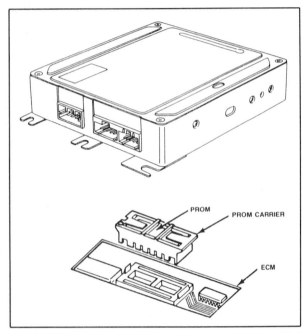

The Electronic Control Unit (ECU), sometimes called ECM (Engine Control Module), or EEC (Electronic Engine Control), is a special purpose computer which can control engine fueling or ignition spark timing. It determines the current engine state via sensors, determines a strategy (action), initiates the next event via actuators (such as injectors), and then determines the new state of the engine, in an endless loop. Some ECUs are user-programmable via some kind of user interface like a laptop personal computer (PC), while others can only be reprogrammed by changing the Programmable Read-Only Memory (PROM), which contains data tables that affect the operation of the ECU's internal logic. A newer strategy for re-directing engine management operations is to use a second computer or "black box" to intercept sensor or actuator data from the main ECU, and to change it. Some black boxes do not interfere with the operation of the ECU, but add fuel independently via separate injectors.

computing injector pulse width and other actuator events (output calculation), directing the operation of the actuator (output to actuators), and beginning again, all the while evaluating what may have changed via new sensor data, recomputing pulse width, and so on—endlessly.

There are many interrelated variables affecting engine operation. The ECU's control logic cannot anticipate every actual running condition with infinite granularity. ECUs frequently fail in their goal to achieve perfection in engine operation. Perhaps a sensor is malfunctioning, or something very subtle is going on in the engine which cannot be detected by existing sensors. Perhaps the control logic is not complex enough (smart enough) to anticipate every possible contingency. Perhaps there is a "bug" (mistake) in the system hardware or microcode.

Perhaps the computer's actuators or sensors cannot react quickly enough. Perhaps, the computer itself is slow enough that it views the engine status in "snapshots" rather than viewing it constantly in "real time." In such a case, the computer, sensors, and actuators are too slow to keep up with changing conditions in the engine so by the time the system can react and produce a fuel injection management event, conditions have changed so much that now the system is forced to overreact in a different direction.

We've all seen an engine "hunting." Future ECUs will have the speed required to consider the state of all engine sensors in real time. This, coupled with fast sensors and fast engine actuators, would eliminate hunting problems by allowing the system to treat the engine as if it were standing still (this is approached but not achieved by current equipment). It would also reevaluate conditions and make corrections much faster than conditions could change.

ECU builders design their systems around a microprocessor. Electronic circuits, and especially the microscopic circuits in the microprocessor, are sensitive to heat, which can cause them to fail. The faster the circuitry, the more sensitive it is to heat, which must be dissipated in order to keep circuitry running right. Emitter-coupled-logic and other fast microcircuitry build up a lot of heat. The problem is made worse when microprocessor logic is so fast that a few extra inches of distance, even at the speed of light, will slow things down too much. In this case, circuitry must be packed together more densely. Most large, high-speed computers have been designed to operate at about 68 degrees Fahrenheit—plus or minus a few degrees! In the past, many large computers have been water-cooled or even freon-cooled, unlike the Macintosh PC used to word-process this book, which is air-cooled and designed to operate at around room temperature, and is fine anywhere between about 50 and 90 degrees.

Consider the harsh environment of an automobile engine. The engine compartment may easily heat up to several hundred degrees on a hot day when the engine is working hard. Even the passenger compartment can heat up to temperatures approaching 150 degrees Fahrenheit or more with the windows shut on a hot, sunny day.

In the wintertime, the temperature might be well below zero when the engine first starts. Vibration may be extreme, and the system is subject to high humidity and possibly dust. Thus, the microprocessor controlling the engine must be *very* rugged. Military electronic equipment (which must be shielded against a possible nuclear electromagnetic pulse that would immediately render inoperative all vehicles with ordinary ECUs), farm tractors, and offshore boats constitute an even harsher environment than the ordinary car. This is why the Intel 80X86 and Motorola 680X0 chips used in personal computers aren't practical for ECUs. They're not sturdy enough.

ECUs have used rugged microprocessors that run at relatively slow clock speeds to minimize logic errors due to heat failure and processor errors due to speeds that vary with temperature changes. Although fast microprocessors can perform many millions of instructions per second (MIPS), automotive-type microprocessors generally work at slower speeds. Consequently, some ECUs are approaching their limit in handling sequential injection (with a granularity of a few ten thousandths of a second) plus ten or fifteen other engine actuators and sensors on an engine that can rev to 10,000 plus rpm—like a motorcycle or Indy car.

The Ford EEC-IV, using a proprietary special-purpose microprocessor, is designed specifically for automotive use and considered by many experts to be one of the best original equipment ECUs (Ford calls it an electronic control *module*). The EEC-IV is built for Ford by Intel, the same company that makes most of the chips for DOS-type PCs. The EEC-IV microprocessor operates at a frequency of 15–18 megahertz and is capable of operating at "pretty close to real time" speed, evaluating the engine in a feedback loop that takes 15-40 milliseconds. This ECU is used in all Ford cars, running various subsets of engine management software and 15k–56k memory, depending on the complexity of the engine.

In order for the microprocessor to manage engine control devices, the ECU must contain circuits called latches (something like relays), which respond to a control signal from the microprocessor by turning on, for example, a 12 volt signal with a square wave format, to activate injector drivers. Other circuits convert the constantly varying analog voltage signals from sensors to

digital format for the microprocessor. Today, these A-D converters are usually integrated circuits, and may in fact be built into the microprocessor itself (as on the Ford EEC-IV ECU, which uses a ten-bit A-D converter on the microprocessor chip). The microprocessor contains multiple I/O "channels" which enable digital data—perhaps from an A-D converter—to be stored directly in the microprocessor's memory.

Injector drivers like the Motorola MC3484 can produce 4 amps of current in less than a millisecond (thousandth of a second) to bang open an injector quickly *(peak)*. In 200 microseconds (millionths of a second) the driver then drops the current back to 1 amp to *hold* the injector open. Peak and hold drivers take advantage of the fact that it takes much less current to hold open an injector once the solenoid is initially energized. They don't require as much power as drivers that hold at full voltage, yet open the injectors very fast. The MC3484 uses five leads: for power in, power out, ground, trigger, and reference voltage. Anytime voltage in the trigger exceeds the reference, the

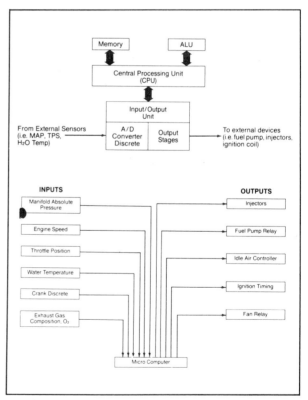

ECU computer system schematics. All sensor data undergoes analogue to digital conversion before presentation to the input-output system of the ECU and transfer into the CPU. Digital data from the CPU must be converted to analogue form in order to control actuators. Sensors provide input while actuators handle outputs.

driver will immediately route voltage from power in to power out, which can be used to fire an injector.

A running ECU is endlessly executing its way through a loop of software "code" to sample sensors, evaluate their status, make output calculations, and activate control devices. If-then-else branching causes the microprocessor to execute various section codes in the loop, by-passing others, depending on conditions.

Data affecting microprocessor operation comes from internal look-up tables (fuel maps, VE tables, and so forth) and sensors. Various sensing strategies are used to evaluate engine airflow, which impacts the internal ECU data structures. Most aftermarket ECUs are speed-density systems which deduce the number of air molecules entering the engine (and, hence, fuel requirements) from engine speed and manifold pressure—or by using speed and pressure and temperature as indexes into look-up raw fueling tables. The Air Sensors ECU, the first aftermarket unit, directly measured air mass via an airflow meter, and could calculate fuel requirements based on this by consulting VE tables. A few ECUs like the Haltech F7, the Holley Pro-Jection, and certain racing versions of the EFI Technology and the Zytek systems deduce air entering the engine by speed and *throttle position.*

Virtually all OEM ECUs and some aftermarket units have the ability to operate in closed-loop mode, which means they can factor in the actual air-fuel mixture achieved in the last injection event, as measured by an exhaust gas oxygen sensor, to influence pulse width in future injection events (necessary to meet emissions requirements). Some ECUs modify their base fuel data tables as they learn what is working in a particular engine (perhaps with a particular driver!), and as injectors and other parts age or wear out (disconnecting the battery may erase this learned behavior).

Volumetric Efficiency Enrichment

A fuel injection computer's PROM is loaded during the initial setup or configuration with a table of numbers that correspond to the engine's volumetric efficiency (VE) over the entire operating range. This table might be modified when the ECU is tuned so old data is lost and the changes are permanently available for future operations. In some cases, the original values are maintained in the table, but a separate table of modifications is built.

Each VE value is directly utilized by the microcomputer as an amount of fuel enrichment or enleanment required at a certain combination of rpm and engine loading. There are, of course, theoretically an infinite number of such values; in reality, the VE table might contain from several dozen to several hundred values logically arranged in rows and columns corresponding to rpm and engine loading. These values may indirectly be entered into the microcomputer's PROM by literally typing them into a PC on-line to the fuel injection ECU. The PC may save you the trouble of physically entering *all* the data, by allowing you to enter a few values and then estimating other values in between (as in the Haltech Version 4.0 Programmer "Fill" feature)—as a person might use a ruler to draw a continuous line through several points.

In many cases, engineers or inventors configure one set of data for a certain car's PROM, and simply duplicate the data over and over for other vehicles of the same type. This data is often referred to as an engine "map." If you have a common sort of hot rod engine, you'll probably find maps for your engine already available from the fuel injection manufacturer. For the hot rodder designing his or her own unique engine configuration, it is possible to modify fuel injection engine maps by laptop PC while the engine is *running,* enabling you to see immediate changes in the way the engine performs in response to the map changes. Factory fuel injection systems (not designed to be easily user-programmable) require a device called an emulator for on-line changes. An emulator plugs into the PROM socket of the OEM injection microcomputer and contains a socket to accept the stock PROM. The emulator enables an operator to interactively modify PROM data, instantaneously testing the effect of changes.

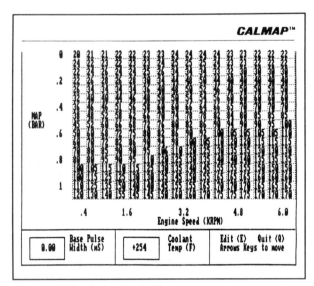

Accel/DFI's Base Fuel Map matrix corresponds to engine volumetric efficiency (VE) for each engine speed and loading "breakpoint."

Let's take a slightly harder look at what is going on behind the scenes with the VE table section of a fuel injection microcomputer's map.

The stoichiometric air-fuel ratio of 14.7lb of air to 1lb of gasoline is theoretically ideal for combustion. Under the right conditions, this mixture will burn to release all chemical energy stored in the fuel, leaving no unused oxygen and no unburned hydrocarbons. Theoretically and under ideal conditions, stoichiometric combustion produces energy, carbon dioxide, and water vapor, all nonpolluting and harmless. This naturally assumes factors like enough *time* for combustion to finish completely, perfectly mixed air and fuel, and so on.

But what if our goal is to produce maximum fuel efficiency, especially at part throttle? In the real world of fires burning at high speeds among the swirling mass of air and fuel atoms in the combustion chamber of an engine, it is easy to miss a few atoms of fuel or oxygen here and there—particularly when throttle position and engine speed are changing rapidly and the air and fuel will *not* be perfectly mixed.

If the goal is maximum *power output* from an engine, you want to be sure there is enough fuel present in the air-fuel mixture so *every molecule of oxygen* that has managed to be drawn into a cylinder gets used in combustion. In this case, you should enrich the mixture with extra fuel to shorten the odds that you don't miss using any of the oxygen. (It's a little like inviting extra girls to a dance to improve the odds that every boy will find a partner!)

In the same way, if you're trying for maximum *efficiency,* you definitely don't want to waste any unburned fuel by blowing it out the exhaust. So to make sure every molecule of fuel gets burned, you'd like to lean out the mixture (increase the ratio of oxygen to fuel) to improve the likelihood of making use of every last fuel molecule (like inviting extra boys to the dance).

There is a logical correspondence between volumetric efficiency and enrichment. The engine operates at a higher volumetric efficiency (cylinders fill more completely) when working harder (wide-open throttle), which is exactly when you want *best power*. At part throttle and lower speeds, the engine operates at a lower volumetric efficiency—just when you'd like *best economy*.

It is a simple matter to construct a microcomputer-based table of volumetric efficiencies (VE) at various engine rpm and loading values. The microcomputer reads rpm and engine loading from its sensors and uses them to index into the VE table whose values correspond exactly to enrichments or enleanments required at a certain rpm and engine load. When the engine is operating at rpm or load points that fall in between set points in the VE table, the computer is able to locate the closest VE table values and use geometric formulas (linear interpolation) to estimate exact VE and, therefore, mixture adjustment required. The VE table values can be exaggerated at the extremes to produce extra richness or leanness.

A carburetor approximates this sort of VE-based air-fuel adjustment by sizing the main jet to regulate fuel delivery to the venturi. Air corrector jets and emulsion tubes of precise size are selected to progressively dilute the main-jet fuel stream with air. (Otherwise, fuel flow would increase faster than airflow as engine speed and loading increase.)

A "power valve" in the carburetor opens under high manifold pressure (high VE) to allow additional fuel to by-pass the main jet and flow to the venturi. As you can imagine, these physical correction systems in a carb are a blunt instrument compared to the precision of a fuel injection computer.

Choking Enrichment

The microcomputer's PROM-based fuel tables also contain a second table of "choking" values that correspond to *special enrichments* required when a driver starts a cold engine under conditions in which fuel would not vaporize completely (anytime the engine is not at full operating temperature). These choking values are subdivided into cold-start enrichments, after-start enrichments, and warmup enrichments. The computer adds this enrichment to normal injection pulse width.

Carburetors provide cold-start enrichment utilizing a choke plate located above the venturi

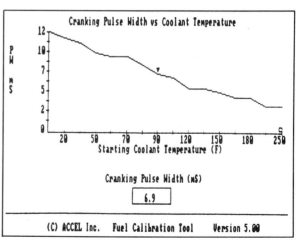

Some programmable ECU offer several different enrichment parameters for cold running operation. Accel/DFI's ECU provides cranking enrichment based on coolant temperature.

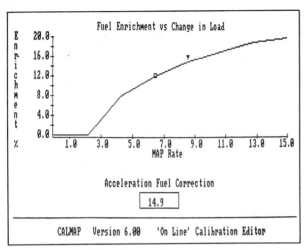

Accel/DFI's EFI has the sophistication to allow acceleration enrichment based on manifold pressure changes in addition to throttle position changes. This is particularly useful on multiple throttle body systems in which tiny throttle angle changes can provide large changes in air flow and where conventional acceleration enrichment based on throttle position may be insufficient.

like a second throttle, designed to physically restrict airflow through the carb. Cold air activates this choking action based on its effect on a bimetallic spring (thermostat) connected to the choke plate. The closed choke plate increases vacuum in the area of the venturi to create *additional* pressure differential there compared to atmospheric—thereby forcing additional fuel out of the float chamber and into the inlet air stream at the venturi (producing a vastly enriched air-fuel mixture).

Acceleration Enrichment

A third table in the microcomputer PROM contains, in the first dimension, values corresponding to enrichment required on *acceleration*. A second dimension of enrichment values in this table indicates specified rates of decay in enrichment after the throttle plate is no longer turning. This enrichment prevents a "flat spot" on sudden acceleration. Most carburetors provide transient enrichment with a diaphragm pump activated by the throttle shaft, which squirts raw fuel directly into the throat(s) of the carburetor.

Enrichment values stored in tables in PROM, therefore, include choke enrichments, acceleration enrichments, and volumetric efficiency enrichments (and enleanments). These values together represent a fueling map for a certain engine. Density enrichments or enleanments for air temperature and altitude (not needed in MAF sensor systems like SPIF), and exhaust gas oxygen sensor enrichment and enleanment values originate in the electronic *sensors*, not in tables.

(However, the ECU may contain translation tables for these.) The microcomputer sums all enrichment values to arrive at a total enrichment for the current fuel injection event which is represented by "G" (for the Greek letter *Gamma*).

The total enrichment (or enleanment) is an offset from the theoretical (stoichiometric) air-fuel ratio based directly on air mass.

Equations (don't panic!)

The representative (based on Electromotive system documentation) basic equation that the microcomputer solves to compute injection pulse width is as follows:

$$PW = G * MAP * FIC$$

(Note: In equations, I use the FORTRAN asterisk (*) for multiplication, and the solidus or slash (/) for division.)

Pulse width is obtained by modifying the MAP sensor value (air mass) by the enrichment value G, and modifying the result by a fuel injection constant (FIC)—a "fudge-factor" which converts the equation to actual pulse width based on engine size and injector flow rate. FIC values range from 20 to 100 percent (0.2–1.0).

This is a slightly simplistic view of things.

In reality, the microcomputer actually *corrects* MAP values to *mass* airflow by multiplying the MAP value by K/(R * T) in which T is temperature in degrees absolute and R is the universal gas law constant.

Of course, on MAF systems, like SPIF, this is unnecessary since the MAF value is already mass airflow. The computer always adjusts pulse width to include injector turn-on time (ITO) and change in ITO due to changes in the system battery voltage (BTO) by directly summing ITO and BTO into pulse width. Since the dynamic range of an injector is limited on the low end by the minimum time it can reliably turn on before injector spray becomes inaccurate, and on the high end by the maximum time available for injection (limited by the time of crankshaft rotation at high rpm), in engines with a very high speed range, pulse width may require "scaling" to prevent digital computer resolution problems (rounding error) from adversely affecting injection times. This scaling factor, TOG (time for one gamma) makes certain very fine enrichment values are not lost.

Therefore, the complete pulse width equation is:

$$PW = (MAP * (K/(R * T)) * G * FIC * TOG) + ITO + BTO$$

Whew!

PROMS

Programmable Read-Only Memory (PROM) and Electrically Erasable Programmable Read-Only Memory (EEPROM) are used to store data and instructions for use by a computer's central processing unit. All microcomputers without a disc drive must have PROM or EEPROM to store the instructions and data they need to begin doing work on power-up. This includes all ECUs running fuel injection systems.

Typically, the ECU is configured with the code (machine instructions that are executed over and over again when the engine is running) and certain data tables already stored in PROM. The code routines make use of this data in calculations. Clever software routines can be designed to be very data dependent in their operation. Sections of code will be executed only conditionally, on the basis of *data* values. In the case of aftermarket EFI computers, there is usually some interface method that can be used to get additional data into the EEPROM look-up tables, often from a laptop DOS computer, or perhaps a special keypad/display that is bundled with the ECU. This lets the user customize the system's data to the engine's individual configuration.

Software routines will use certain data for EFI calibration computations, and treat other data as switches. Based on the value of a certain byte or bit of data, code may or may not be executed to handle, for example, computation of additional fuel enrichment for nitrous injection. ECUs are very data dependent, that is, they will behave differently depending on the data in their PROM or EEPROM.

When General Motors designed their Tuned Port Injection, they were kind enough to design the PROM so that it could be easily changed. GM PROMs plug into a socket that is accessible without even violating the ECU's enclosure. Ford's EEC-IV uses a PROM that is soldered in place, and therefore not easily replaceable; however, the ECU includes a multi-pin diagnostic plug which can be used to load code and data in place of the onboard PROM.

Some aftermarket entrepreneurs have designed small modules with replacement PROM chips that plug into the EEC-IV diagnostic port and supersede the onboard EEC-IV PROM or modules that connect inline between the EEC-IV and the stock EFI wiring harness connector.

OEM fuel injection system PROMs are often set up from the factory in a way that causes them to behave very conservatively. They are designed to be foolproof and to keep negligent or ignorant operators from hurting their engines with poor driving methods, poor quality gasoline, and poor preventive maintenance. Take the case, however, of a knowledgeable operator who is willing to take more care, willing to operate a little closer to the edge, use good gas, avoid lugging the engine, willing to suffer degraded gas mileage and/or emissions. This owner will discover it's often possible

TPIS Proms

Tuned Port Induction Specialties (TPIS) in Chaska, Minnesota, sells replacement high-performance PROM chips for GM vehicles with the 5.0 and 5.7 liter V-8s. The TPIS staff says it is very important to develop a PROM for each *gear ratio* (with the exception of the 2.59 and 2.73 ratios, which will work with the same PROM).

TPIS points out that accelerating a car in low gear (a high rate of acceleration) requires different ignition and fueling than accelerating in a higher gear (a low rate of acceleration). TPIS claims that its PROMs improve throttle response at all rpm levels.

The TPIS staff finds that computer-controlled cars are not all created equal: about one in twenty cars is very fast, while three in twenty are very slow, and may be difficult to work with. TPIS bases its test results on average cars (sixteen out of twenty).

to make more power available via a higher state of tune than stock—which can be arranged by substituting a PROM with revised data. The ECU code is designed to take into account many different individual (and data-dependent) characteristics of engine management. If the operator has made major changes to engine internals, it is *mandatory* to change the PROM data so that the injection system will operate properly.

It is essential to understand the envelope of a specific set of tuning parameters for a computer-controlled car. Factory EFI cars are designed with states of tuning that provide some built-in flexibility for the *actual* volumetric efficiency of an

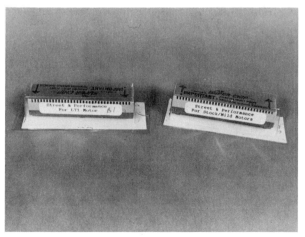

Street and Performance offers multiple PROMs for various sizes of GM engines and to serve various performance levels of the engines.

individual engine. Minor changes to the VE, perhaps a low-restriction air filter, will probably work OK, particularly with a MAF-based EFI system, since the computer has some ability to compensate for slight VE changes. But an *aftermarket* PROM may be operating very close to the edge, and a change in VE or other engine characteristics may cause it to operate badly.

You, the operator, without access to system documentation, have no idea what the envelope looks like, and where the system's flexibility ends. Thus it is essential to consult with the people who know, such as factory experts at the Ford Motorsport Hotline, or aftermarket wizards who have reverse engineered or otherwise acquired internal system knowledge and have tested modified parts and PROMs on dynos and on the street. The whole package must work together; you may end up worse off than how you started if you tamper in any way with a factory EFI vehicle, either in PROM changes or in engine changes.

Many aftermarket entrepreneurs offer packages of replacement PROMs and parts that are designed to work well together on a specific car. An increasing number are approved for legal use on the street, which is nice, considering that all parties concerned—from manufacturer to jobber to user—are potentially liable for any vehicular tampering that might affect emissions.

"Our first-level package is the easiest to get started with," said a representative of Tuned Port Induction Specialties (TPIS) in Chaska, Minnesota, "because it involves inexpensive parts and simple techniques. But if you're looking for more muscle, check out Levels II, III, or IV. And when you're ready to blow the doors off everybody in town, look into Level V, which is completely customized to *your individual car.*"

Aftermarket PROMS like those from TPIS offer a higher state of tune for stock vehicles, or appropriate fuel and ignition curves for modified vehicles. In many cases, it is possible to upgrade to a different PROM as a user makes additional modifications to an engine—for a small upgrade fee. Most of the companies selling PROMs offer phone consultation to users to help them get the correct combination of parts and PROM.

Typically, a first-stage PROM might work well with a low-restriction air filter, a low-temperature thermostat, a throttle-body air foil, removing MAF screens, and modifying the air filter housing. A 20hp gain is possible with these modifications, according to TPIS, translating to a 0.6 second faster quarter mile with 2 miles per hour (mph) faster top end.

It is very important to use a new PROM with lower temperature thermostats, since the ECU may otherwise assume that the car is still warming up, and keep warmup enrichment activated.

(Like having a choke on all the time, it wastes fuel, cuts power, and wears out the cylinders fast from wetting down the cylinder walls.)

Typically, Stage One PROMs affect wide-open throttle, advancing the timing and improving the mixture (which, in cars like the 5.0 liter Mustang, involves *leaning* the mixture that is too rich with factory fuel curves). Stock engine management tuning is very conservative (read, safe) and results in fewer warranty claims. Engineers may choose an overly rich wide-open-throttle fuel map in order to protect the engine from knocking and thermal stress, and to guard against aging fuel pumps and injectors eventually producing dangerously lean conditions. In addition to retuning fuel and ignition curves, a replacement PROM chip may also change the circumstances under which torque converters lock up, eliminating jerkiness in shifting into or out of high gear.

With a few more minor pieces and a Stage Two PROM, power gains can become as much as 45hp, cutting off a second in the quarter mile.

A third level might involve low-restriction exhaust (headers, free-flow mufflers, and possibly removal of the catalyst for off-road use), additional MAF modifications, and yet another PROM change.

The next level improves the breathing with intake porting, larger TPI runners, higher lift rockers, and a new PROM, yielding an extra 100hp, knocking 2 seconds off a quarter-mile run. Driveability is still excellent, with across-the-board performance improvements at all rpm levels.

A Stage Five package might add ported heads, a hotter cam, and an appropriate PROM, resulting in 130hp over the stock 305 or 350ci Chevy TPI motor, with quarter times in the low 12s and 112.5mph in a Corvette. These sorts of modifications will work well with 383 or 406ci Chevy small-block motors, which need the improved breathing and fuel.

TPIS says its demonstrator Corvette gets almost 23 miles per gallon (mpg) at speeds as high as 80–100mph, yet turns 12.1 seconds at 112.5mph in the quarter with a stock displacement 350 motor.

With a new PROM or module in place, it is essential to treat the vehicle like the more highly tuned beast that it has become, listening for knock and giving the vehicle excellent maintenance. It is also essential to check with the manufacturer before assuming that any replacement chip will work with a different engine-vehicle combination (such as an HO Camaro chip in an LG4 or stand 305 engine). And it is essential to know what type engine you have, which sometimes requires checking the Vehicle Identification Number (VIN) that contains a code indicating the engine installed at the factory. If engine changes have been made, check with the PROM manufacturer, and have all internal and external engine documentation available.

PROM Installation

PROMs can be installed in less than thirty minutes using a small flathead screwdriver, a Phillips head screwdriver, a 1/4in socket, and sometimes 7mm and 10mm sockets.

Locate the electronic control module (ECM) and remove the mounting screws for easier access, and pull out the ECM. GM computers have a small cover that allows access to the PROM. Remove it and *gently* unplug the stock PROM from its socket. (It is very easy to bend or break the multiple prongs, especially without a PROM puller tool.) Plug in the new PROM and reinstall the cover plate. Now go have fun!

In the case of Ford vehicles, you can add a power module from companies like Hypertech that plugs into the diagnostic port on the EEC-IV computer, superseding the stock chip, which stays in place. This procedure requires the same tools as a GM PROM change, plus maybe a 9mm or 10mm Torx bit. Locate and dismount the ECM. Remove the service port cover and side screw from the computer (this is on the end of the computer with the warranty label). The power module plugs into the end of the ECM, and includes longer screws which hold it in place using the side screw holes. Reinstall the computer in its place, and go have fun.

Multiple PROMs

An ECU gathers data from engine sensors and makes engine management decisions many times per second. The computer is controlling spark timing, air-fuel mixtures, converter lockup, emissions device controls, and so on. Changing PROMs can be very effective in changing the computer's behavior for modified and special-purpose vehicles. However, changing the parameters used by the ECU to control the engine involves tradeoffs.

PROM "burners" use ultraviolet light to program computer PROMs, after which their data cannot be changed electronically, but must be re-blown in the PROM burner.

Improving the vehicle's performance under some circumstances may make it worse in others. The ECU will not have the ability to know when you want maximum power no matter how bad the fuel economy degradation—and when you want maximum economy—or when you are running racing fuel versus low-octane fuel, or when you are pulling a heavy trailer on a hot day versus a lighter load, or possibly even when you are at high versus low altitude.

To eliminate these tradeoffs, it is now possible to install devices that permit instantaneous switching between multiple PROMs, each optimized for certain conditions. PROM switching can be controlled manually, or according to throttle position, manifold pressure, turbo boost, temperature, rpm, altitude, or anything that can be converted to a voltage.

Multi-PROM switching units are designed to switch instantly "without a stammer," according to testing by Ken Dutweiler, as reported in *Turbo* magazine.

Chapter 5

Sensors

An engine management computer makes decisions about fuel injection and ignition events based on data. The data may exist as tables of numbers in memory, such as a "chart" of volumetric efficiencies for a specific engine. This data doesn't change except when someone reprograms the ECU.

Data may also exist in memory in the form of numbers or values that are more or less constantly being refreshed according to the status of various engine sensors. Sensors assign an electric voltage to external events such as the cylinder head temperature. This voltage is converted from an analog physical magnitude to a discrete digital number by A–D circuitry (usually onboard the microprocessor) and made available in Random Access Memory (RAM) for processing, exactly like the table data already discussed. This data heavily impacts which software instructions are exe-

cuted by the microprocessor and the results of the instructions that are executed.

Let's take a look at sensor operation and the effect on engine management. Sensors are the "eyes and ears" of the computer.

There are several sensors used for engine management. They include the exhaust gas oxygen sensor or Titania oxygen sensor, coolant temperature sensor, air temperature sensor, manifold absolute pressure (MAP) sensor, mass airflow (MAF) sensor, throttle position sensor, and barometric pressure sensor.

Exhaust Gas Oxygen Sensor

The exhaust gas oxygen sensor (also called Lambda or EGO or O_2 sensor) is godlike to modern factory fuel injection systems. That's because its data enables the electronic control unit (ECU) to constantly tune the engine on-the-fly in a feedback or closed-loop mode. In this mode, it can instantly evaluate the effect of changes to engine operating parameters and make corrections—resulting in improved emissions and fuel economy. The O_2 sensor operation is so important that some technicians routinely replace the sensor before doing any further tuning. It's not that expensive, and O_2 sensor problems can be confusing and waste a lot of time.

The computer leans the mixture when a lack of oxygen indicates a rich mixture, and enriches the mixture when a relative presence of oxygen indicates a lean mixture. The oxygen sensor could actually be considered an "air battery." In the lead-acid battery used to start a car, an acid medium induces a current flow between two dissimilar metals, freeing energy stored in the acid. The chemical composition of the medium changes as the battery discharges, affecting the output or voltage of the battery. One could therefore deduce the chemical composition of the acid (state of charge) based on the battery's output voltage.

The zirconium dioxide element in the tip of

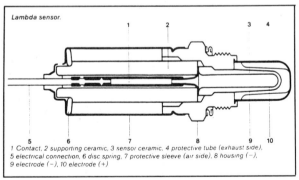

Lambda sensor.

1 Contact, 2 supporting ceramic, 3 sensor ceramic, 4 protective tube (exhaust side), 5 electrical connection, 6 disc spring, 7 protective sleeve (air side), 8 housing (−), 9 electrode (−), 10 electrode (+)

Exhaust Gas Oxygen (EGO) sensors, also called O_2 sensors or oxygen sensors, should be installed in the exhaust manifold where they measure a mixture of exhaust gas from various cylinders. The location should maintain the sensor at a minimum of 200 degrees Celsius. In cases where the sensor must be mounted at a colder location, such as long tube header engines or far downstream of turbochargers, electrically-heated sensors may be required. Bosch

the O_2 sensor similarly produces an electric voltage that varies according to the *difference* in oxygen content between the atmosphere and the exhaust gases. In a lean mixture, there is a surplus of oxygen (not enough fuel for all oxygen molecules to participate in combustion). The opposite is true in a rich mixture. The higher the concentration of unburned oxygen, the less differential there is in the zirconium element of the sensor, and the lower the voltage output of the sensor.

The sensor's output varies continuously from a lean value of 0.1volt to a rich value of 0.9 volt. The "perfect" 14.7 stoichiometric air-fuel mixture produces a sensor voltage of 0.5volt. By design, the sensor bounces from rich to lean every few seconds, but an average of 0.5volt indicates a correct stoichiometric mixture.

Bosch and others have developed extended-range O_2 sensors for closed-loop operation at wide-open throttle. The problem with wide-range sensors is that as the mixture moves farther away from stoichiometric, subtle changes in exhaust gas oxygen content occur very quickly in the rich direction; there is little or no oxygen in the exhaust. Beyond this, additional richness adds more unburned fuel to the exhaust gases, hardly affecting the oxygen content. Existing air-fuel mixture diagnostic equipment makes use of very expensive EGO or UEGO (Universal Exhaust Gas Oxygen) sensors, which offer very fast operation over a wide range of mixtures; the problem for production use in cars has been the expense.

There are a number of drawbacks with the oxygen sensor. It will not function until its temperature reaches 600 degrees Fahrenheit–which means it won't work immediately on startup when the engine is producing the most pollution. Some oxygen sensors contain heating elements to help the sensor reach operating temperature sooner and to keep the sensor from cooling off too much at idle.

Tetraethyl lead will rapidly kill a conventional platinum and ceramic O_2 sensor, but Lucas Industries, Bosch, and others have recently introduced sensors resistant to lead contamination, for racing use. According to Sutton Engineering, special Bosch oxygen sensors for European use with leaded fuel can tolerate up to 0.4gram of lead per liter, which is a lot.

Oxygen sensors can also become clogged with carbon or fail prematurely due to solvents from some RTV silicone sealing compounds.

An oxygen sensor normally lasts 30,000–50,000 miles. As it ages, driveability problems can result from the sensor losing its ability to react quickly to changes in exhaust gas oxygen, resulting in improper mixtures producing loss of

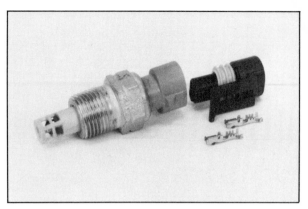

A typical temperature sensor. Temperatures increase the resistance in the sensor to electrical flow. Electronic circuitry relays this value to the CPU, which has internal tables relating coolant and air inlet temperature to full enrichment requirements. MSD

power, rough idle, bad gas mileage, and high emissions.

The computer's ability to correctly deduce air-fuel ratios from exhaust gas oxygen can be adversely affected by air leaks in the inlet or exhaust manifold, by malfunctioning injector(s), or even a misfiring spark plug. One or two cylinders misfiring or running significantly leaner or richer than the rest can fool the O_2 sensor and computer about overall air-fuel ratio, causing the computer to make wrong closed-loop adjustments.

Oxygen sensors produce a "sawtooth" voltage which can be useful to the ECU in the one to two millisecond time range with clever computer algorithms; however, as the ECU makes injection pulse width corrections, the pulse width and actual air-fuel mixture tend to hunt, varying around the stoichiometric mixture in a wave pattern.

The computer believes the oxygen sensor before any other sensor. The ECU is constantly making judgments about the accuracy of various sensors, and actually builds a correction table (of K-factors) for each sensor in memory. When the battery is disconnected, the K-factors are reset and reevaluated as the engine runs. This correction table enables the system to function reasonably well in spite of aging equipment and manufacturing tolerances. When racers attempt to tamper with sensor data in order to "defeat" performance limitations of the EFI system, the computer will work against them in correcting suspect sensor data in order to bring the system back to EPA-legal calibration.

Titania Oxygen Sensor

Some late-model vehicles use oxygen sensors with a titania element. These sensors operate effectively at lower temperatures and not referenced to outside air, as is the case with zirconium sensors, so there are no atmospheric vents to become blocked. Due to the lower operating temperatures, titania oxygen sensors warm up in as little as fifteen seconds, allowing the system to begin closed-loop (feedback) operation almost immediately. They don't cool below operating temperature at idle, and can be located further downstream from the engine or used with turbochargers, which bleed off a lot of heat from the exhaust gases.

Titania sensors do not generate a voltage like zirconium sensors; rather, they change resistance dramatically as the mixture changes from rich to lean. The change is not gradual. The sensor changes from low resistance of less than 1,000ohms when the mixture is rich, to high resistance of over 20,000ohms when the mixture goes lean. Therefore, the ECU supplies a 1volt reference signal which passes through the titania sensor and is then evaluated by the ECU. The effect of the sensor is such that at rich mixture (and low resistance), the computer reads back a voltage of nearly 1volt; as the resistance dramatically increases with the change to lean mixture, the voltage switches suddenly to 0.1volt. This type of sensor is therefore binary: the sensor tells the ECU that the mixture is either too rich or too lean—and not by how much.

However, a clever ECU can make educated guesses as to actual mixture based on pulse width changes required to flip rich or flip lean. But the titania sensor is obviously not as well suited to closed-loop operation at non-stoichiometric mixtures (such as wide-open throttle in turbocharged vehicles when 14.7 may be too lean).

Coolant Temperature Sensor

The coolant temperature sensor is used by the ECU to deduce engine operating temperature and therefore the applicability of cold-operation enrichment.

Engine temperature may also determine the following: when the computer will enter closed-loop operation (not while the engine is cold, but as soon as it warms up in order to keep emissions low); operation of emissions control devices such as early fuel evaporation (EFE) heating grid or thermactor systems; control of ignition timing (full advance not possible while cold); EGR flow (not while cold to improve driveability); evaporative canister purge (not while cold); transmission torque converter lockup; and fast idle (only while cold).

On water-cooled engines, the main temperature sensor usually protrudes into the coolant water jacket through the head or intake manifold. Thermistor-type sensors accurately and predictably change resistance with temperature, modifying a 5volt reference signal from the computer which is then evaluated by the computer to determine engine temperature. The sensor resistance is high when cold, dropping 300ohms for every degree rise in temperature. Obviously, the sensor should be located where it accurately reflects the actual engine temperature, not at a hot or cold spot in the cooling system, or at the very least, should be proportional to the engine temperature.

A faulty coolant temperature sensor or circuit will probably cause a variety of symptoms, given the sensor's effect on so many engine functions. Symptoms may include: stalling when cold from wrong mixture; retarded timing or slow idle speed; poor cold idle from wrong mixture; lack of heated inlet air or EFE enhancement; stumble or hesitation from lack of EFE or too early EGR (exhaust gas recirculation); poor gas mileage due to extended cold mixture enrichment; lack of closed-loop operation; and failure to activate full spark advance when warm.

Some vehicles also use switch-type coolant temperature sensors which open or close at a certain temperature in a binary fashion like a thermostat—either on or off, for example, to control the operation of an electric cooling fan.

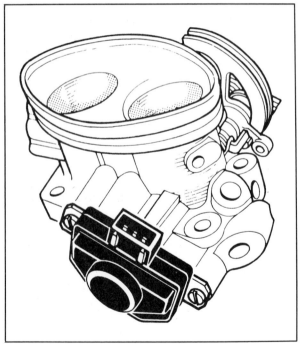

Throttle Position Sensors (TPS) are mounted on the throttle body, and are often linear potentiometers which change resistance as they are rotated by action of the throttle shaft. The ECU may provide acceleration enrichment based on changes in TPS, and may sometimes detect idle or wide open throttle based on microswitches in the TPS. Some TPS units only provide indications of idle and wide open throttle.

Modern ECUs often incorporate limp-home mode strategies in which the ECU will disregard sensor data that it decides is suspect. In the 1970s, ECUs could be fooled into fuel enrichment by grounding out temperature sensors and such; these days, a sensor too far out of range too suddenly may hardly cause a hiccup in engine operation as the computer's trouble strategy takes effect.

Air Temperature Sensor

Some fuel injection systems measure the temperature of inlet air in order to deduce its density. Bosch L-Jetronic EFI systems use a pressure vein air meter to measure the *velocity* of air entering the engine, converting this to *mass* airflow by correcting for altitude and air temperature (colder air is denser than hot air, containing more molecules of air per volume). The air temperature sensor is a thermistor sensor like the coolant sensor. Naturally, placement of the sensor is critical. It's important to place it after the turbocharger and intercooler and in a position where it will not be rendered inaccurate by heat soak from into the mounting surface.

Many aftermarket and factory speed-density EFI systems measure inlet air temperature.

Throttle Position Sensor

The throttle position sensor (TPS) is a variable resistor potentiometer that changes resistance as a shaft is physically turned. When linked to the butterflies of a carburetor or throttle, a TPS indicates the position of the throttle via the specific voltage output. Furthermore, by evaluating the change of throttle position over *time,* the computer can determine the *rate* of throttle opening or closure.

Some older fuel injection systems such as the Lucas-Bosch EFI on early Jaguar V-12s also incorporated throttle microswitches that indicated idle (closed throttle) or wide-open throttle. The TPS is usually bolted onto the exterior of the throttle body on fuel injection systems.

On virtually all modern emissions-controlled passenger cars, the TPS is used to activate transient enrichment on sudden throttle opening, in order to prevent bog—like the accelerator pump on a carburetor—or enleanment or fuel cutoff on deceleration.

On some naturally aspirated aftermarket EFI systems (such as the Holley Pro-Jection) and certain racing EFI systems (so-called Alpha-N or throttle position EFI systems), the ECU combines throttle angle with engine speed sensing to estimate air entering the engine (and, hence, fuel requirements). A big throttle angle for a given engine speed implies higher manifold pressure and higher engine loading (and, therefore, more

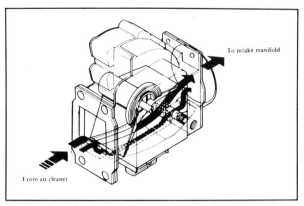

Air flow sensors include the velocity air meter, which measures the force of inlet air rushing past a spring-loaded door using with a device like the TPS. This measurement must be corrected for temperature and altitude to equal air mass.

air entering the engine). Throttle position EFI systems tend to be very responsive and therefore good for racing.

This system has no ability to automatically correct for changes in engine VE, however, and is entirely unsuitable for turbocharging applications where a given throttle angle and engine speed cannot distinguish between a wide range of possible engine loadings.

Exact TPS calibration is critical on Alpha-N systems. The system specification requires a specific voltage signal which tells the computer that the throttle is closed. Calibration procedures at closed throttle require loosening the TPS and rotating it while watching the TPS resistance with an ohmmeter. At the correct voltage, the tuner tightens down the TPS mounting screws. On some speed-density systems, such as the Haltech F3, the TPS does not require calibration since the sensor is only used to detect *changes* in throttle position for transient enrichment, not *absolute* position. Some ECUs *require* a *linear* potentiometer TPS, which is more expensive than the nonlinear version where TPS resistance changes rapidly with initial increments of change in throttle angle, changing *less* per additional angle change the farther the switch moves toward wide-open). Other ECUs can understand nonlinear TPS data; a mathematical function corrects the nonlinear voltage from the TPS to accurate specific throttle angles for use in fuel injection pulse width calculations.

MAP Sensor

Given engine speed and displacement, manifold absolute pressure (MAP) sensors indicate absolute (not relative to changing atmospheric pressure) air pressure in the intake manifold, which corresponds to engine loading and enables the computer to deduce how much air is entering the engine. The computer then makes adjustments to fuel injection pulse width and ignition timing.

The computer is able to deduce engine volumetric efficiency by using rpm and loading to index into a VE table which, for example, will cause the computer to lean the mixture and advance spark timing under low-load, high-vacuum conditions for best fuel economy. On the other hand, high-loading, high-manifold pressure will result in enriching of the fuel mixture like a power valve to produce best power, and retarded spark timing to prevent knocking like a vacuum boost-advance retard unit on a conventional distributor.

The MAP sensor is plumbed to the inlet manifold by direct mounting or hose. A pressure-sensitive electronic circuit in the sensor generates an electrical signal that changes with air density. The sensor is not influenced by ambient atmospheric pressure like the DPS or VAC sensors, which read the difference between manifold and atmospheric pressure and are influenced by altitude and weather. The MAP sensor is pre-calibrated in such a way that it measures absolute pressure regardless of other factors.

Barometric pressure—or BARO or BP—sensors sense atmospheric air density. Sometimes a

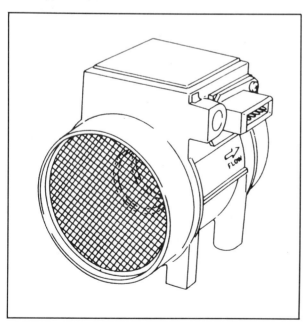

In contrast, the newer Mass Air Flow (MAF) sensors directly measure air mass by considering the cooling capacity of inlet air rushing past a heated wire connected to circuitry designed to measure how much electric current is required to keep the wire at a fixed temperature. Some MAF sensors now use thin film instead of wire.

combination of a DPS and BP are used to determine absolute pressure in the manifold; these two functions have occasionally been combined in one sensor, as in the BMAP used by Ford in EEC-III and early EEC-IV systems.

The MAP sensor is obviously critical to correct engine system functioning, since any accuracy problems may affect both spark timing and fuel mixture. A bad sensor, wiring problems in the circuit connecting the MAP sensor to the ECU, or air leaks in the manifold or plumbing connecting the MAP sensor to the manifold can result in bad MAP data. This can cause driveability problems of detonation from lean mixture and excessively advanced spark, or power loss and poor economy due to retarded spark and too rich a mixture. Knock sensors may *mask* problems of lean mixture and advanced spark by retarding the spark under detonation. By watching engine timing via a strobe while banging on the block with a hammer, it may be possible to determine if the knock sensor is functioning properly.

Air Metering Sensors

Air metering sensors fall into two categories. Velocity air meters measure the force of air rushing into an engine against a spring-loaded door in an air tunnel. A linear potentiometer, much like a TPS, measures the angle of opening and sends an electrical signal to the ECU that changes as the door opens more or less. The ECU can deduce airflow into the engine based on this value—after making some corrections.

The problem is, the force against the door is a function of two variables, the weight of the air and the speed of the air. And the ECU cannot distinguish, for a given door angle, whether the air is less dense—but traveling faster—or more dense (heavier), but traveling slightly slower. In other words, air velocity must be corrected for air density (temperature and barometric pressure) in order to reflect air *mass* (actual number of air molecules entering the engine per unit of time). Velocity air meters have been used on common OE systems such as the older Bosch L-Jetronic.

Air mass entering the engine can be directly measured by the second type of air flow meter, the mass airflow (MAF) sensor. The pre-1991 GM TPI systems, typical of MAF-sensed EFI systems, use a tiny electrically heated wire, suspended in an air tunnel, to estimate mass airflow into the engine by measuring the amount of electrical current it takes to keep the wire heated to a certain fixed temperature. The cooling effect of air on the wire is exactly proportional to the mass of air flowing past the wire.

Some MAF sensors use a thin film to measure air mass.

MAF sensors must be designed aerodynamically to maintain a smooth flow of air over the wire that is proportional to total flow through the air tunnel. In other words, the MAF sensor would be inaccurate if there were turbulence in the tunnel that caused a disproportionate amount of air to *miss* the wire. Consequently, there is some tradeoff between accurate air measurement at low speed, and restriction at high speed. Revision pulses from "wild" cammed engines can also cause problems with MAF accuracy, and MAFs do not react instantly to changes in air flow.

Aftermarket MAF sensor makers such as Professional Flow Tech use patented aerodynamic designs to build accurate high-flow MAF units that outperform factory sensors. Professional Flow Tech points out that engines run with a steady airflow only below 1/3-full throttle. In this realm, where all pressure drop from atmosphere to cylinder is produced by the throttle plate, all air meters seem to perform well. And it's in this range from idle up to 1/3-full throttle that 50 percent of all driving is done.

According to the company, "in the remaining throttle range, the air pulses wildly from actual reverse flow (caused by valve overlap, pneumatic hammer, and acoustic resonance) to a maximum of four times the swept volume of each cylinder (the intake stroke happens in 1/2 crank revolution and the piston is moving at two times the average piston speed). For a 302 engine with eight cylinders (37.75ci each=0.02185cu-ft) at 5000rpm, the intake air peak value will be a maximum of 437cfm (5000rpm * 0.02185cu-ft cylinder displacement * 4in maximum swept volume per cylinder)." If any part of the intake system limits this maximum flow, there is a potential for performance improvement.

Professional Flow Tech also states that because of multiple screens and poor fluidics design, the mass air meters being produced have pressure drops in the order of 12in-24in of water. This reduces maximum horsepower by 5-7 percent due to the drop in engine volumetric efficiency (the engine can't breath as well!). It's made worse by higher altitude, which reduces efficiency by 0.7 percent per thousand feet.

Velocity air meters tend to be even worse than MAF sensors in restricting airflow so that there is a greater pressure drop past the sensor which reduces engine VE. See the troubleshooting chapter for more details.

Knock Sensor

The knock sensor is a microphone that continuously listens for engine pre-ignition knocks and ping. ECUs with the ability to adjust spark timing can retard timing when this sensor detects knocking, and can also advance the maximum spark timing to take advantage of higher octane fuels and altitude changes (higher altitude results in lower cylinder pressures and less tendency to knock). Some ECUs and stand-alone knock sensors have the ability to selectively retard spark timing on just the individual cylinder(s) that exhibit knock.

Chapter 6

Actuators

Actuators are electromechanical devices that enable the computer to make things happen in the world. In the realm of EFI, these may include electronic fuel injectors, electric fuel pump(s) and relay(s), nitrous oxide solenoid, turbo wastegate or EGR valve , idle speed control, torque converter lockup, engine fan control, spark advance, warning and diagnostic lights, and so on.

Electronic Fuel Injectors

Imagine a nozzle on the end of a hose on a windy day. Squeeze the handle on the nozzle, and water sprays out and mixes with the air. Release the handle, and the flow of water spray stops. If you imagine several nozzles on the same hose, you are visualizing the situation in a port fuel-injected engine. Electronic fuel injectors open and close, spraying gasoline into air that is rushing into a spark ignition engine. This provides an explosive mixture of fuel and air that can push against pistons and cause the engine to run.

Although the fuel enters the air in bursts or pulses, by the time the fuel and air are in the cylinder and compressed, they are thoroughly mixed (some of this vaporization occurs inside the hot cylinders). The injector nozzles contain tiny valves operated by electromagnets that overcome the force of a spring and pull the valves open. Once open, fuel pressure in the supply line leading to the injectors causes fuel to spray through a tiny orifice and mist out into inlet air rushing past the injector(s). The injectors are usually aimed directly at the intake valve(s).

The Robert Bosch Corporation, based in Germany, which long ago licensed the rights to build electronic injection systems as invented by an American company called Bendix, has built more than 150 million electronic injectors and currently dominates this market.

Several other companies make electronic injectors, the most important of these to aftermarket engine designers or racers being Lucas

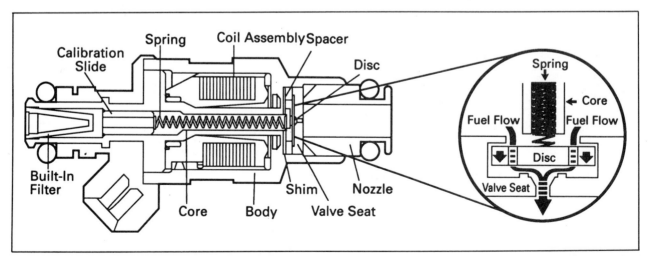

Lucas D-Series injectors use a unique disc valve to meter fuel, which gives the injector high dynamic range *compared to pintle designs, and high resistance to clogging. Lucas*

Industries and AC Rochester, Having long been a force in mechanical fuel injection, Lucas has targeted the aftermarket EFI niche and is freely supplying technical data about its injectors, including electrical characteristics and fuel flow rates at specified pressures. Lucas also provides several injectors that are original equipment on vehicles like the TPI Camaro and Corvette.

Apparently for reasons of liability, Bosch will not reveal injector flow rates and other specifications to the public, but will only specify injectors designed for certain engines on specific vehicles. (Actually, Bosch injector performance data are

well known by companies like Sutton Engineering, which manufactures equipment to test and clean injectors. This book includes such observed data, although, naturally, this information is not guaranteed to be correct.)

For the hot rodder or racer, easier access to official injector specifications alone makes Lucas more attractive than Bosch, but Lucas injectors are also preferred for other reasons. According to Sutton, the Lucas injector's disc-based design gives it several advantages, and in addition, it has a more universal external design that allows more part number overlap than Bosch. Bosch offers many injectors, mostly with subtle differences from one model to the next. Lucas currently covers the entire range of injector applications with just twenty-seven part numbers.

The Bosch injectors use mainly a pintle design (see sidebar). Consequently, the Lucas injector moving parts weigh 1/8 that of the Bosch, which Lucas claims gives the injector faster response time and better metering down at the very low one- to two-millisecond range.

MSD sells injectors with very high flow rates—up to 96lb/hr. Injectors like these shown here can each make 140hp or more. MSD

Gigantic Holley throttle body injectors such as this supply the fueling needs of big block engines with two or four injectors.

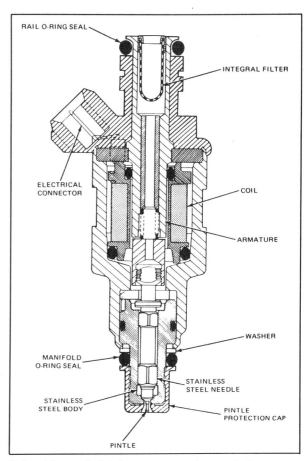

RAIL O-RING SEAL
INTEGRAL FILTER
ELECTRICAL CONNECTOR
COIL
ARMATURE
WASHER
MANIFOLD O-RING SEAL
STAINLESS STEEL NEEDLE
STAINLESS STEEL BODY
PINTLE PROTECTION CAP
PINTLE

Solenoid-type fuel injectors use an internal electromagnet to pull open a spring-loaded valve, allowing high-pressure fuel to spray into the intake manifold.

With no pintle valve protruding into the intake port as on the Bosch injectors, the Lucas disc injector is not as susceptible to clogging.

Injector Fuel Flow and Selecting Injector Capacity

Injector fuel flow is measured in pounds per hour at a given pressure, or in cubic centimeters (cc's) per minute at pressure—either statically (injector open continuously) or pulsed at a certain duty cycle. The amount of fuel that actually enters an engine from an injector depends on several factors.

The first factor is the amount of time the injector remains open for each engine cycle (or for each combustion event). The longer the injector is open, the more fuel sprays out, which maxes out at a point when the injector is open all the time. (Since energizing of injector windings causes heat buildup, injectors may fail if operated above 80 percent duty cycle.) Theoretically there is no lower limit to the length of time an injector could be opened, but practically, injectors do have a lower limit. This occurs at a point (usually somewhere between 0.001 and 0.002 second) when the injector is open so briefly that random factors

Comparison of Pulse Injector Designs

Injectors consist of a valve housing and a valve assembly. The assembly consists of the valve itself, and its solenoid armature. The housing contains the solenoid winding and its electrical connection. With no voltage applied to the winding, a helical spring assisted by fuel pressure forces the valve against its seat in the valve assembly, preventing any fuel from passing through the injector. When the solenoid winding is energized, the valve lifts by approximately 0.06 millimeter (varying according to design), and fuel rushes through the valve body and sprays out of the injector.

The valve assembly in a Lucas injector consists of the armature attached to a disc with six tiny holes drilled around the outside. In a closed position, the disc rests on a seat, the center of the disc covering a hole in the middle of the seat which prevents any fuel from passing through the injector. When the armature is pulled open as the injector is energized, fuel passes through the six outer holes, through the hole in the seat, and sprays out of the injector.

In the Bosch-style injector, the armature is connected to a tapered needle. The valve housing narrows to form a seat upon which the needle rests when the injector is closed, effectively choking off fuel flow. A pintle assembly attached to the end of the valve needle protrudes out the end of the injector through a plastic chimney and is beveled at this end; the beveling and chimney are designed to improve the spray pattern. The flow of a Lucas disc injector is determined by the size of the six holes drilled in the disc. Bosch injector pintles and seats are always the same size; Bosch determines flow by varying the size of the bore after the seat.

A low-resistance (usually 2.4ohms) or high-resistance (usually 15.9ohms) solenoid winding may be fitted to the injector valve assembly. High-resistance injectors can be triggered directly by the ECU driver stage; with low-resistance windings, a series resistor may be necessary to protect the injector and driver stage of the ECU unless a current-regulated driver stage is used—the point being

that not just any injector can be used with any ECU (more on this later). A current-regulated driver stage combined with a low-resistance injector results in reduced opening time.

According to Bosch, injectors are designed with the following goals in mind:
• Precise fuel metering at all operating points
• Accurate flow at narrow pulse widths—with deviation from linearity within specified tolerances
• Broad dynamic flow range
• Good fuel distribution and atomization
• Valve leak tightness
• Corrosion resistance to water, "sour gas," and ethanol mixtures
• Reliability
• Low noise

Injectors can be divided into the following metering categories:

Annular orifice metering, which uses a pintle to optimize the atomization via a conical-shaped spray pattern, and which meters fuel by the size of the gap between the pintle and the valve body.

Single-hole metering, in which fuel spray is injected directly from the drilled passage in the valve body downstream of the needle valve (atomization is not as good as with a pintle design, at worst case producing a "pencil beam").

Multi-hole metering (C-version), which forces fuel through a stationary drilled plate located at the end of the valve body orifice, downstream from the needle valve. This design, which normally includes four precisely spaced and aligned holes, results in a good conical spray pattern.

Multi-hole metering for multi-valve engines is similar to the C-version, but aligns the metering holes so a separate spray of fuel hits each intake valve.

Disc metering uses a drilled disc that moves off a flat seat with the armature. Claimed benefits include resistance to deposit buildup and clogging (thus no cleaning is ever required), wider dynamic range for improved idle, quieter operation, lighter weight (which improves response), and operation with alternate fuels like natural gas, propane, methanol, and ethanol.

tending to cause slight variations in injector open time and fuel flow each time the injector fires, become significant in comparison to the planned duration of open time. As a result, the consistency of the open event begins to suffer—you will not get a good, clean, *repeatable* spray pattern.

A second variable affecting injector fuel output is how much fuel pressure exists in the line supplying fuel to the injector. The lower the pressure, the less fuel that sprays out of an open injector. Again, limited by a low pressure beyond which repeatability suffers, most port injectors are never operated below 2 bar (28psi). The fuel flow on the high end begins to suffer from diminishing returns as pressure increases. It is absolutely limited when the injector's internal electromagnet can no longer overcome fuel pressure to open, and/or when the spring pressure tending to close the injectors cannot consistently overcome the high-pressure fuel rushing through the injector valve. Many experts recommend 72.5psi as a maximum fuel pressure. Most injectors operate around 40psi.

A third important factor affecting the amount of fuel injected into an engine is the size of the injector's valve or orifice through which fuel must flow. Most electronic injectors are rated in pounds of fuel per hour that will flow at a certain pressure (flow rate). Injector maximum size is practically limited by the increasing weight of its moving parts. Larger weights have more resistance to moving quickly, and thus require increasing power to activate them. (This follows the physical laws concerning momentum, which describes the resistance of stationary objects to movement and the resistance of moving objects to stopping.)

Large-flowing injectors get very expensive. As injector size increases, each opening event has a greater effect on the hydraulics of the fuel supply system, implying larger fuel pumps, fuel rails, fuel line size, and higher pressures. And the larger an injector is, the higher the minimum flow possible. It is limited, as described, to the amount of fuel that flows in one or two milliseconds at a given pressure. This is particularly important on engines with a high dynamic range.

An example of an engine with a high dynamic range is a small, high-output turbocharged engine where the fuel required at maximum horsepower is *very* high in comparison to that required at idle. On many engines, the dynamic range of the injectors is increased by increasing the fuel pressure along with load, usually by fuel-pressure regulators referenced to intake manifold pressure. On some very large displacement engines or smaller engines with large dynamic range, it may become necessary to use multiple smaller injectors that are staged.

All of these factors have to be considered when you are selecting injectors for an engine that differs from those with factory predetermined injector requirements.

Lucas offers the following formula designed to allow high-performance-oriented customers to determine which injector (flow rate) they will need for a specific engine based on horsepower output:

Flow Rate = (HP * BSFC) / (#Injectors * Maxcycle)

Flow Rate is in pounds per hour of gasoline

HP is projected engine horsepower (this may increase with port injection); for the formula to be useful, this must be realistic

BSFC is brake specific fuel consumption in pounds per horsepower-hour, generally 0.4 to 0.6lb (possibly higher) at full throttle. Start with 0.45lb for naturally aspirated engines, 0.55lb for turbo-supercharged engines

 # Injectors is the number of injectors you're using

Maxcycle is the maximum duty cycle of the injector. According to Lucas, this is 0.8 (80 percent) for a typical OEM ECU; above this, the injector will begin to overheat, which can cause it to lose consistency—or even fail completely!

Example: 5.7 liter V-8

Flow Rate = (240hp * 0.65) / (8 cyl. * 0.8)

or

Flow Rate = 24.37lb per hr injectors required—*at rated pressure!*

Lucas points out that their part number 5207011 injector, rated at 23.92lb per hour, is close. They warn that the only problem with this equation is that to get a completely accurate answer, you need to instrument and measure the *exact* engine configuration in question, which means a dynamometer with full instrumentation.

Turbo magazine suggests using 0.55lb as the

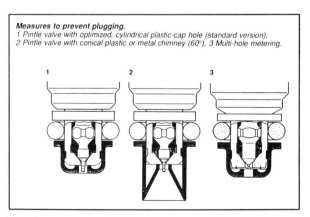

Bosch measures to prevent plugging, including (from left): pintle valve with optimized, cylindrical plastic-cap hole (standard version); pintle valve with conical plastic chimney (60 degree); and multi-hole metering. Bosch

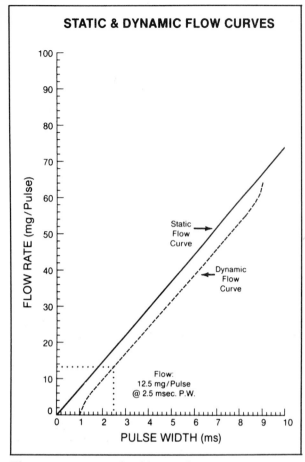

STATIC & DYNAMIC FLOW CURVES

Static Flow Curve

Dynamic Flow Curve

Flow:
12.5 mg/Pulse
@ 2.5 msec. P.W.

Electronic injectors should never be open 100 percent of the time (called "going static") due to the possibility of damage from overheating and the fact that the ECU's control strategy can no longer be effective in regulating flow, but static flow rates are useful in understanding the absolute upper limit of injector flow. DFI

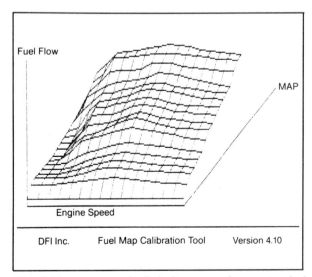

Fuel Flow

MAP

Engine Speed

DFI Inc.   Fuel Map Calibration Tool   Version 4.10

This DFI projection of 3-D fueling map plots engine fuel flow as a function of engine speed and Manifold Absolute Pressure. DFI

BSFC for a turbocharged or supercharged engine. In the case of a 530ci stroked Cadillac V-8 with turbocharging that outputs 800hp, the figures would look like this:

Flow Rate = (800 * 0.55) / (8 * 0.8) = 68.75lb per hr injectors

Injectors this big are expensive and might not idle well on some engines. In this case, a designer might decide to use two smaller injectors per cylinder, staged such that only one injector per cylinder is operating at idle with the other phasing in as engine loading and rpm increase.

Gasoline contains a certain amount of chemical energy that is released when it is burned (oxidized). If all the energy in gasoline could be converted to work, a gallon of gas could make 45hp for one hour. Internal combustion engines are notoriously inefficient, so the actual horsepower

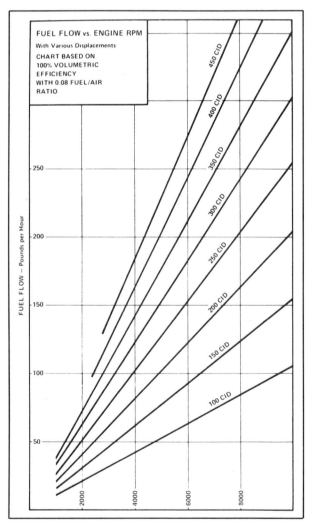

FUEL FLOW vs. ENGINE RPM
With Various Displacements
CHART BASED ON
100% VOLUMETRIC
EFFICIENCY
WITH 0.08 FUEL/AIR
RATIO

Multiply RPM by volumetric efficiency you expect from the engine to estimate fuel flow. Chart assumes full-power air-fuel ratio of 12.5 to 1, assumes 100 percent VE. Holley

you can expect to make from a certain injector is way less than theoretical. The following formula is a revision of the above equation, rearranged to yield the maximum horsepower that a given injector can make at a specified fuel pressure.

Horsepower = (Flow Rate * # Injectors * Maxcycle) / BSFC

213 = (20lb * 6 * 0.8) / 0.55

I conclude that the injectors on a stock Jaguar 4.2 liter six-cylinder motor could make 213hp at the specified pressure.

Injector Pressure Changes

Altering the system fuel pressure is a good and inexpensive way to increase the dynamic range of any fuel injector, which is why this is done on many original equipment injection systems. The normal method is to reference the fuel pressure regulator to manifold vacuum. As manifold vacuum rises and falls with decreasing and increasing engine loading, the vacuum is used to increase or decrease the effect of the regulator spring which presses against the regulator's diaphragm, and which dynamically changes the pressure of fuel that can force its way through the regulator. This means that fuel pressure is lowered at idle (high vacuum) and raised at wide-open throttle (WOT) when there is zero vacuum.

On an engine with high vacuum at idle, system pressure might be 39psi at WOT, 25psi at idle. Some regulators are not manifold vacuum-referenced, but have an adjustable bolt or screw that can be turned to increase or decrease regulator spring pressure against the diaphragm to alter fuel pressure.

As we'll see in a minute, the static flow rate of a fuel injector is directly proportional to the change in system pressure.

In the case of a turbocharged or supercharged engine, one atmosphere of boost (14.7psi) against a manifold pressure-referenced regulator would raise the system fuel pressure an equal amount *above* that at zero vacuum—assuming the fuel pump has the capacity to provide the fuel. Therefore, fuel pressure on a forced induction engine would vary from 25 at idle to roughly 55psi at full 15psi turbo boost. At equivalent injector pulse widths, this fuel pressure change causes a tremendous difference in the amount of fuel injected into the engine. The long and short is that referenced regulators enable larger injectors to idle better, smaller injectors to produce more high-end power.

Glen Grissom, formerly of MSD in El Paso, Texas, offered the following formula in *Turbo* magazine to calculate the effect of changing fuel pressure on injector flow:

(SQR [SysPs / SysP1]) * Statflow1 = Statflow2

SQR means take the square root of the value in parentheses.

SysP2 is the proposed new system pressure (psi).

SysP1 is the specified pressure for the injec-

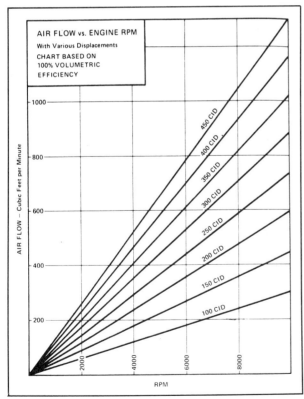

To estimate an engine's maximum air flow requirement, select max RPM, displacement, and find CFM on the left side of the chart. Multiply this value by the actual VE you expect from the engine. Holley

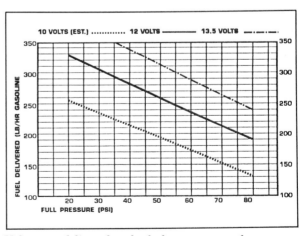

Voltage as delivered to the fuel pump can make an enormous difference in fuel flow. MSD found that changing voltage at the pump from 10volts to 13.5volts raised fuel flow from 220lb/hr to 340lb/hr, the difference between 440 and 680hp. Turbo Magazine

tor's rated flow (psi).

Statflow1 is the rated static (nonpulsed) injector flow rate.

Statflow2 is the calculated new static flow rate.

For example, the Jag 4.2 Bosch injector is rated at roughly 20lb per hour at 39psi; at 25psi it is calculated as follows:

(SQR (25/39)) * 20 = 16lb per hr at 25psi! (a 20 percent difference)

On the other hand, considering the same injector at 55psi:

(SQR (55/39)) * 20 = 23.75lb per hr at 55psi (a 19 percent difference)

Therefore, simply by changing fuel pressure based on manifold pressure, the maximum flow of the injector is changed by 40 percent! Most experts suggest 70psi as a maximum system pressure, particularly if the ECU is not programmable; very high pressures begin to affect the ability of the injector's internal spring to force the injector closed against fuel pressure flowing through it, and may also affect the ability of the armature and windings to open the injector. As a consequence, the opening and/or closing time and/or the repeatability of flow during the open event can change and become unpredictable. Furthermore, as mentioned previously, flow gains with increased system pressure offer diminishing returns. MSD discovered the following effects when varying the pressure of 72 and 96lb/hr (at 43.5psi) injectors using 85 percent duty cycle:

The compact Holley fuel pump supplied with Pro-Jection throttle body injection systems maintains up to 22psi at the injectors. Holley

Cartech EFI turbo systems often use a high-pressure Bosch fuel pump (left) and a special Cartech regulator (right) to increase injector flow during boost conditions by increasing fuel pressure 10psi for every pound of boost. Note that injectors should not normally be pressurized above 70-80psi, at which point injector performance may be adversely affected by the high pressure. Cartech

Injector Flow Rates

This chart from *Turbo* Magazine shows changes in injector flow rates as a function of fuel pressure. Fuel flow at pressure is a function not only of the capacity of the fuel pump, but of the capacity of the plumbing between the pump and fuel rail, including any restrictions from fuel lines, fittings, and filters. The two sets of pulsed flow readings were made with two different models of fuel pumps.

Fuel Pressure (psi)	Pulsed flow (lb/hr) P/N2014	Pulsed flow (lb/hr) P/N2015
30	56	72
40	64	84
50	71	93
60	76	101
70	76	106

Source: Turbo Magazine

In the same *Turbo* article, MSD points out that the ability of the injector to realize high flow rates depends upon the ability of the *fuel pump* and plumbing to supply enough fuel. As the fuel pressure increases, the pump is able to supply progressively lower volumes of fuel. In addition, it is worth pointing out that the fuel pump can be limited by the hydraulics of the supply line(s) size, filter(s) restrictions, restrictions posed by bends and turns in the supply line, and restrictions and pressure differentials in the fuel rail. The pump's ability to supply fuel is also affected by the vehicle's electrical system voltage (more about this in the section on fuel pumps).

When adding turbocharging to engines with stock fuel injection systems, the ideal situation would be to maintain stock injection characteristics under low-load conditions, adding some sort of fuel enrichment during the relatively rare bursts of turbo boost. This is exactly the approach taken by Cartech of San Antonio, Texas, and several other turbocharging specialists. Cartech supplies a special fuel regulator inserted in the fuel return line, which raises fuel pressure roughly 7lb per pound of turbo boost, automatically causing the injectors to provide enrichment. Under naturally aspirated conditions, the regulator is dormant. Given the fact that most injectors do not function well above 70 to 100lb of fuel pressure, starting with nominal fuel pressure of 40psi, this enables fueling for turbo boost in the 5 to 7psi range.

Injector Electrical Characteristics

Another factor to consider when selecting injectors has to do with the varying electrical power requirements of various fuel injectors—which must be compatible with the electrical output capabilities of the electronic control unit (ECU) that drives them. (In addition, when combined with the electrical requirements of all other onboard equipment, the system's power requirements must fall within the constraints of the vehicle's battery or charging system's electrical output.)

Most car people intuitively understand plumbing systems. They understand what pounds per square inch means, they understand the concept of pounds or cc's per minute, and they understand discussions of injector valves and fuel lines and supply restrictions. Electrical properties affecting fuel injectors and ECUs are similar to plumbing concepts, but the terms used to describe them are different.

Voltage is used to describe electrical pressure, as psi is used to describe fuel pressure. *Amperage* is used to describe electron flow, as pounds per hour describes fuel flow. Resistance in *ohms* describes how easily current flows through something like a wire, which is similar in concept to the varying resistance to water flow through a small pipe versus a large pipe. Ohm's law states:

Current = Electromotive Force / Resistance, or Amperes = Voltage / Ohms

Since injectors are activated by electromagnetic force, each injector contains a magnetic coil with a particular resistance to the flow of electricity through it—also referred to as the impedance, which is rated in ohms. A coil of wire rated at 16ohms has much greater resistance to current flow than a coil with 2ohms. Many port fuel injectors are rated at roughly 16ohms. A 16ohm coil will not allow nearly as much current to flow through it for a given voltage as a 2ohm coil.

Very large port injectors and throttle-body injectors (usually huge in comparison to port injectors) may require more current to produce enough magnetic force to operate the injector quickly and reliably. (According to Bosch, very large injectors require large springs to force the injector armature and needles closed against such a large volume of fuel flowing through it.) This can be achieved by lowering the resistance of the injector coil windings to flow more current and by designing the ECU injector driving circuits so that they can safely provide enough current to drive the low-impedance injectors–and there's the rub: ECUs designed to drive low-resistance injectors can easily provide the lower current needed to drive high-impedance injectors.

The Holley pressure regulator is integral to the Pro-Jection throttle body assembly. The Pro-Jection kit also includes a high-pressure fuel filter designed to handle system pressure of 12-20psi. Holley

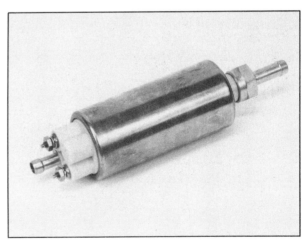

MSD specializes in high-performance EFI components. MSD designed and manufactured the Holley Pro-Jection ECU. An MSD roller-vane fuel pump is suitable for supplying systems large and small. MSD

The MSD pressure regulator is adjustable for system pressure. MSD

But ECUs designed for high-resistance port injection systems may encounter problems if you change to low-impedance injectors. For example, if you decide your modified Buick GN turbo needs larger injectors because the injectors are already running close to the limit in duty cycle (on all the time, or nearly all the time), you may find that larger flow injectors readily available are *low resistance only.* (Bosch, Lucas, and others are constantly introducing new higher performance injectors, so this may no longer specifically apply to the GN.) The ECU power supply may be able to provide additional current, but the transistors and integrated circuits in the driver section of an ECU could blow out trying to regulate the higher electrical draw of a low-resistance injector. Or, since electrical circuits are often overdesigned to an extent, the ECU may work fine for a time, but with a *shortened life.* It is essential to match injector resistance to the capabilities of the ECU driving them.

Injector Physical Layout

The final factor to consider has to do with the physical layout of the injector, which must be compatible with the connections on the fuel supply or rail, and which must allow the injector to plug into the bosses on the intake manifold or elsewhere on the intake air plumbing system or on the throttle body itself. The injector's metering or spray pattern must also be compatible with the application in terms of single-hole metering, annular orifice metering, multi-hole metering, or multi-hole metering with two sprays. Lucas has introduced a line of disc injectors in the last sev-

eral years that are designed to replace Bosch pintle injectors.

Fuel Supply Systems: Pumps, Fuel Lines, and Regulators

Fuel injection systems require a reliable and stable fuel supply. In the absence of a sufficient and accurate fuel supply, the ECU's precisely calculated injector pulse width will not provide accurate fueling for actual engine conditions. The fuel pump must be capable of providing adequate fuel at worst condition, which is wide-open throttle (WOT) at high rpm and maximum manifold pressure. Fuel pumps, actuated by computer-controlled relays, are rated to provide a certain fuel flow at a certain pressure.

Be aware, however, that there will be pressure losses in the fuel line, through the fuel filter, and in the fuel rail. Naturally, the pressure regulator must be capable of bleeding sufficient excess fuel at idle, when the engine needs the least amount of fuel. Haltech recommends checking the actual fuel delivery by supplying a specified vacuum/pressure to the regulator and collecting the fuel that would normally return to the fuel tank in a safe container of known volume, and timing the event. This will yield the maximum amount of fuel available to feed injectors without bleeding fuel rail pressure below the specification. The method takes into account any restrictions in the fuel supply plumbing which affect the specified fuel delivery of a known new fuel pump. It also tells you the capacity of an unknown pump or a used pump that may have suffered inefficiencies due to wear.

This fuel supply calculation can be worked backward or forward. You can start with a known engine fueling spec, calculating a minimum fuel pump capacity to provide adequate fueling. Or you can start with a pump spec, calculating the maximum horsepower engine it can supply. Suppose you have a 300hp engine:

Flow Rate = Horsepower * BSFC

Assuming this is a turbocharged engine, most experts suggest using 0.55 (see previous section) as BSFC (brake specific fuel consumption in pounds per horsepower hour). Therefore:

Flow Rate = 300hp * 0.55lb per hp/hr

Flow Rate = 165lb of fuel per hp/hr

Convert pounds to gallons by dividing 165 by 6 (gasoline weighs slightly more than 6lb per gallon). The answer is 27.5gal. Therefore, the fuel pump must supply 27.5gal per hour at injector-rated pressure, which is slightly under 1/2gal per minute. Doing a little mathematics, we can figure that at full throttle, this engine requires a quart of fuel every 33 seconds; it is clear that any pump that could fill a container through the outlet of the regulator in *less* than this will do the job. The mathematics looks like this:

27.5gal per hour / 3,600 (seconds in an hour) = 0.00763888gal per second of fuel required.

Dividing 1gal by 0.0076388 tells how many of this volume it takes to make 1 gallon, or, looking at it another way, how many seconds of this flow it takes to make a gallon (130.9090909...). Dividing this figure by four (quarts in a gallon) yields the number of seconds of this flow it takes to fill a quart container (convert this to metric on your own).

MSD Ignition offers a roller vane-type electric fuel pump designed for port fuel injection which supplies 43gal per hour (282lb per hour) at 40psi and 12volts of power, which would be adequate for the 300hp engine discussed above. Many normally aspirated engines use fuel injection designed to run at 40psi at full load, which means zero vacuum. But suppose you turbocharge this engine to 10lb of boost? It is critical to understand that the pump will deliver *less* fuel at 50lb of fuel rail pressure than it would at 40psi (50psi is what a nominally 40psi manifold pressure-referenced regulator will produce in the fuel rail at 10lb of boost).

How much horsepower can the MSD pump support? At 40psi with 12volts of power, the MSD pump will flow 282lb per hour.

Horsepower = Flow Rate / BSFC

Assuming a BSFC of 0.55 (turbo motor), the equation becomes:

Horsepower = 282 / 0.55 = 512

The pump can support 512hp at 40psi.

Many fuel rails are equipped with a connection allowing attachment of a fuel pressure gauge. This allows a mechanic or EFI designer to actually observe the fuel pressure while operating the vehicle. Clearly, the pressure should either remain constant under all engine conditions (never falling) or, if the regulator is referenced to

The Idle Air Control (IAC) device uses a stepper motor under ECU control to open the IAC valve, allowing air to bypass the throttle plate to change idle speed. This prevents stalling under sudden deceleration. Accel/DFI

manifold pressure, vary in exact correspondence with manifold pressure.

The performance of an electric motor increases with voltage and decreases with a voltage drop. Experiments by MSD as reported in *Turbo* show that at 40psi, the MSD part number 225 electric pump flowed 220lb per hour, while at 13.5volts, the flow increases to 340lb per hour.

The voltage delivered at the fuel pump will be a function of the capacity of the battery and charging system, limited by the resistance of the wiring circuitry connecting the pump to the battery. You will get the most voltage at the pump by running a large, low-resistance wire directly from the battery to the pump and switching this wire with a low-resistance relay controlled by the ECU.

Nitrous Solenoids

A nitrous solenoid is like a giant injector that stays open constantly when activated. ECUs from DFI, NOS, Emtech, and Electromotive have the capability to examine a triggering signal from the arming switch of a nitrous system, and under specified conditions, to activate the nitrous solenoid, simultaneously providing fuel enrichment for the nitrous through the fuel injectors (as opposed to traditional nitrous systems which provide nitrous fueling via a second solenoid through a spray bar or port nozzles). Appropriate nitrous solenoids are provided by nitrous kit suppliers, and ECU suppliers have documentation regarding fuel enrichment and wiring.

ECUs without this specific capability can potentially provide enrichment via a relay which triggers a false temperature sensor signal to the ECU, triggering a special temperature enrichment. (This applies for an engine coolant temperature that would seldom or never be encountered, such as minus 20 degrees Fahrenheit in southern California, or a high engine temperature, like 250 degrees Fahrenheit on an engine with a 180 degree thermostat.) This would be relatively simple with a programmable ECU like the Haltech which enables you to specify temperature-based enrichment, but potentially possible on an older OE ECU which, unlike late-model ECUs, doesn't detect and reject sudden temperature sensor changes as suspect.

Engine Fans

DFI's electronic control unit has the capability to turn on a fan based on coolant temperature similar to stock GM ECMs.

Electronic Wastegates

Currently, only the EFI Technology/NOS Race ECU (and many OE ECUs) have the capability to control electronic wastegates.

Exhaust Gas Recirculation (EGR)

All OE, and the DFI and EFI Tech units can control EGR valves.

IAC Stepper Motor

DFI, Electromotive, Edelbrock, and most original equipment ECUs allow programmable control of idle speed based on several parameters, such as coolant temperature, closed- and open-loop mode, and threshold engine speed.

Ignition Spark Advance

Most late-model OE ECUs, including those manufactured by Electromotive, DFI, Edelbrock, Emtech, NOS, and EFI Technology, allow programmable control of spark advance based on engine rpm, loading, and/or throttle blade angle. The Edelbrock system is a complete kit with everything needed to handle ignition spark and appropriate advance. The Electromotive TEC units are available with direct-fire coils (one per pair of cylinders via waste spark). The DFI and NOS units require a coil driver and coil, such as the MSD 6 and 7 series. Most provide rev-limiting capability (through spark retard and fuel cut) and programmable boost retard, and can be triggered by a combination of crank sensor, cam sensor, or various electronic distributors. See DFI and NOS installations in a later chapter. Electromotive and DFI provide programmable detonation sensor-based ignition retard. Spark advance and retard occur based on a large matrix of numbers specifying advance at various load, rpm, and throttle angle cells with interpolation between cells.

Transmission Control

DFI and many original equipment ECUs provide programmable control over torque convertor lockup, activating lockup based on rpm, manifold pressure, and throttle position.

EFI Injector Selection Chart

Flow	Pressure (bar)	Style	Application	Mfr.	Part #
145	2.7	5 (hose)	323 BMW	Bosch	0280150208
147	2.7	2 (O-ring)	1.6 Ford	Lucas	5207007
164	3.0	2	Buick 3.0	Lucas	5207003
188	2.5	5	280 ZX	Lucas	5208001
188	2.5	2	Chev. 5.0	Lucas	5207002
195	2.7	2	BMW	Bosch	0280150203
201	2.7	2	4.0 Jeep	Lucas	5207013
214	2.5	5	4.2 Jag	Bosch	0280150157
218	3.0	2	Chev. 5.7	Lucas	5207011
237	2.5	5	Chyr/BMW	Lucas	7208005
237	2.5	2	Ford 98ci	Lucas	5208004
260	2.5	5	300ZX Turbo	Lucas	5206004
299	2.5	2	Buick 3.8T	Lucas	5207009
323	2.7	2	Ford 2.3T	Lucas	5207006
340	2.7	2	Porsche 914	Bosch	0280150009
368	2.7	2	Ford 2.3T	Lucas	5207008
390	2.7	5	Porsche 944T	Bosch	0280150803
422	2.7	2	(Aftermarket)	Lucas	5208010
480	2.5	5	Porsche 928	Bosch	0280150036
503	2.7	5	(Aftermarket)	Lucas	5207005
503	2.7	2	(Aftermarket)	Lucas	5207601
540	2.7	2	(Aftermarket)	Lucas	5207602
560	2.7	2	Judd Race	Bosch	0280150351
720	2.0	2	RX-7 SE	Nip	N304132500
800	2.5	2	BMotorsport	Bosch	280412911

Notes:

1. Convert cc/min to horsepower/cylinder by multiplying by .1902044. Example: 150cc/min = 28.5hp/cylinder or 228hp on a V-8 engine.

2. Convert pounds/hour of fuel to horsepower by doubling. Example: 14.26lb fuel/hour = 28.5hp/cylinder

3. Convert cc/minute to gallons/hour by multiplying by .0158503. Example: 150cc/min = 2.378gal/hour

4. Convert gallons/hour to pounds/hour by multiplying by 6. Example: 2.378gal/hour = 14.26lb/hour

5. One gallon of fuel can produce 2700hp for one minute, or 89,000,000ft-lb of torque. Most engines operate at about 27 percent thermal efficiency and 70-100 percent volumetric efficiency.

6. 1.0bar equals 14.7psi.

Chapter 7

Hot Rodding Your Fuel Injection

This chapter discusses methods to increase the air or fuel flow into a fuel-injected spark ignition engine. But before making modifications to a fuel-injected engine, we need to examine the effect on engine performance of spark timing, valve timing, temperature, air density, compression ratio, and exhaust backpressure. We will then examine specific methods of hot rodding fuel-injected engines. Final sections of this chapter deal specifically with hot rodding Chevrolet and Ford fuel injection systems.

Effects of Internal Engine Changes on Fueling Requirements

Spark Timing

Spark timing and advance have a large impact on the efficiency and exhaust emissions of an engine. As an engine turns faster, the spark plug must fire sooner. It must allow time for the mixture to ignite and achieve a high burn rate and maximum cylinder pressure. All of this must be done by the time the piston is positioned to produce best torque at roughly 15 degrees past top dead center.

This was traditionally accomplished with a centrifugal advance mechanism in the distributor which incrementally turned the distributor's cam mechanism by action of a set of spring-loaded rotating weights so the points opened sooner as rpm increased.

There is an independent variable affecting the need for spark advance as rpm increases. That is the need to modify ignition timing corresponding to engine loading and consequent volumetric efficiency variations—due to throttle position effects on cylinder filling and corresponding variations in air-fuel mixture requirements with the changing manifold pressure.

A denser mixture burns more quickly, and a leaner mixture requires more time to burn. Traditionally, a spring-loaded canister attached to a metal rod progressively retarded spark advance with increased manifold pressure by rotating the points breaker plate and points. Most carburetors have special ports for timed spark which deliver full manifold vacuum at all speeds except idle, during which the port source is covered by the throttle plate. This means that referencing a distributor vacuum advance to this port will not yield vacuum advance at idle (but will produce a surge of advance [and power] as the throttle opens).

In the 1970s, automotive engineers began to detune engines to meet emissions standards that were increasingly tough. They began to *retard* the ignition timing at idle, for example, sometimes locking out vacuum advance in lower gears or during normal operating temperature, allowing

The Chevrolet Corvette LT-1 engine uses EFI strategy to make high RPM power with short, large intake runners, compared to the TPI strategy which used long, relatively narrow tuned runners and was designed to make low and mid-range torque.

more advance if the engine was cold or overheating. Since oxides of nitrogen (NO_x) are formed when free nitrogen combines with oxygen at high temperature and pressure, retarded spark reduces NO_x emissions by lowering peak combustion temperature and pressure. This strategy also reduces hydrocarbon (HC) emissions. However, retarded spark combustion is less efficient, causing poorer fuel economy and higher heating of the engine block as heat energy has more time to escape through the cylinder walls into the coolant. The cooling system is stressed as it struggles to remove the greater waste heat during

retarded spark conditions, and fuel economy is hurt since some of the fuel is still burning as it blows out the exhaust valve, necessitating richer idle and main jetting to get decent off-idle performance. (If the mixture becomes too lean, higher combustion temperatures will defeat the purpose of ignition retard, producing *more* nitrous oxide.)

Inefficient combustion under these conditions also requires the throttle to be held open further for a reasonable idle speed, which, combined with the higher operating temperatures, can lead to dieseling (not a problem in fuel-injected engines which immediately cut off fuel flow when the key is switched off). By removing pollutants from exhaust gas, three-way catalysts tend to allow more ignition advance at idle and part throttle.

Valve Timing

Valve timing has a great effect on the speeds at which an engine develops its best power and torque. Adding more lift and intake and exhaust valve opening overlap allows the engine to breath more efficiently at high speeds. However, the engine may be hard to start, idle badly, bog down on off-idle acceleration, and produce bad low-speed torque. This occurs for several reasons. Increased valve overlap allows some exhaust gases still in the cylinder at higher than atmospheric pressure to rush into the intake manifold when the intake valve opens exactly like EGR, diluting the inlet charge—which continues to occur until rpm increases to the point where the overlap interval is so short that reverse pulsing is insignificant. The charge dilution of reverse pulsing tends to make an engine idle badly.

Valve overlap also hurts idle and low-speed performance by lowering manifold vacuum. Since the lower atmospheric pressure of high vacuum tends to keep gasoline vaporized better, racing

The Street and Performance LT-1-type Chevrolet engine is designed for higher RPM power. Note the lack of TPI runners. Street and Performance

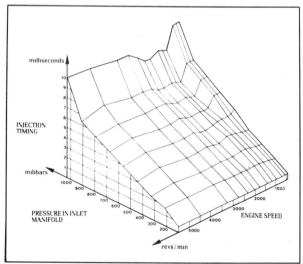

The EFI fuel map for the Fenix-equipped 2.2liter Renault engine shows a basically linear rise in fuel quantity when manifold pressure is increased. Jan P. Norbye

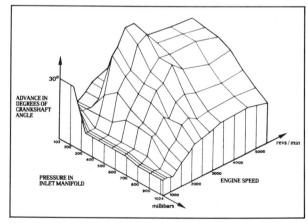

The spark-timing map for the Renault engine shows the greatest spark advance under high load-conditions in the maximum-torque range. Jan P. Norbye

cams with low vacuum may produce distribution problems and a wandering air-fuel mixture, which may require an overall richer mixture in order to keep the motor from stalling. Carbureted vehicles with hot cams may not have enough signal available to pull sufficient mixture through the idle system, leaning out the mixture, and thus requiring a tuner to increase the idle throttle setting (which may put the off-idle slot or port in the wrong position, causing an off-idle bog!). This is not a problem with fuel injection.

At higher engine speeds, reverse pulsing of racing cams tends to enrich the carb mixture where reversion gases pass through the venturi *twice*. Naturally, this is not a problem with fuel injection. Hot cams also may produce problems for carbureted vehicles when changed engine vacuum causes the power valve to open at the wrong time. Changed vacuum could affect speed-density fuel injection systems, but would have no effect on MAF-sensed EFI.

Temperature

Temperature affects fuel injection (as it does carburetion) for three reasons: colder air is denser than hotter air, colder air inhibits fuel vaporization, and colder air affects combustion temperatures. EFI systems normally have sensors to read the temperature of inlet air, and adjust the pulse width of injection to compensate. Engines will make noticeably more power on a cold day because the cold dense air increases engine volumetric efficiency, filling the cylinders with more molecules of air. This is bad news for a carb, which has no way of compensating other than jet changes (one size per 40 degrees). Airplane pilots must always know the ambient air temperature in order to estimate takeoff distance (much *short-*

Pressure variation in combustion chamber at various degrees of ignition advance.
a Ignition (Z$_a$) at correct point.
b Ignition (Z$_b$) too early.
c Ignition (Z$_c$) too late.

Combustion chamber pressure as a function of ignition spark advance: a, ignition at correct point; b, ignition too early; c, ignition too late. Ideally pressure rise should maximize at 15 degrees after TDC. Bosch

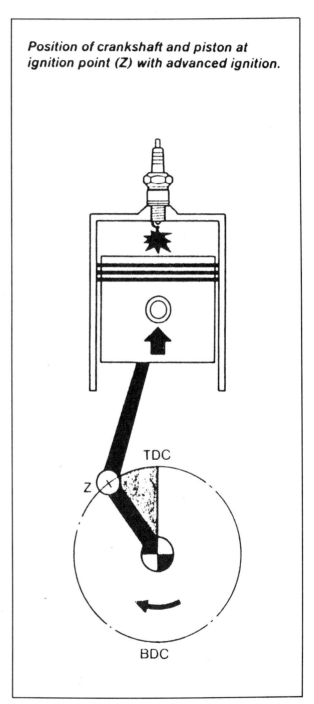

Position of crankshaft and piston at ignition point (Z) with advanced ignition.

Crank position with advanced ignition. Bosch

er on colder days). As you'd expect, racing automotive engine designs always endeavor to keep inlet air as cold as possible, and even stock streets cars often make use of cold air inlets, since each 11 degrees Fahrenheit increase reduces air density 1 percent.

On the other hand, gasoline does not vaporize well in cold air. (The oil companies, however, change their gasoline formulation to increase the vapor pressure in cold weather—which can lead

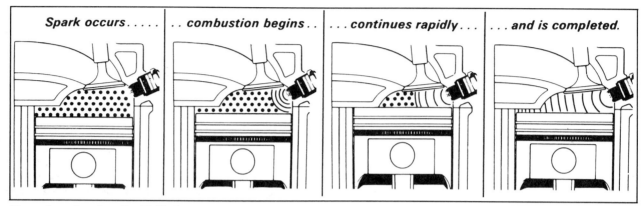

Normal combustion. Jan P. Norbye

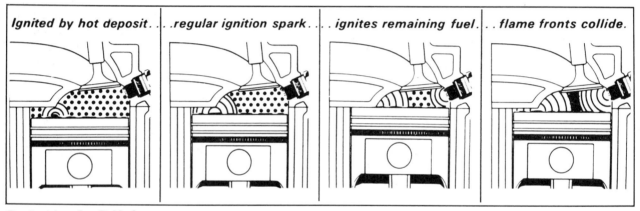

Pre-ignition. Jan P. Norbye

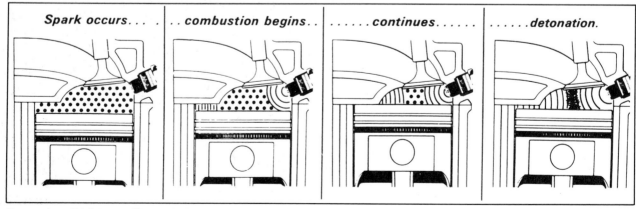

Detonation. Risk is smaller with fuel-injected than carbureted engines, allowing EFI engines to run higher compression ratios. Jan P. Norbye

64

to a rash of vapor lock in sudden warm spells in winter.) Choking systems in carbureted vehicles and cold-start fuel enrichment systems on EFI are designed to produce a rich enough mixture to run the vehicle even when much of the fuel exists not as burnable vapor, mixed with air, but as drops of nonburnable *liquid* fuel suspended in the air or resting on the manifold walls. Most air pollution is produced by cold vehicles burning mixtures as rich as 3.0:1 or 4.0:1 (even 1.0:1 during cranking!). EFI systems sense coolant temperature in order to provide cold-start enrichments (cranking, after-start, and warmup). EFI systems usually inject fuel straight at the intake valve into the swirling turbulent high-velocity air that exists there—which greatly improves atomization and vaporization. EFI does not normally need the exhaust gas-heating that carbs require in order to provide acceptable cold-start operations. EFI manifolds may use coolant heating of the manifold to increase vaporization at idle in very cold weather.

Unlike carburetors, which are susceptible to fuel starvation if ice forms as vaporizing fuel removes heat from the air and metal parts of the carb, EFI systems will deliver fuel even if ice forms in the throttle body. EFI is not as susceptible to icing since fuel vaporizes (stealing heat) at the hot intake valve, not at the throttle body. And EFI systems don't require a choke stove to heat inlet air for cold-start driving, like carbureted vehicles.

Another benefit of electronic fuel injection systems is that they are not susceptible to hot weather percolation—in which fuel boils in the carburetor in hot weather when a hot engine is shut down, flooding into the manifold. This can be aggravated by high vapor pressures produced by fuel boiling in the fuel pump or fuel lines, forcing additional fuel past the float needle. Similarly, vapor lock—produced by mechanical fuel pumps

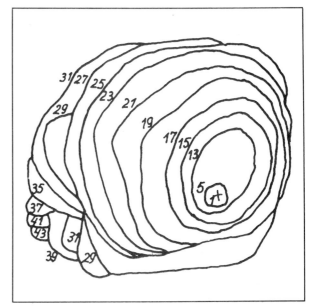

Flame front begins at X, the point of ignition at the spark plug. Plot is from a Mercedes Benz engine using canted overhead valves and fuel injection, filmed through a "window" into the combustion chamber. Numbers indicate progress in milliseconds, indicate a critical slowing in the quench area near the intake valve. Jan P. Norbye

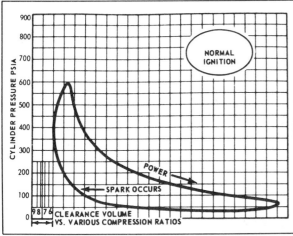

Theoretical four-stroke engine pressure volume diagram. Intake stroke takes place at lower right. Moving left from there, the compression raises pressure, and spark ignition causes the pressure to increase massively. Pressure and temperature decline during the power stroke until the exhaust valve opens. Heat and friction losses keep this diagram theoretical, but EFI engines come closer than carbureted designs. Jan P. Norbye

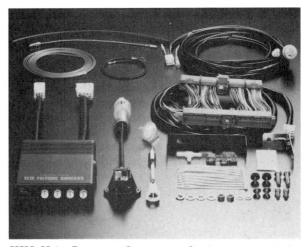

HKS Vein Pressure Convertor eliminates restrictive MAF sensors, converting speed-density air flow estimates to MAF-format data for the ECU. HKS

supplying a mixture of gas and vapor to a carb and eventually uncovering the main jets as fuel level drops–is not a problem with EFI.

Air Density

Air density varies with temperature, altitude, and weather conditions. Hot air, with greater molecular motion, is less dense. Air at higher elevations also is less dense, as is air with a higher relative humidity. Air is less dense in warm weather, but air that is heated for any reason on the way into the engine becomes less dense and will impact the injection pulse width required to achieve a correct air-fuel ratio.

Intake system layout can have a great effect on the volumetric efficiency of the engine by affecting the density of the air the engine is breathing. Air cleaners that suck in hot engine compartment air will reduce the engine's output, and should be modified to breath fresh cold air from outside. Intake manifolds that heat the air will produce less dense air, although a properly designed heated intake manifold will very quickly

be cooled by intake air at high speed and will probably improve distribution at part throttle and idle.

High Compression Ratios

High compression ratios (CR) squash the inlet air-fuel mixture into a more compact, dense mass, resulting in a faster burn rate. Turbochargers and superchargers produce *effective* compression ratios far above the nominal compression ratio by *pumping* addition mixture into the cylinder under pressure. Either way, the result is a denser mass of air and fuel molecules that burns faster and produces more pressure against the piston. The peak pressures can also produce more NO_x pollutants.

High compression ratios also tend to produce more hydrocarbons (HC) because they imply more combustion chamber surface area per volume, meaning more cooling can occur, which makes more HC. Lower CRs raise the fuel requirements at idle because there is more clearance volume in the combustion chamber which dilutes the intake

The Cartech Miata turbo motor uses a second set of outboard injectors and Haltech ECU to provide fuel enrichment under boost. The engine now makes 215hp at 8psi boost.

This Arizona Speed and Marine Firebird uses large runners on a 406ci GM TPI engine to straighten out the roads of Arizona.

charge. And because fuel is still burning longer as the piston descends, lower CRs raise the exhaust temperature and increase stress on the cooling system.

Until 1970, high-performance cars often had compression ratios of up to 11.0:1 or 12.0:1, easily done with the vintage high-octane gasoline that was readily available. By 1972, engines were running compression ratios with 8.0:1 to 8.5:1. In the 1980s and 1990s, ratios in computer-controlled fuel-injected vehicles were showing up in the 9.0:1 to 10.0:1 area based on fuel injection's ability to support higher compression ratios without detonation, coupled with the precise air-fuel control and catalysts required to keep emissions low.

Higher compression ratios or *effective* compression ratios demand higher octane gasoline to resist knocking—which can literally shatter pistons and rings at worst case. Traditionally, gasoline contained additive tetraethyl lead to slow down its tendency to explode (knock). Environmental concerns caused Congress to outlaw gasoline lead in the early 1990s, completing a trend of many years toward unleaded gasoline requirements in cars. Precisely controlled mixtures in all cylinders via port fuel injection are a key tactic in avoiding lean cylinders with increased tendency to knock.

Power Modifications

What are the *technical* solutions to increasing the power output of a fuel-injected vehicle?

Essentially, engines are limited in torque and horsepower by the amount of air they draw into the cylinder (volumetric efficiency). Improvements to VE require improvements in fueling

capability. For reasons of emissions, driveability, and warranty considerations, OE fuel injection systems have air and fuel flow bottlenecks that can be removed by the enthusiast or racer.

Eliminating Injection System Airflow Bottlenecks

The air metering section of the injection system itself may be a bottleneck to higher horse-

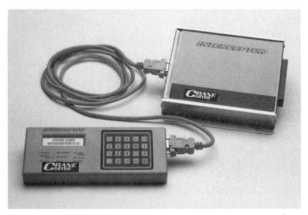

The Crane Interceptor modifies the outgoing signals to injectors, giving them a plus/minus change. Built-in user interface makes the unit very user friendly. Crane

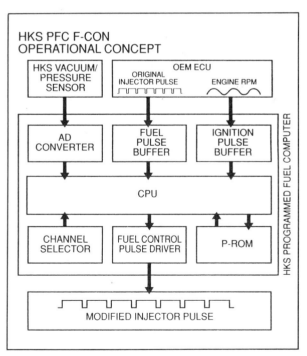

The HKS Programmed Fuel Computer (PFC) works around soldered-in PROM chips on Japanese original equipment (OE) ECUs. HKS is the largest manufacturer of speed equipment in Japan, and has an American subsidiary based in Torrance, California. HKS

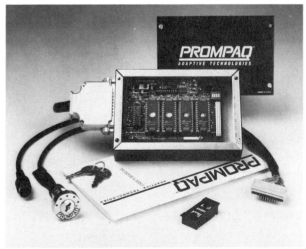

Adaptive Technologies Prompaq allows manual or automatic switching between multiple PROMs on GM engines to handle nitrous fueling and turbocharger fuel enrichment instantly.

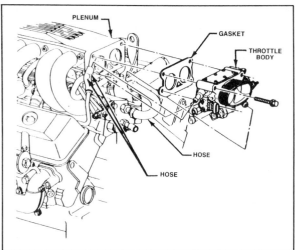

This GM TPI schematic shows the EFI throttle body mounting on the plenum. Many aftermarket firms sell higher-flow TPI parts such as larger throttle bodies, MAF sensors, TPI runners, and more.

power by restricting airflow into the engine, thus hurting volumetric efficiency.

EFI systems that directly measure airflow usually estimate mass airflow (MAF) by considering the cooling effect of inlet air on a hot wire or film suspended in an orifice of fixed size through which all inlet air must flow. Or—in the case of the velocity airflow meters—they measure the pressure of inlet air against a spring-loaded door suspended in the inlet air stream. If there is a significant pressure drop across the air metering device, then the cylinders will not fill as well with air, lowering power output. There are several ways to eliminate this airflow restriction.

Converting to an aftermarket speed-density EFI system, which measures manifold absolute pressure (MAP) and engine speed and deduces airflow based on these parameters without requiring an airflow metering device, enables a hot rodder to completely remove the metering system bottleneck. Haltech, DFI, NOS, Edel-

This 1000cfm Accel/DFI system, or systems like it, is available for all Chevrolet V-8 engines of all port configurations, using either the stock ECU or Accel's own unit, available with GM wiring harness connections. Accel/DFI

High-flow runners need a larger, lower manifold such as this to work well (or at least port-matching). TPIS

Tuned Port Induction Specialties (TPIS) offers a variety of large runners, siamesed runners, and short runner super/mini ram-type EFI manifolds for all Chevrolet V-8 motors. Here's a look at a plenum following porting that resulted in siamesed runners. TPIS

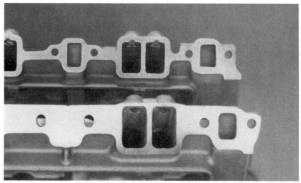

A comparison of TPIS lower manifold size (bottom) versus stock TPI manifold (top). Note the thinner walls of the TPIS unit. TPIS also has air foils designed to improve the performance of throttle bodies on TPI Chevys by eliminating turbulence in air entering the throttle body. TPIS

brock, and Electromotive fuel management systems all use the speed-density method. Some of these systems are extremely sophisticated with capabilities equal to, or, in some cases, exceeding factory engine management systems. In later chapters, this book shows how to replace factory air-metering fuel management systems with speed-density systems—in the case of a Jaguar and a Lotus which originally used Bosch L-Jetronic EFI systems with restrictive airflow meters. Pre-1990 GM TPI can be converted to speed-density control, eliminating the MAF.

All that is necessary in many cases is to replace the computer and sensors (including the air meter). The stock injectors, throttle body, and manifold, and many other systems remain stock.

The main disadvantage of replacing the stock fuel injection system is that it may not be legal (for emissions reasons), and the replacement may not preserve all the capabilities of the original system. HKS, of Torrance, California, sells a device called the Vein Pressure Converter (VPC), with which you can retain the stock EFI electronic control unit while eliminating the air metering system. The VPC is a auxiliary computer that combines data from an add-on MAP sensor referenced to intake manifold pressure with engine speed and air temperature data, to estimate mass airflow for a specific vehicle. It then sends this information to the stock ECU in the proper electrical format that exactly simulates the action of an airflow meter, but without the airflow restriction of the air meter.

Increasing Turbo Boost and Fuel Enrichment

With the many vehicles that are factory turbocharged, if is often a simple matter to increase power output by increasing the maximum boost—which is generally possible if there is a way to

For high-RPM and high-output performance, short runners and large plenum are the way to go. Keep in mind that large-runner systems need larger gaskets, and an engine with large runners sometimes needs higher fuel pressure from an adjustable fuel pressure regulator. TPIS

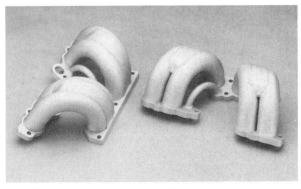

ASM's semi-siamese runners offer an option in between TPI and Super Ram manifolds. They raise the RPM capability of a ported-head engine by eliminating restriction in small runners. ASM

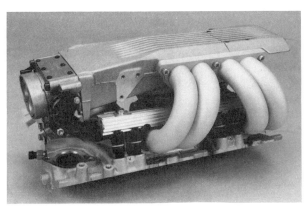

ASM TPI makes use of larger runners plus a ported and matched lower manifold and gives any size of GM small-block engine more power. ASM

An ASM 52mm 750cfm throttle body such as this is good for improving power of most big-block V-8s. ASM

raise the pressure at which the wastegate opens to cut off further increases in turbo boost. This is like making the engine bigger. Or like increasing the engine's VE by internal engine modifications such as bigger valves and cams, headers, and so on, that increase the engine's breathing capability—standard hot rodding techniques for many years.

HKS sells the Electronic Valve Controller (shown on the triple-turbo Jaguar in a later chapter), which fools the stock wastegate by feeding it an erroneous manifold pressure signal under electronic control. Mechanical means of increasing boost include mini regulators which restrict man-

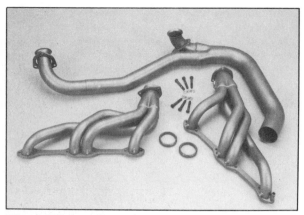

The ASM four-into-one headers for F-body cars (Camaro and Firebird) from 1985-1992 allow TPI engines to breathe. They should be used with MAF-based TPI engines or speed-density units with a custom PROM since they will change engine volumetric efficiency. ASM

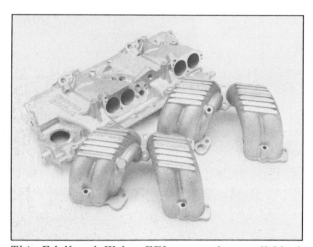

This Edelbrock-Weber EFI system for small-block Chevys works with a package of cam, headers, and EFI to provide a fairly radical street engine which still has closed loop mixture control for clean emissions. Edelbrock

ifold pressure to the stock wastegate, pressure bleeds that prevent full manifold pressure from arriving at the wastegate actuator, adjusting the spring pressure of certain stock adjustable wastegates, and finally replacement wastegates and/or larger turbochargers.

The question now is, can the stock EFI system provide the extra fuel for the engine's increased breathing?

EFI Fuel Enrichment

If an engine uses a MAF sensor, then the additional air entering the engine at a given speed will automatically call for more fuel; most stock EFI systems can deliver *some* additional fuel at a given speed.

The Mustang 5.0 liter MAF system and the GM TPI (tuned port injection) systems can deliver a small percentage of extra fuel—like 10 or 15 percent. That's enough extra fuel for minor modifications like small cam changes, air filter changes, and so on, but not enough to support fueling for significant turbo boost.

The situation is more complicated if the EFI system is not programmable and uses a speed-density system. Changing cams may alter the manifold pressure for a given engine air flow, causing the ECU to be confused or wrong about estimating how much air the engine is consuming and therefore injecting the wrong amount of fuel. There are several solutions to this problem. The first is to convert to an *aftermarket programmable ECU*, which can then be programmed to inject fuel correctly based on the new manifold pressure values. Installing a new ECU (and maybe new larger injectors and sensors) offers the advantage that a user can use any size injectors, and compensate perfectly for any engine hot rodding modifications. The ECU may have the ability to control ignition timing, and may do away with the need for a distributor.

The disadvantage of an aftermarket ECU is that the system may not be legal for street use—and, depending on the skill and the time invested by the programmers, may not be as clean or efficient or even as powerful as a factory unit. It almost certainly will not have the ability (at the time this book was written) to control add-on emissions devices. (DFI and EFI Technology can control the EGR valve.)

The second possibility is to purchase a *new PROM* for your stock ECU, one that has different look-up tables of data used to fuel the engine based on the new engine parameters. Clearly, this requires detailed knowledge of the internal data structures of the stock ECU and PROM, and requires special equipment not available to hot rodders. The PROM would have to be set up correctly for the exact equipment on the correct engine to work properly. If you have a Chevy small-block with common internal engines changes, you're in luck. Otherwise, the right PROM may not be available off-the-shelf, although there are suppliers (see chapter 4) who have the ability to make custom PROM chips.

A third possibility is to use one of the new *add-on black boxes* from HKS, Crane, and DFI which modify the *pulse width* of the electrical signal from the stock ECU to the injectors and can shorten or lengthen the injector-open time. The stock ECU knows nothing of this black box, continues fueling as always. But now a user can program the black box to provide more or less fuel under certain conditions to compensate for the changed volumetric efficiency and manifold pressure of the new hot rodded engine—by lengthening or shortening the injector pulse. Such units include the Crane Interceptor for Ford EFI, the HKS PFC for various Japanese systems, and the DFI Power Processor for GM computers.

But what if the fuel injection system is already at its limit; that is, the injectors are already open continuously or nearly continuously? There are several ways to handle this problem. The first is to *change injector size* so the new injectors flow more fuel for a given pulse width and pressure. The problem is that the ECU has no knowledge of the new injector size, so a new PROM is required, or a programmable ECU or black box as mentioned.

A simpler option is to *raise the fuel pressure* transiently so the fuel pressure increases above normal only when the engine needs additional fuel. Companies like NOS of Cypress, California,

Cartech of San Antonio, Texas, and Vortech of Simi Valley, California, make special regulators that can do this. The trick is to increase the pressure the precisely correct amount at the right time.

Another option is to add *additional injectors* that are controlled by a special add-on black box which senses engine conditions and kicks in the extra injection capability when it is needed and in the right amount. Miller-Woods sold the Turbogroup Fueler for several years, and HKS more recently brought out their additional injector controller (AIC). The additional injectors are not usually installed in the individual ports, but at a single point somewhere upstream of the throttle body (preferably at least 9-12in upstream).

Norwood Autocraft of Dallas managed to acquire a prototype GM twin-turbo EFI system for a TPI engine. This small-block Chevy reportedly makes 600-plus horsepower!

This Norwood Autocraft stroker 454ci uses 16-injector Haltech EFI with twin-cam Batten heads. The block is an aluminum Donovan 600ci block.

EDELBROCK E.F.I. SYSTEM SCHEMATIC

The speed-density system for the small-block Chevrolet engine was ahead of its time in the seventies. The Edelbrock Pro-Flo EFI system shown in this schematic uses the latest digital circuitry and sensors and a proprietary LCD display to provide add-on EFI for any 265-400ci Chevrolet V-8. Edelbrock

Dual-Fuel Injection—
A Motorhead's Guide to Cheating

Inventors have long recognized the advantages of a vehicle that could run on multiple fuels. Pickup trucks in eastern Arizona 20 years ago frequently had both gasoline carbs and Impco Propane carbs—one mounted on top of the other! Gasoline started the vehicle more easily, made more power, and you could get it at any gas station. But Propane was way cheaper for use around the huge irrigated farms of Cochise County. A dashboard switch manually activated solenoids that could affect fuel changeover at any time.

That was in the days of carbs. The more recent advent of programmable electronic fuel injection has given the concept of dual-fuel vehicles new life. Dallas Supercar builder Bob Norwood has applied the dual-fuel concept to a recent Supercar project which involved turbocharging an Acura NSX. By retaining the stock internal engine parameters—including 10.2–1 compression ratio—the Norwood turbo NSX retains the stock fuel injection system under all driving conditions, yielding excellent drivability including great low-end crispness and torque, plus emissions compliance, and the economy and convenience of street gasoline. Under turbo boost, an auxiliary Haltech F3 computer activates two huge 1600cc Indycar fuel injectors which inject super high "octane" Methanol for air-fuel mixture enrichment and detonation control, enabling the car to safely run 9psi boost. The NSX runs an auxiliary 5gal Methanol tank and a totally separate fuel supply to a high pressure fuel rail which supports the two single-point injectors, each of which fires three times per engine revolution near the throttle body. The F3 computer controlling the additional injectors is virtually "sensorless," reading only engine speed and manifold pressure to provide timed injection. The car looks normal from the outside, idles normally, but as they say, step on the gas, she goes wild.

Norwood has now extended the dual-fuel injection concept to other vehicles with intermittent injection of 106 octane race gas, and even Nitromethane. The dual fuel injection scheme makes sense from many points of view: Exotic fuel cost and availability, detonation control, emissions compliance, improved power, and improved dynamic range of injection.

Consider emissions: The automotive aftermarket has been feverishly working to build legal add-on or modified parts or parts kits with legal California emissions Exemption Orders. And this is one reason auxiliary computers and injectors enter the picture: It is often a far more simple task to use one or more auxiliary computers to modify the behavior of the factory engine management system—under the relatively limited circumstances during which add-on modifications such as turbochargers change engine fueling or spark requirements—than to start from scratch building an entirely new set of engine control parameters with the precision required to pass emissions testing. Why reinvent the wheel when the car factory has already done all the work to pass emissions? Since many performance modifications only make a difference at full throttle (which is not part of the Federal Test Procedure for emissions compliance) the add-on auxiliary computer is a potent weapon in the hands of nineties tuners. And when you have secondary injectors, it is relatively easy to supply them with a different fuel.

There are power advantages to dual fuel injection. The fact that Methanol contains 10 percent oxygen helps support additional combustion—a little like shooting nitrous oxide into a motor. Nitromethane contains even more oxygen, acting nearly like a monopropellant such as Thermoline, a rocket fuel which will burn without air—which is why Nitro can be incredibly dangerous. Multiple-injector Norwood auxiliary fueling systems plumb additional injectors into individual runners and provide an

continued on next page

This 16-injector Norwood engine—"Charlie Brown II"—uses twin turbos to pressurize the manifold of Chevy big-block and dual fuel injection of "river gas" under ordinary conditions, with 106 octane race gas injected by Haltech-controlled additional injectors under high boost for "lake burnouts."

The turbo NSX built by Norwood Autocraft used "dual fuel injection" that consisted of two 1600cc/minute injectors under Haltech F3 control, injecting alcohol under boost conditions and allowing retention of the stock compression ratio of 10.2-1.

entirely separate fuel supply. Norwood has used up to three electronic injectors per cylinder for Nitro or alcohol, producing prodigious amounts of power on demand, while offering precise computer control of both fuels. If emissions compliance is not necessary, electronic controllers like the F3 can *stage* dual fuel injection, providing basic engine fuel control under all circumstances, while activating an *additional* set of dual fuel injectors at a specific RPM or manifold pressure—which has the added benefit of extending the dynamic fueling range of the stock injectors to much higher power levels while allowing the engine to idle properly at the other end of the scale. Norwood "tunes" the dual fuel mix of such a system by balancing the size of the primary and secondary injector nozzles, since all injectors are currently limited to firing at equal pulsewidths when controlled by a single computer. An auxiliary computer, as on the turbo NSX, has no such limitation, firing dual fuel injectors entirely independently. Norwood has used dual fuel injection on naturally-aspirated engines, switching at a pre-programmed RPM entirely to alternate fuel, for example 3000-4000rpm in a roundy-round type of car. A Norwood twin-turbo dual-use powerboat normally runs on river gas, with a separate tank of 106 race gas for lake "burnouts."

Exotic fuel availability can be a serious problem for any dual-use vehicle—even if you don't care what it costs. Vehicles like power boats and club race cars do not require super high octane fuel except under heavy loading conditions. Running on pump gas vastly extends the practicality of such a car or boat. At the same time, controlling detonation is essential. Racers buy race gas and run it constantly, while street cars are happy on 87 or 92 octane. For the lunatic fringe that require a dual-use street-mannered vehicle with incredible horsepower on demand, dual fuel injection is a free lunch.

Pulse Width Modification Black Boxes (Crane and HKS)

Most original equipment (OE) EFI systems have the ability to compensate for variations in engine fueling requirements. These variations are due to small differences in engine operating characteristics resulting from climate, wear, driving style, and even how "blueprinted" an individual engine happens to be.

Original equipment ECUs are constantly computing how much air is entering an engine based on stored tables and sensor data, then estimating fuel injection requirements. After the injection event, they evaluate the accuracy of the air-fuel mixture via the oxygen sensor data. If the estimated injection pulse width is wrong, the ECU has the ability to make adjustments.

(This is usually *not* true at full throttle; existing sensors and ECUs are generally not capable of reacting quickly enough to changing fuel requirements to operate in closed-loop [feedback] mode at full throttle, where the consequences of mistakes in mixture might very quickly become disastrous—so they work from existing fuel maps without attempting to make adjustments based on exhaust gas oxygen content.)

This built-in flexibility at idle and cruise may allow the EFI system to continue delivering accurate fueling after minor performance modifications increase the airflow through an engine.

Obviously, internal fueling maps do not abruptly end *exactly* at the loading or rpm points that define the boundaries of *expected* engine operating parameters. ECU-engine combinations—especially those with mass airflow metering—will be able to detect accurately how much air an engine is flowing even after substantial performance modifications, and will compute fuel requirements correctly. They will, that is, up to the point when performance modifications result in combinations of rpm and airflow that go past the edge of the stored fuel map tables. Memory space in ECUs is often tight; obviously, Ford is not going to store base fuel map data for 30lb worth of turbo boost airflow into a 5.0 liter engine at 1500rpm on a factory naturally aspirated engine. You get the idea.

And of course, at some point the stock fueling system reaches its physical limit, given the size of the injectors and the capacity of the fuel pump. You can easily compute the upper limit of fueling capacity or a vehicle's injection system by looking at injector squirt capacity at 100 percent duty cycle, correcting this for brake specific fuel consumption to yield a theoretical maximum horsepower.

What additional fueling can an OE system handle beyond stock? The only way to know this for sure in the absence of proprietary OE system documentation is trial and error. Equipment needed in this testing includes: digital pulse width analyzers, heated oxygen sensor air-fuel ratio meters, highly accurate manifold absolute pressure and rpm gauges, exhaust gas temperature (EGT) meters, test equipment to monitor the activity of detonation sensor activity, equipment to monitor all air temperatures, and horsepower dynos to monitor the engine status.

You make your performance mods and see what the stock ECU does. However, this is obviously not within the scope of capability for many enthusiasts.

Several companies are offering modified PROMs for use with modified engines. This is easy and cheap with GM computers with their removable PROM chip. Ford PROMs are not removable, however, and aftermarket Ford PROMs must include a PROM and circuitry that plugs into the diagnostic port on the EEC-IV control unit. In either case, the new chip *will* modify the stock fuel curve in certain respects under certain conditions; the chip will react the same way under the same conditions. At least one entrepreneur has brought out the Prompaq to enable the user to instantly select from several PROMs mounted on the Prompaq circuit board, depending on driving conditions.

The DFI Power Processor, the Crane Interceptor, and the HKS Programmed Fuel Computer F-CON are black boxes that plug into an OE injection wiring harness to enable modification of stock fuel curves—anything from minor enrich-

ment or enleanment to the radical pulse width changes needed to support larger injectors and forced induction and/or increased fuel pressure. The idea is to keep some or most of the highly developed factory fueling map, modifying only those parts necessary to provide correct fueling for modifications such as increased turbo boost (or larger turbo), addition of turbo to naturally aspirated engine, and so on.

The Crane Interceptor is currently designed for use with the 5.0 liter Ford engine. HKS offers multiple control maps for the PFC for use with various engines based on extensive testing. The unit is not generally sold for universal applications, although HKS will work with manufacturers of performance goods outside the range of HKS' own specific product line to supply PFC maps for the new applications.

The PFC and Interceptor are designed to plug into the factory EFI wiring harness, and require no fabrication or "surgical skills" to install. Once installed, PFC internal dip switches allow selection of gross richer or leaner percentage of the basic program, plus selection of nine separate condition programs.

Beyond that, the Graphic Control Computer (GCC) option gives the user a second black box with pots to adjust individual load points of 500, 2000, 3500, 5000, 6500, and 8000rpm, each of which can be adjusted to deliver up to 16 percent more fuel or 12 percent less fuel than the base map. The GCC averages values between the adjustable points for smooth fueling.

HKS offers a further optional black box called the Electronic Valve Controller to raise turbocharger maximum boost levels by electromechanically altering boost pressure levels as seen at the factory wastegate/controller. And to work with this, they offer the Fuel Cut Defenser

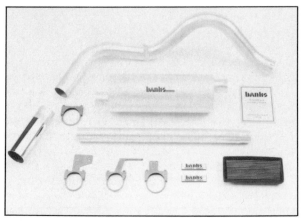

A Banks 460ci Ford breathing kit like this works well on late-model 460 EFI trucks. Banks

These Cartech hop-up parts include a gigantic V-8 manifold with short-runner plenum-ram configuration designed to run twin front-mounted throttle bodies. Cartech

The Cartech cross-ram on 5.0liter engine uses twin side-mounted throttle bodies. Note the IAC motor/valve in foreground. Cartech

74

(FCD) black box to defeat factory fuel shutdown with overboost or high rpm for use with modified engines where such limits are dysfunctional.

The Crane unit plugs into the Ford EEC-IV computer, and is programmed with a twenty-key pad. You can then increase or decrease the fuel and spark and/or monitor engine operational status via monitor mode which displays rpm, timing, injector percent of duty cycle, air-fuel mixture, and percentage of throttle opening via the TPS sensor. Monitor mode will also list certain trouble codes on the display. The Crane unit allows a user to modify idle, part throttle, and full throttle in three rpm scales, plus extended rpm scale for operation beyond the stock 6250rpm rev limit. A user can design three different programs: stock, EEC-IV, or set up for racing, fuel economy, trailer towing, high altitude, nitrous operation, and so forth. The user can instantly compare the effects of changes to one program by switching to another (perhaps the stock EEC-IV program) on the fly. Crane offers an optional boost harness to allow custom fuel and spark adjustments under forced induction conditions.

Installation of the Interceptor is easily done in less than a half hour. On a Mustang, it involves access to the EEC-IV via the passenger-side kick panel; removal of two screws enabling the computer to drop down for access. Remove a bolt that holds the stock harness to the computer and then connect the harness to the Interceptor, which, in turn, connects to the EEC-IV, which would normally be reinstalled in stock position. Then mount the keypad/display controller in a convenient place and find a mounting position for the Interceptor, perhaps under the passenger seat.

Crane supplies suggestions for possible modifications to stock fueling and ignition for basic performance increases and maximum performance with turbos, nitrous, and high rpm—and a method for making and testing small changes to yield a good final result. With a simple setup change, the Interceptor will work on speed-density as well as MAF air metering vehicles. Like the ZR-1 Corvette, an Interceptor-equipped car provides a "valet-mode" lockout of high-performance operation via passcode, and allows removal of the controller.

Chevrolet Tuned Port Injection (TPI)

GM TPI is so important that this book devotes a special chapter to a tutorial on the TPI engine and TPI engine swapping.

Chevrolet designed Tuned Port Injection (TPI) for a 305ci engine modified for street use. Design goals included responsive acceleration with an automatic transmission in a heavy car under average driving conditions (which means

JLJ Racing's twin turbo aluminum 5.0liter Ford engine made 1032 dyno horsepower on gasoline! Note the cross-ram manifold with 16 injectors, plus twin air-water intercoolers.

low to medium rpm), plus good fuel economy and emissions (which implies tall gears). As it should with these goals, the TPI system makes great low-end torque that dies out rapidly above 4000rpm. This is a situation that leaves hot rodders and racers looking for ways to make more power at higher rpm on a TPI-injected Chevy.

It's important to keep in mind that torque is what makes a car fun to drive. Horsepower is a measure of how much work an engine can do at a certain speed, such as lifting a weight of a certain size. Torque measures the moment of a force, that is, its tendency to produce torsion and rotation around an axis. In other words, twisting force—the kind of force that causes a car to leap forward when you nail the gas because of the instantaneous rotational force of the engine's crankshaft.

Torque is critical to an engine's ability to accelerate. Peak torque usually occurs at the engine's point of highest volumetric efficiency. Both race and street engines need to accelerate well from a variety of speeds; therefore, good torque over a *broad range* is important, not just peak torque. High horsepower achieved at high engine speeds over a narrow range (way above the peak torque at low VE where the cylinders are no longer filling as well, just more often) tends to produce cars that aren't flexible or fun to drive—you have to drive the car like you're mad at it to get any performance.

Tuned-runner port injection is great at making torque, but there are tradeoffs with various manifold and runner designs, just as there were with intake manifolds designed for carburetors. Port EFI manifolds do not have to deal with keeping fuel suspended properly in air as wet-air carburetor or throttle-body injection manifolds must do. This gives designers more flexibility with runner length, geography, and cross section—that is, the ability to tune the intake for the best torque curve for a given application. However, it is a fact that intake runner length and cross section (as well as *exhaust* port and header length and cross section) do impact the torque curve of an engine. There are tradeoffs. Longer, narrower runners accelerate air to high velocities with high momentum which produces higher air pressure at the intake valve. If the engine is turning slowly, time is not a critical factor in cylinder filling and VE is higher with longer, narrower runners. At higher rpm, time is critical. There is not time for a long column of air to accelerate and enter the cylinder in time to fill it well. The narrow cross section of a runner implies less volume and more pressure drop at high rpm. Again, less cylinder filling. Bigger, shorter runners are the hot ticket for high-RPM performance.

If the motor is stock, and always will be, it is hard to beat the GM TPI system, which works well up to 4600rpm. But stock TPI manifolds negate the effect of better heads and cams and headers for higher rpm power. If the motor is not stock and/or you need power above 4600rpm, the stock TPI manifold will have to be modified with larger runners and larger throttle body or a completely new manifold. (Equipment is available from Arizona Speed and Marine in Phoenix, Arizona, Accel (DFI), TPIS, and others.)

You'll need an aftermarket ECU *or* a modified PROM in the stock GM computer that is matched to the new engine modifications. And if the engine changes again, you may need yet another PROM. An alternative may be the Accel/DFI Power Processor, an auxiliary add-on computer designed to work with and change the ECM's calibration. With new intake equipment, the heads will become the flow bottleneck. As always, every part of the complete system must be designed to work well together or some unexpected bottleneck can negate the effect of other expensive modified parts. A mild stock 305 engine is well matched to the stock TPI system.

But let's say you've improved the cam a little, and installed headers, perhaps even upgraded to a crate 350 High Output (HO) motor with somewhat better cam and heads, designed to make roughly 350hp. It's easy to install runners from Arizona Speed and Marine or TPIS, and a matching larger throttle body. Typically, the TPIS runners are 0.190in in diameter larger than stock and 0.325in longer, which adds considerable higher rpm torque and power from 3000rpm up. (One test showed 75 foot pounds [lb-ft] over stock across the board from 3700rpm on up to redline!)

Runners are available not only in larger sizes, but with adjacent ports siamesed together so a cylinder can share two runners for better breathing at high rpm (which hurts lower rpm power and torque). Serious hot rodders may decide to Extrude Hone the manifold base to match the flow capabilities of the new runners and higher cubic-feet-per-minute throttle body—or switch to a large manifold base like the TPIS Big Mouth, with its round 1.750in entry sizes and 1.960-1.200in exits.

A serious big-displacement Chevy small-block motor—one with a good 240 degree duration 0.550-0.600in cam, compression over 10:1, and some seriously ported good high-rpm aftermarket aluminum heads—will require a completely new manifold to take advantage of this configuration's ability to make high-rpm power. Accel, TPIS, and others make such manifolds designed with considerably shorter and fatter runners and much higher volume plenums. The Accel SuperRam runners are over 3in shorter than the stock TPIS (4.125in vs. 7.250in), incorporating D-section geometry of 1.878in x 1.970in (versus stock 1.470in round runner). The one-piece TPIS Mini-Ram is a serious high-rpm manifold with still shorter runners (3.5in) and huge 2.600in x 1.350in entry, tapering to 1.960in x 1.200in exits.

Properly sized carburetion can make as much maximum horsepower as port EFI; unfortunately, by sizing the venturis in such a way that they are not restrictive on a hot motor at high rpm, the carburetor(s) will provide terrible low and mid-range power and torque. Good, big-runner TPI manifolds, and even short-ram EFI and stock TPI manifolds, will be making 100lb-ft more torque at 2500rpm, compared to a higher rpm carburetor and manifold! This is power you can *feel* as well as measure.

The Cartech 5.0liter Mustang twin-turbo kit replaces the top of the stock EFI manifold with a twin throttle body plenum. The kit uses an aftermarket ECU and large port injectors to make 500-600hp.

Ford Multi Port Injection (MPI)

Professional Flow Tech builds the Pro-M 77 mass airflow (MAF) air sensor, a patented high-flow (1,000cfm) unit for pumped Ford 5.0 liter engines, as well as EFI test equipment and systems capable of wait-time testing, other troubleshooting, and Ford and GM EFI calibration.

Professional Flow Tech's president, Bob Atwood, has worked with fuel system products for twenty-two years, as a consultant and engineer for Rochester Products, Ford Motor Company, and Professional Flow Tech. Atwood is considered an expert on Ford EEC-IV ECU-based products. In order to get the 5.0 liter Ford V-8 air metering to work properly in low-range airflow, Ford restricted the high end, says Atwood. The Pro-M 77 utilizes patented aerodynamics which use resonation effects to get excellent metering at low airflow while handling 1,000cfm on the high end—which translates to a bolt-on 15-20hp on the 5.0 liter engine. The Pro-M 77 will work on any MAF EEC-IV engine, including the Mustang, the Supercoupe, and the SHO Taurus. The company is currently designing a system for Ford speed-density EFI trucks which converts the system to Mustang high-output programming, including a high-performance MAF.

Many of the same principles that apply to GM TPI also apply to the Ford 5.0 system. It is designed to make good low-end and mid-range torque. But like the TPI systems, there are many parts available to pump your 5.0, with a good place to start being Ford, whose Motorsport program offers high-performance GT-40 upper and lower intake manifold pairs, as well as GT-40 iron and SVO aluminum heads, which will increase the breathing of a 5.0.

Other common mods on Mustang 5.0s include cams, 77mm mass air kits, Pro-M 77mm complete conversion kits (with wiring, computer, and 77mm sensor), SVO complete mass air conversions, 65 and 75mm throttle bodies, 24 and 30lb injectors, adjustable pressure regulators, the Crane Interceptor, shorty headers, cat back exhaust systems, and high-volume fuel pumps.

Cartech, Vortech, Spearco, and others offer turbocharger and supercharger kits for the Mustang, some of which are even street legal in California. Most of these kits use add-on fuel pressure regulators which massively increase fuel pressure under boost to provide adequate fueling and enrichment.

The problem in modifying Ford 5.0 engines is that maximum horsepower is limited by the stock injection components: The 19lb/hr stock injectors can make 300hp at 45psi. The stock fuel pump will supply sufficient fuel for 300hp at 45psi (the SVO pump will supply 375hp), and the stock MAF meter will supply air (and voltage signal to the EEC-IV) for 310hp. The limit with stock EFI components is roughly 300hp. Any strategy to increase power levels above this must address these limitations.

EEC-IV PROMs are not replaceable, but ADS offers a performance module to alter the OE computer's performance by inserting the module between the EEC-IV and the wiring harness. Other devices reprogram the EEC-IV by plugging into the diagnostic port.

Chapter 8

GM Tuned Port Injection

TPI was GM's high-performance fuel injection system from the mid-eighties into the nineties, installed exclusively on GM's High Output Corvettes, Camaros, and Firebirds, with horsepower rating to 245hp. Although the new non-TPI LT-1 and LT-5 (ZR-1) Corvettes make 300 and 400hp with higher revving capabilities, multiple overhead cams, and four-valve combustion chambers, these engines are rare and expensive. TPI engines have been produced in great numbers, and what's more, parts are readily available to build TPI engines that easily exceed the power output of the exotic LT-series GM engines.

TPI Tutorial

Certain information in this section is based on data provided by Fuel Injection Specialties of San Antonio, Texas, in a tutorial they provide about GM Tuned Port Injection. FIS provides special TPI wiring harnesses and modifications, as well as consulting and parts for high performance modifications to TPI fuel injection.

History

Tuned Port Injection appeared in 1985 on certain GM F-Body cars (Firebird and Camaro) and on the Corvette. This is a multi-port fuel injection system using long tuned runners to produce high performance in GM small block V-8s, producing 30-35 percent improvement over carbureted V-8s in horsepower, torque, and efficiency. TPI also made impressive gains compared to previous GM EFI systems. The GM 350 (5.7L) V-8 eventually went from 205hp in the Cross-fire Injection twin throttle body injection Corvette to 245 with the addition of TPI and valve train improvements, a twenty percent gain.

Over the years, GM has modified the original 1985 EFI system. The electronic control module (computer module) has changed several times, as have peripheral electronics. The 1985 TPI with #1226870 ECM used a Mass Air Flow sensor (MAF) and controller module to measure air flow into the engine so the ECM could determine fuel injector open time. In 1986 the MAF controller module was deleted as a separate peripheral device and the ECM changed to #1227165. In 1989, the auxiliary cold start injector was deleted in favor of cold start enrichment through the main injectors. In 1990, GM changed from MAF air flow metering to Speed-Density air flow estimation based on engine speed and manifold pressure as measured by a Manifold Absolute Pressure (MAP) sensor. The new system used ECM #1227730 for F-Body cars and a hardened ECM #1227727 for the Corvette which could survive in the engine compartment.

ECM Chart (F= F-Body Camaro and Firebird, Y= Corvette)

Vehicle	Model Year	GM Part #	Engine
F, Y	1985	1226870	5.0L, 5.7L
F, Y	1986-89	1227165	5.0L, 5.7L
F	1990+	1227730	5.0L, 5.7L
Y	1990+	1227727	5.7L

Note: These ECMs are not interchangeable—i.e., a 1227165 will not plug into a 1226870 harness and operate. To work correctly, the harness would have to be modified.

GM uses plug-in PROM chips in the ECM to provide specific information to the ECM and its internal programming about the particular engine and vehicle it is operating. GM calls the PROM (and data!) a "calibrator." This calibrator enables identical internal programming logic, for example, to operate both 305 and 350 engines. The data being used in calculations differs based on the calibrator. In addition to raw fueling information, emissions control data, transmissions information, and Vehicle Anti-Theft System (VATS) are contained in the calibrator. Rear axle ratio information may be located on a separate chip on the calibrator module. GM uses many different calibrators. Aftermarket outfits offer additional calibration options for high performance vehicles on their own custom PROMs.

Some post-1987 calibrators include anti-theft countermeasures (VATS) which prevent the engine from starting without the properly encoded key in the ignition—at which time the VATS system informs the ECM that it is OK to start the car.

1985 TPI vehicles use a 32K PROM for calibration. From 1986 to 1989, GM used a 128K PROM, and the latest ECMs use a 256K PROM.

Calibration and Learning

In order to maintain the best possible performance as vehicles age and to correct for minor variations in production of new vehicles' engines and fuel systems, TPI systems have the ability to adjust engine management as you drive—in other words, to *learn*. The ECM uses two features to organize its "learning." The first is the Integrator and Block Learn (I & BL), the second the Block Learn Memory (BLM) cell. The I & BL is normally set near 128. Higher values indicate the ECM is temporarily adding fuel to the base fuel calculation because the ECM thinks the engine is running lean. Lower values indicate the ECM is reducing fueling due to a perceived rich-running engine.

The BLM is a longer term correction strategy. If the I & BL stays non-128 for a "long" period of time, the BLM has up to 16 cells it can modify to provide fueling corrections—depending on engine status during the longer term calibration error—factoring in RPM, MAF or MAP values, air condition status, and so forth. The BLM calibration comes into play at the appropriate time only. The BLM is intentionally based in volatile memory so it is reset to default values any time the battery is disconnected or run down far enough. Once reset, the ECM has to relearn everything again by observing what engine management corrections are required while the vehicle is driving. Learned calibrations typically change parameters for injection pulsewidth, fuel cutoff, spark advance/timing, and will stabilize idle, calibrate the engine for best fuel economy at idle and light cruise, and may modify spark advance and increase fuel flow during hard acceleration.

TPI Engine Management

1985-88 TPI ECMs use the following sensors and actuators:
Mass Air Flow Sensor (MAF)
Manifold Air Temperature (MAT)
Coolant Temperature
Exhaust Gas Oxygen Sensor (EGO or O_2)
Throttle Position Sensor (TPS)
Cold Start Switch
Cold Start injector

Space constraints at the throttle-body inlet area made installation of this TPI engine in this 1978 Chevrolet Caprice a challenge. Fuel Injection Specialties

Fuel Injectors
Idle Air Control Valve (IAC)
Distributor
Electronic Spark Timing Module (integral to distributor)
Electronic Spark Control Module (ESC)
Knock Sensor

The ECM uses cool running strategies during startup and warmup periods. Early TPI systems activate the cold start injector when the coolant temperature is less than 100 degrees. Under control of the cold start valve, the cold start injector sprays raw fuel into the air stream near the throttle plate such that it is distributed to all cylinders. After start, the ECM uses stored data to provide fuel enrichment based on temperature and warm up tables until the O_2 sensor reaches 600 degrees, at which time the system enters Closed Loop mode, possibly still providing cold-running enrichment until the engine coolant reaches operating temperature. In Closed Loop mode, the system looks at exhaust gas oxygen to estimate whether the the engine is running richer or leaner than the chemically perfect (14.7-1) stoichiometric air-fuel ratio.

During normal running, the ECM incorporates information on engine air flow, coolant temperature, air temperature, exhaust gas oxygen content, and throttle position in order to calculate injector open time (pulse width) and spark advance, as well as operation of emissions control devices. This process occurs continuously in an "infinite loop," with the ECM constantly striving to optimize fueling and spark advance, checking how it is doing via the O$_2$ sensor and the knock sensor.

TPI systems are complex enough that it makes sense to work with a complete matched engine and all components where possible, even in an engine swap situation. Certain components must be matched for best performance. These include the Distributor/EST module, ESC module, knock sensor and ECM calibrator, and these components are *not* interchangable between 5.0L and 5.7L engines.

Fuel Injection Specialties recommends using 5.7L components for 327ci-400ci engines, and 5.0L components for 265ci-305ci engines. If you are adapting TPI to non-TPI engines, particularly where the cam and displacement are non-original, you should know what you are doing or get help from someone who does. You should almost certainly be using the earlier MAF system, and you should have test equipment available to verify that the engine is operating correctly (such as gas analyzer, EGT probes, etc.). You may need a custom PROM chip. Expect to invest time and energy getting the non-standard engine sorted out, and don't try it unless you are mechanically adept.

After 1989, GM eliminated the cold start injector on TPI systems, the calibrator providing a fatter pulsewidth on startup to all injectors.

In 1990, GM changed to Speed-Density air flow estimation. Since air flow is no longer measured, but rather estimated based on assumptions about the correlation between manifold pressure at speed and air flow *for a specific engine with a specific cam and other equipment,* the new system does not have the ability to correct for air flow changes into the engine resulting from modifications that screw up the factory-assumed relationship between manifold pressure/vacuum and air flow at speed. The new Speed-Density system may simplify routing air into the throttle body on a TPI engine swap, since there is no longer a big clunky MAF sensor to mount near the front of the engine.

Systems from 1990 and later years use the VATS to foil car thieves, requiring a special key with an encoded resister for the car to start.

Peripherals

1985-86 TPI *intake manifolds* will fit all older GM small-block engines. Later TPI heads were designed with vertical bolt taps for the two center bolts on both sides of the intake manifold. As I discuss later in the section on TPI engine swaps, you will have to drill newer TPI manifolds to fit older heads. For all practical purposes, the TPI manifolds are interchangeable for all small block engines. The TPI manifold plenum is interchangeable between all years, although 1990 and later models are tapped for the MAP sensor required on earlier models. Intake runners are also interchangeable, although 1989 and later left-side runners delete the Cold Start injector mounting.

Fuel Rails differ in that earlier rails have a fitting on the left side near the firewall to attach the cold-start injector fuel line. See the chart in this section for identification of the TPI system via the number stamped on the rail, which will tell you whether the system was on a 350 or 305, and identify the injectors on the rail.

TPI Fuel Rail Identification

Stamped Number	5.0	5.7	Bosch	Injectors Multc.	Roch.	Vehicle	Year
17085052	X		X			F	85-87
17087264	X			X		F	85-87
17089024	X				X	F	89
17090100	X				X	F	90-91
17085050		X	X			Y	85
17085019		X	X			F, Y	86-87
17086106		X	X			F, Y	86-87
17087265		X		X		F, Y	87-88
17087266		X		X		F, Y	87
17088065		X		X		F, Y	88
17089025		X			X	F, Y	89
17089026		X			X	F, Y	80
17080101		X			X	F, Y	90-91
17080102		X			X	F, Y	90-91

1985-1986 TPI systems used a GM HEI *distributor*, keyed differently from earlier models. 1987-1991 F-Body systems use a small diameter distributor with external coil, while Corvettes still used the HEI unit. Either unit will work, although the connectors are different. The 1985-86 5.0L HEI distributor is stamped with 1103679 at the base, while 1985-91 5.7L HEI units are stamped 1103680. The small diameter later F-Body non-HEI distributor is stamped 1103749.

TPI *fuel pumps* are high-pressure units located in the tank designed to provide 24gal per hour at 50psi. FIS sells a 30gal/hr at 60psi unit made by AC Delco. By comparison, carbureted systems operate at 3-6psi using a mechanical pump to fill the float chamber, while Throttle Body Injection systems use electric fuel pumps supplying roughly 12psi pressure. FIS suggests TPI systems require 5/16 or 3/8in fuel supply lines, and 5/16in fuel return lines.

GM has used several different brands of *fuel injectors* in an attempt to handle injector clogging problems, including units from Lucas, Bosch, AC Rochester, and Multec. Bosche uses a pintle injector design, Lucas a disc design, Rochester a ball/disc design, the Multec an inverse conical nozzle, all supplying 4.05 milligrams of fuel with a 2.5ms pulsewidth—or 18.13lb/hr at roughly 36psi. The 5.7L injectors must supply 4.83 milligrams in a 2.5ms pulse, or 23.92lb/hr at 43.5psi. Injectors varying in price from $60 to $100 or so. The TPI closed loop system can correct for minor differences in flow. The GM ECM is designed to power 16ohm injectors.

1985 *wiring harnesses* provide a connection for the MAFS module in the vicinity of the ECM connection. Early systems require the Mass Air Flow control module, which mounts piggyback on the ECM. ESC and fuel pump relay mount together on a bracket in the engine compartment. 1986-89 harnesses have three relays and ESC module together in the engine compartment. The 1989 harness has no connections to control a Cold Start injector, and all early systems require the MAF. Connectors on early systems are the same, but *not* interchangeable between 1985 and other systems. The ECMs are *not* the same. 1990 and later systems include the ESC module in the ECU, and have no MAF sensor, instead having wiring connections for the MAP sensor on the intake manifold. The EST module in the distributor, and the knock sensors are different on late systems and must be correctly matched. Late systems are cheaper to manufacture without the delicate MAF sensor, but cannot compensate for volumetric efficiency changes from higher lift/longer duration cams on modified engines. Late ECMs in Corvettes are hardened for mounting in the engine compartment (#1227727), while the F-

Body cars use #1227730 with compatible electronics but different enclosure and connectors. Calibrators are interchangeable, according to FIS. Note that the Assembly Lined Diagnostic Link (ALDL) is not normally part of the factory engine harness, but is part of the instrument harness. The factory harness includes some connectors for devices not absolutely required for off-highway use or on older vehicles, including connections for Air Management, Transmission, EGR, Electric Cooling Fans, Instrument Panel Oil Pressure sender, Air Conditioning high pressure switch, and VATS. Some people have run TPI engines without the VSS, but note the warning in the swap section regarding the VSS deletion.

Harness Modifications

Fuel Injection Specialties (FIS) can modify factory wiring harnesses to remove certain connectors, as well as installing the ALDL connector and interconnecting leads to existing vehicle electrical systems for switched (ignition) power, bat-

These components make up a TPI system, and this photo includes the elements of the wiring harness. Missing are the lower manifold and runners. Fuel Injection Specialties

tery power, fuel pump, A/C compressor (which tells the ECM to speed up idle when A/C on), and crank signal (connection to starter solenoid). All other TPI harness connections are for self-contained TPI devices. FIS and other venders also supply new "off-road" TPI harnesses which delete air management, EGR, transmission control and sensing, VSS, instrument panel, fans, and vacuum purge cannister. Street legal harnesses from FIS and other venders retain all emissions devices. FIS stocks OE parts for GM TPI and TBI systems, as well as parts, harnesses, and harness modifications for GM big-block and Ford EFI systems. FIS supplies performance PROMs (calibrators) and can modify stock calibrators for VATS bypass. Other FIS products include adjustable fuel pressure regulators, power pulleys, throttle body air foil, and lower temperature fan control switches.

TPI Performance

Many people want to know whether they can increase TPI performance by simply increasing the intake runner size. FIS explains that the intake runners are already larger than the intake ports in the heads of a TPI engine. If you are dong head work, then it makes sense to think about increasing the TPI runner size. Similarly, it makes no sense to simply bolt on a larger throttle body to a stock engine, since the stock GM throttle body, flowing 600cfm, is good to 5500rpm— which is well beyond the breathing capability of the stocker. According to FIS, the stock runners on a 350ci motor will make over 340lb-ft of torque at roughly 2500rpm, peaking at 370lb-ft at 3200rpm; larger runners will reach 340lb-ft at 3200rpm, peaking at 380lb-ft at 4500rpm. Peak horsepower on the stock motor is better at high rpm with big runners, but the torque peak is shifted upward, and the car will probably be *slower*. FIS recommends larger runners as part of a package on larger motors running over 5500rpm. For improved performance, FIS recommends higher compression, bigger cam with a little more duration, port polishing/matching, and headers— and TPI calibration to go with it.

People often ask FIS whether changing to 350 injectors on a 305 engine will improve performance. Simply changing injectors will almost certainly make the motor run badly. If you are hopping up the rest of the engine, it may need more fuel, but with a new PROM (calibrator), the stock injectors can deliver more fuel for a higher output engine. Once the stock injectors are maxed out (continuously open) you could increase fuel pressure to get more fuel, or change injectors.

FIS is sometimes asked to supply a wiring harness and sensors for engines other than the Chevrolet small-block. If you have an intake man-

ifold that will accept port fuel injectors, a higher pressure fuel delivery and return system, a matching electronic distributor, a throttle body with TPS, and an Idle Air Control valve, FIS can supply the right harness.

FIS has converted big-block throttle body injection motors to port injection in the following way: 1) remove the throttle body injectors from the stock throttle body; 2) install injector bosses at each port by milling holes (see the chapter on installation Do's, Don'ts and Maybe's); 3) connect fuel rails to the injectors; 4) install a high-pressure fuel pump; 5) install a pressure regulator in the fuel return line to supply 43-50psi fuel; 6) install FIS harness with matching ECM, distributor, and sensors.

Particularly where engine swapping results in space problems around the MAF on an older TPI engine, it is possible to convert from MAF-sensed to later Speed-Density injection. As discussed in the section on TPI engine swapping, this will require the new ECM and PROM, and modifications to the harness. FIS can supply the modified harness, or modify yours, and provide the ECM and calibrator module.

Where it is impractical or undesirable to use a Vehicle Speed Sensor (VSS), FIS can supply a relay kit to lock up the 700R4 torque convertor when the car is in fourth gear with the brakes not applied.

TPI, TBI Engine Swapping

GM has built thousands of Tuned Port Injection (TPI) and Throttle Body Injection (TBI) fuel-injected small-block V-8 engines since the mid-eighties, and many owners have been kind enough to wreck these cars without destroying the powertrain—meaning 305ci and 350ci EFI engines are becoming more and more plentiful in wrecking yards and are available for engine swaps at reasonable prices—which here in Austin, Texas, means $550-850 for the complete engine, $1000-1,500 for the engine and 700 series overdrive automatic transmission. A wrecking yard here recently had a couple of *brand new* TPI engines in crates for *$1250*! As you'd expect, Corvette engines are much more expensive than 305 or 350 TPI Camaro/Firebird motors, the most recent engine and ZF six-speed transmission combination selling for up to $7,000 in the Bay Area of California. ZR-1 4-valve 4-cam Corvette engines might easily be over $10,000. New ones are reportedly available from Chevy for $18,000.

Swapping in a TPI engine is a great way to fuel inject your vehicle or improve the performance of your existing non-TPI EFI engine.

Advantages of Fuel Injection

Port injection squirts fuel directly at the

intake valve, meaning designers don't have to worry about keeping fuel evenly mixed with air in the intake manifold. Therefore, "dry" manifolds allow greater flexibility of design to make use of ram effects and pulse tuning to increase low- and mid-range torque—which is what makes street cars feel fast and responsive. Port Injection inherently produces virtually perfect mixture distribution to all cylinders, meaning all cylinders produce maximum power or economy under precise computer control. Perfect distribution means more efficient, higher compression ratios are available without spark knock. Coordinated ignition spark advance and precise control of part throttle fuel-air mixtures gives fuel-injected engines the ability to run well and *lug* well at very low RPM. Coupled with automatic overdrive transmissions and locking torque convertors, EFI engines are capable of both excellent fuel economy at part throttle and high output at full throttle. The locking convertor automatic overdrive transmission typically saves 10hp worth of friction drag at highway speeds at light cruise due to the slower running motor. The key to drivability is a matched engine-transmission pairing, with fuel injection and computer-controlled torque convertor lockup. Carbureted engines simply cannot equal the streetable power and economy of EFI. EFI engines always start well in any weather, always idle well, and last longer (typically over 200,000-plus miles) because O_2 sensor-controlled fuel-air mixture feedback loop programming makes sure overly rich mixtures don't wash oil off cylinder walls, causing premature wear. A properly done EFI engine swap makes a hot rod into a daily driver instead of a hanger queen—and it's legal in all states.

Complete Engine vs. EFI Components Swap

If you are dealing with an emission-controlled vehicle for street use (anything newer than about 1967), you need to maintain functionality of all required emissions controls on the new engine. This explicitly means the emissions controls applicable to whichever is *newer,* the engine or vehicle), and all original components (or exempted replacement parts) which can affect emissions—intake manifold, throttle body, exhaust manifolds, air pump, charcoal canister, EGR system, computer and relays, fuel delivery system, air cleaner, air cleaner ducting, vehicle speed sensor (VSS), torque convertor lockup wiring, and virtually all wiring. You could fabricate your own wiring, or buy an aftermarket wiring harness, but all devices in any way affecting or potentially affecting emissions must work properly.

Modified TPI

If the car is not emissions-controlled, you do

This Chevrolet 350ci engine is ready to be swapped into a waiting vehicle, and it is in full compliance with emissions regulations. Corvette engines are somewhat more difficult to swap into other vehicles than are F-body (Camaro and Firebird) TPI engines. Fuel Injection Specialties

not need original smog equipment, and in this case anything goes as far as speed equipment—such as larger TPI runners, bigger cams, heads, and so forth. The thing is, 1990 and later TPI, and all TBI engines base fueling on *engine speed and manifold pressure*, assuming a fixed relationship between these parameters (corrected for temperature and altitude) and engine volumetric efficiency—a relationship which goes away completely, for example, when you switch to a cam that doesn't run as much vacuum. Computer programming on all modern fuel injection systems is set up to provide fuel and spark timing for a particular weight vehicle, with particular drag, particular thermostat, particular induction and exhaust systems, and particular pollution controls. Any changes at all may mean the vehicle engine management is no longer optimal—and radical configuration changes without a PROM change may mean the engine will hardly run at all. Pre-1990 TPI with the Mass Airflow Sensor (MAF) actually *measures* engine airflow into the block, and can compensate for modifications which influence the factory-assumed relationship between manifold pressure, engine speed, and engine air flow—but only to a point (perhaps 15 percent greater air flow than stock). Remember, ultimately injectors max out in fuel flow once continuously open—which is an ultimate limit for a particular set of injectors unless you alter fuel pressure.

If you are making radical changes to an engine for off-highway use (or street use on a pre-1967 vehicle), you should strongly consider buying a programmable aftermarket computer, which will allow you to alter all engine parameters on the fly via laptop PC. Most aftermarket computers will work fine with TPI-type engine sensors, fueling systems, and the tuned port engine air metering system (Speed-Density). The Accel/DFI Electronic Control Unit (ECU) will even plug directly into GM's EFI wiring harnesses, and control everything from raw fueling to the "check engine" light to torque convertor lockup.

Beware of aftermarket "simplified" wiring harnesses which eliminate essential wiring by "fooling" the computer (ECM) into thinking, for example, that the car is always in neutral or park. If you live in California, after an engine swap, you will have to have any emissions-controlled vehicle inspected by a referee at the California Bureau of Automotive Repair—involving both a visual check and a tail pipe sniffer test. You will want all stock systems to be working properly.

TPI Components Swap

Particularly if you have a healthy carbureted engine, you may be considering swapping EFI *components* onto your engine. This can be done, but there are potential problems: "Swap meet" EFI components may be missing parts—and you may not know it. Buying additional parts can be *terribly* expensive! TPI ducting for the MAF sensor and/or remote air cleaner may be incompatible with accessories and/or radiator and hoses on older engines. The stock EFI computer will be calibrated for a specific engine configuration—and if your older engine is different in *any* respect, EFI calibration may no longer be optimal. In addition, 1987 and newer TPI lower intake manifolds have four bolts that are not compatible with older cylinder heads. The newer TPI EFI manifolds must be modified with welding and/or grinding to fit older engines. Plus, the distributor drive gear metallurgy on newer EFI distributors will not be compatible with older cam drive gears, resulting

Here's one version of Fuel Injection Specialties' TPI air filter and ducting. Fuel Injection Specialties

in improper wear unless the gear is changed.

Pre-1990 vs. 1990 and Newer Engines

Older TPI engines computed engine fueling requirements by directly measuring Mass Air Flow into the engine with a hot wire mass air flow sensor, which is mounted upstream of the throttle body. All air entering the engine must flow through the MAF. Since air mass is equivalent to the air's ability to cool a heated wire, electronic circuitry in the MAF simply measures the current required to keep the "hot wire" at a fixed temperature. Post-1990 engines *estimate* engine air flow by measuring air temperature, manifold pressure, and engine speed, and using these parameters to look up fueling requirements for a specific engine in computer memory (Interestingly, while GM switched from MAF-sensed air flow metering to Speed-Density manifold pressure-sensed metering, Ford did the opposite!). From the point of view of an engine swap, Speed-Density EFI is preferable due to the simplified inlet plumbing required in the absence of a MAF sensor. However, the system will not work right if you modify the air flow of the engine—unless you switch to a custom PROM chip (available from suppliers such as Arizona Speed and Marine in Scottsdale, Arizona)—and it may be hard to get a really right PROM unless your engine configuration is *identical* to something with which the PROM manufacturer is familiar. Amazingly, MAF-sensed engines will work fairly well with the MAF *removed* entirely (due to excellent limp-home strategies which disregard suspect sensors and make do with historical data and and data from other sensors in order to *deduce* engine air flow), but will work better if you find the parts to convert to the late model computer and Speed-Density sensors.

What's Involved in an EFI Engine Swap

1) *Get the engine (and transmission) installed and mounted.* Obviously, as in any engine swap, you need the right motor mounts that locate the engine with correct geometry such that everything fits. You may need to relocate engine components or equipment in the engine compartment, alter engine accessories, or even modify the firewall, radiator bulkhead, radiator, or other components to make the new engine fit in place.

2) *Install exhaust system/catalysts.* Emissions-controlled engines must have legal exhaust manifolds with properly located oxygen sensors, legal catalytic convertor(s), and AIR injection. Vehicles with Speed-Density EFI engines may need relatively correct exhausts just to keep the engine Volumetric Efficiency close enough to stock to maintain correct EFI calibration—or a custom PROM chip. Some tight swaps may man-

date custom headers—which can be a gray area for California street driving unless the header manufacturer has a California Exemption Order for the modified parts. Clearly, the closer to stock configuration, the better chance a referee will approve the vehicle.

3) *Mount and/or modify the drive shaft* so it bolts to the EFI-compatible transmission, possibly shortening it and/or replacing one end if the vehicle rear-end is foreign to the transmission. (Standard swap stuff.)

4) *Mount the computer and wiring harness.* Except for certain Corvette EFI computers with "hardening" to survive the harsh environment of the engine compartment (moisture, heat, vibration, electromagnetic radiation, etc.), the engine management computer must be mounted in the passenger compartment or trunk where it will stay cool and dry. You may need to lengthen some wiring in order to locate the computer in an optimal place in the vehicle (and may wish to shorten other wiring for a sanitary installation). As long as you use reasonably heavy gauge wire to extend the wiring harness, and as long as you make excellent quality joints (preferably soldering), sensor and actuator readings to and from the computer will not be affected. If you don't get the wiring harness with the EFI engine, you can probably expect to pay $200-$800 for the complete harness. New aftermarket wiring harnesses are available for roughly $300 or more, but make sure they can connect all components you require on your vehicle (such as torque convertor lockup, Vehicle Speed Sensing (VSS), and so on).

5) *Fit engine accessories.* The AIR pump, air conditioning compressor, power steering pump, and alternator accessory locations for the vehicle must fit with the new EFI engine. TPI engines, with their front-mounted throttle body and (pre-1990) MAF sensor frequently are not compatible with accessories and the radiator in engine swap situations. You will probably have to fabricate air-cleaner/MAF ducting from elbows, pipe, OE ducting, etc. This takes time, ingenuity, and money. In Speed-Density EFI engines, you can mount an open-element air cleaner directly on the throttle body, but you will lose power due to the lack of cold-air inlet. MAF sensors are delicate and require precise aerodynamics to work right, and complicate the swap air inlet plumbing task. TPI engine swappers have often had to relocate or replace radiators, and fabricate new engine accessory mounts to relocate accessories to be compatible with the EFI engines. You may have difficulty with the stock knock sensor location; since the shock wave/sound created by spark knock travels well through metal, this sensor can be relocated fairly easily. If necessary, Teflon tape wrapped around the sensor threads can be used to reduce

the sensitivity of the sensor in the new location.

6) *Handle miscellaneous hassles:* Very late model F-Body vehicles and mid-eighties-on Corvettes have Vehicle Anti-Theft Systems (VATS). A coded resister in the key is compared to data in the computer. Without the right key with the right resister, the vehicle will not start. This can be defeated with a black box from Stealth Conversions in Pleasanton, California.

The Vehicle Speed Sensor (VSS) tells the computer how fast the vehicle is going. The computer makes use of this data in programs to control the lockup torque convertor on AOD transmissions, the EGR valve, the evaporative charcoal canister purge valve, cooling fans, closed loop air-fuel mixture, and idle speed. In order to keep the "Check Engine" light from staying on, some aftermarket wiring harnesses ground the park/neutral wire so the computer always thinks the vehicle is in park. However, there is a lot of internal logic in the computer that depends on the VSS, affecting the operation of the above devices. You should use a VSS if you want the engine to run as well as a stock GM engine.

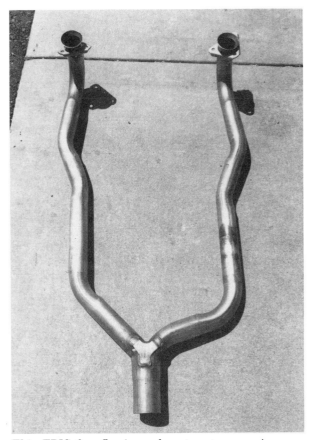

This TPIS free-flowing exhaust system can improve exhaust flow and directs it to a single catalyst. TPIS also has a cat-back system that reduces back pressure.

Depending on your selection of transmission, you will need to make sure the overdrive torque convertor lockup is wired and operating correctly.

EFI wiring is fairly self-contained and operates fairly independently of the rest of the vehicle's electrical system. Other than the check engine light (and on some Corvettes the radio volume, electronic speedometer, etc.), dash gauges are not connected to the engine management computer. 1990-91 Corvettes have a Central Control Module which receives data from several sources including the computer, but does not *feed* data to the main computer, and may be eliminated in engine swaps.

There is usually some wiring included in the factory injection wiring harness for convenience reasons that has nothing to do with fuel injection but operates appliances like windshield wipers that are simply in proximity to EFI wiring and have been routed in the same wiring loom. There are several wires that must be connected to the rest of the vehicle electrical system. Depending on how much of the factory harness you use, or whether you are using an aftermarket harness, these include fuel pump wiring, Torque Convertor Lockup, and power for emissions control devices. In general, fuel injection systems need constant 12v+ power, switched 12v+ power, starter 12v+, tach or crank/cam trigger, and ignition coil, in addition to the EFI sensors and actuators. If you are installing GM EFI onto a non-emissions-controlled vehicle which already uses a Chevy small-block and has a good wiring system, this might be the time to consider an aftermarket EFI wiring harness, since it will only include EFI-specific wiring rather than all engine and related wiring.

You will need to handle throttle linkages, transmission kickdown linkage, or clutch linkage (hopefully you can use a hydraulic clutch, since it will be vastly easier. This is standard swap stuff, except that the EFI throttle body on TPI systems is further forward than a carburetor.

You will have to install an oxygen sensor in the exhaust system as close as possible to the first exhaust "collector" or use a heated sensor if you are not able to use the stock EFI exhaust system (weld-in O_2 sensor bosses are available from companies like K & N).

You will have to consider the total electrical power requirements of the vehicle, including *all* EFI and non-EFI accessories and lights. The alternator must provide sufficient power for worst case (all lights on, A/C on, etc.). Remember, the EFI system will not function reliably if the battery voltage gets much below 8 or 9volts.

7) *Build a Fuel Supply System.* The EFI engine requires high-pressure fuel from an EFI-specific electric fuel pump. Pressurized fuel flows into the injector "fuel rail," while excess fuel beyond that required to supply the injectors at a specification fuel pressure is released by the pressure regulator and returned to the fuel tank. You will probably have to fabricate a fuel return line to route this excess fuel back to the tank unless your vehicle already had some variety of fuel injection. You may also want to construct a mini tank reserve upstream of the high-pressure pump, fed by a low-pressure pump, in order to keep the engine running during high G-maneuvers or on steep hills when the fuel level is low. The fuel return can often be tapped into the fuel filler neck or gauge sender unit. Optimally, the return fuel should dump into the bottom of the tank or spray across the tank to prevent aeration near the fuel pump pickup. This may be difficult to arrange and is not absolutely vital. An original equipment TPI fuel tank will have reserve and return plus fuel damper built into the tank plus a submersible high-pressure pump. Wrecking yards can supply EFI-type in-line external fuel pumps from cars like the 280Z/ZX. You will need adequately sized fuel line for sufficient injection pressure and a high pressure injection in-line fuel filter.

8) *Handle Cooling.* This has nothing to do with EFI, but TPI air cleaner/MAF plumbing may interfere with the radiator and fitting. Depending on the engine-vehicle configuration, you may need to increase the size of your radiator or have it recored for higher cooling capacity.

Summary

GM TPI and TBI engine swaps can result in a powerful and economical street vehicle that operates virtually identically to a GM F-Body or Corvette. In this case, you will need the stock EFI engine and *all* accessories and wiring, and will want to install it with an absolute minimum of modifications. When you are finished, you will have a powerful, modern, efficient powertrain. If you are running off-road or it is an older non-emissions-controlled engine, you can modify the EFI engine's air flow and fuel delivery with high performance parts such as bigger TPI runners and fatter cams and other VE enhancements, and recalibrate the GM computer's fueling and spark timing for the new engine configuration with a new PROM chip—or install a completely new aftermarket programmable computer to handle the job.

A TPI engine swap is not a trivial task. It will probably cost more than you think, and will require more than average ingenuity. If you take your time, start with a complete engine/transmission, and do everything right, the task can be fun, and the result will be a rugged and reliable installation.

Chapter 9

Installation Do's, Don'ts, and Maybes

Selecting or Fabricating the EFI Manifold

Who in his or her right mind would put an Edelbrock 360 Torker manifold on a big four-wheel-drive Jeep project vehicle? Don't you want lots of low-end torque on four-wheelers and trucks—and, in fact, on *most street vehicles* where the goal is fun-to-drive?

Yes. Of course. The Torker 360, for example, which is a single-plane large-port manifold designed to make mid-to-high end power, would be a mistake on any *carbureted* vehicle that isn't ultralight. However, when converting to programmable multi-port injection on a vehicle—which may require fabricating injector bosses on a carburetor-type manifold—it's a whole different story.

Engines with high-rpm manifolds do not usually idle well with carbs. The inlet air velocity is slow at idle, which can allow fuel to condense on the port walls and randomly tear off in sheets and reenter the air stream, producing fluctuating and uneven air-fuel mixtures in the various cylinders. Port fuel injection solves this problem by squirting the fuel directly at each intake valve where high air velocities and swirl are optimal for quick atomization, and where perfect fuel distribution is guaranteed. Slower charge velocities with reduced ram effects tend to hurt low-end torque in high-rpm manifolds by lowering the volumetric efficiency due to reduced cylinder filling at low engine speed. Port EFI offsets this with across-the-board increased torque produced by accurate air-fuel mixtures, lack of venturi flow restrictions, faster response to throttle inputs due to a shorter path once fuel enters the air stream, and the ability to run higher compression ratios without detonation. The larger ports are free to produce better mid-range and high-rpm power. This is a win-win situation, resulting in an EFI engine with greater dynamic power range than an identical carbureted engine.

The bottom line is that a single-plane large-port carb manifold can be a good choice for high-performance fuel injection systems, even on 4x4 applications. A single-plane manifold has the advantage that the runners are all at an equal height as they approach the heads. This conveniently simplifies constructing a nice-looking EFI fuel-rail system.

Tull Systems of San Antonio begins a single-plane four-barrel-type V-8 manifold conversion by milling a hole in each of the eight runners from the underside so fuel injectors fitted to each hole will point directly at the intake valves, usually straight downward. Tull welds aluminum bosses fabricated to hold O-ring-type fuel injectors into the milled holes from the bottom. Injector bosses of aluminum or steel are available from several sources.

Except in very high output cars like the 1992 Corvette LT-1, factory EFI systems almost always utilize small-port long-runner manifolds designed to optimize low-end torque. Since multiport EFI manifolds need only handle dry air, the design usually places a two-barrel throttle body at the end of a log-type plenum, with long tuned-length runners exiting from the plenum at a right angle and flowing air to the head at such an angle that port injectors can be aimed directly at the intake valves for optimum atomization. EFI manifolds are subject to the same laws of airflow, and benefit from the same tuning procedures as carbs in which short ports produce better top-end performance and longer runners enhance low-end performance. However, EFI manifolds don't have to worry about the differential flow of fuel and air when negotiating turns in a runner.

It is essential to match ports so that there are no interruptions in the smooth flow of air into the engine. If you are fabricating a sheet-metal manifold from scratch, you should have it checked and perhaps cleaned by an expert with a flow bench to guard against uneven airflow to various cylinders. Intake ports do not require the rough surfaces that are sometimes helpful in keeping fuel suspended in air in carbureted or throttle-body injection systems. Porting intake systems is beyond the scope of this book. However, note that smooth runners do *not* always produce the highest airflow. Under some circumstances, "dimpling" the intake manifold will improve airflow by preventing laminar flow from producing higher pressure "boundary conditions" in the runner that choke off airflow. Extrude Hone offers a service that improves a manifold's flow by forcing an abrasive paste through it under great force.

Port injection manifolds, unlike manifolds for throttle bodies and carbs, handle a dry mixture. Therefore, their task is simpler than that of a wet manifold, and there is greater flexibility of design possible with performance advantages. An injection manifold has to get equal amounts of air to all cylinders, but it does not have to keep fuel suspended in the air. OE port injector manifolds typically make use of this by building long ram-type runners from a large plenum to the cylinders.

These cylinders are sized in length and diameter to achieve better low- and mid-range torque by utilizing the momentum and resonation or pulsing of gases rushing down the runners to improve the cylinder filling (VE) of the engine and, therefore, torque at certain rpm. Long runners also minimize adverse effects of reversion from big-overlap cams when a pulse of residual exhaust gas enters the intake runners when both valves are open (a pulse also reflects toward the carb when the intake valve closes).

By matching header length and intake runner length, tremendous torque increases are possible—at certain rpm. There can be sharp corners where runners exit the plenum which are of no concern for dry mixtures. Since the fuel is injected in precise amounts at the intake valve, designers also do not need to worry about air-fuel separation in large-port manifolds, as already discussed in the Tull Systems Jeep project.

While carb manifold floors must typically be mounted parallel to the ground to avoid gravity upsetting the mixture to some cylinders (typical-

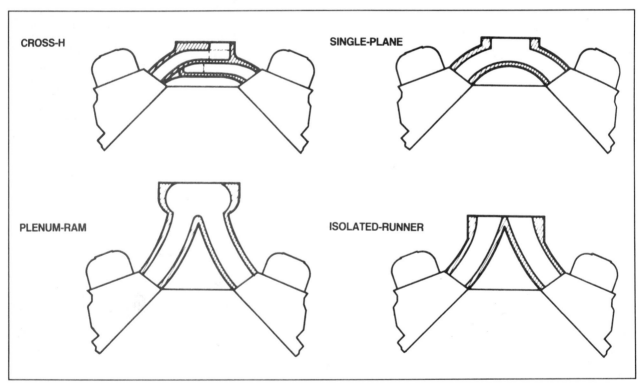

V-8 manifold configurations include: the Cross-H, two-level manifold (top left), which is actually two manifolds in one, feeding half the cylinders from one side of carb, the other half from the other with two completely unconnected sets of manifold runners; a single plane manifold (upper right) feeds all cylinders from a common chamber or plenum, and is the most common type of EFI manifold; a plenum-ram manifold (bottom left) has a common chamber between sets of runners between intake ports and carb or throttle body; and an isolated runner manifold (bottom right) uses an individual throttle bore of carb of EFI throttle body for each cylinder. There is no interconnection between runners in the latter example, although speed-density EFI systems may require balance tubes from each runner to a miniature plenum which then provides a stable manifold pressure single to a MAP sensor. Holley

ly, some liquid fuel is moving around in a carb manifold, and must be controlled, often with sumps, ribs, and air dams), this is not necessary with dry manifolds. EFI manifolds do not require heating like wet manifolds.

In summary, virtually any carburetor manifold can be adapted for EFI and perform at least as well as the carburetor. Performance advantages are possible with ram manifolds and large-port carburetor manifolds. There is no point in using two-plane manifolds of any type with port EFI. Big-tunnel ram and high-rise manifolds will work well with port EFI without the same degree of low-end problems due to uneven mixtures you'd have using carburetors. Independent-runner manifolds tend to cause problems due to the fact that every runner must have individual fuel metering sufficient for high-speed requirements

in a situation in which the metering capacity of each venturi is not shared at all.

Carburetion systems for such manifolds must deal with severe reversion problems which cause a cloud of air-fuel to stand above the carb since fuel is added to air flowing *backward* through the carb during reversion; port EFI has no such problems with individual-runner manifolds, which, with the addition of a plenum, is the preferred system. Single-plane manifolds and big cams with EFI can still affect the idle quality and peak torque rpm as they would with a carb. There is still more air mass to get moving with single-plane-type designs, thus throttle response would tend to be theoretically worse with single-plane manifolds converted to port EFI. In practice, the faster response of injection at the intake valve tends to eliminate this problem.

Tull Systems of San Antonio, Texas, modifies an Edelbrock Torker for EFI use, milling holes for injector bosses, and welding from below.

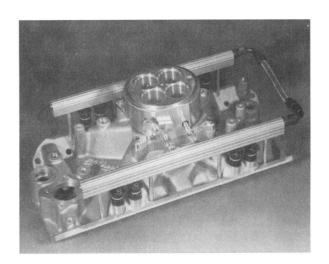

An AMC 360ci engine was used on a Superlift Jeep project vehicle.

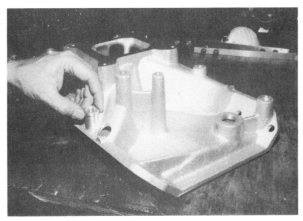

Tull Systems fits injector bosses into a manifold after milling.

Fuel Rails

A unique feature of the Tull Systems single-plane manifold conversion is the method for mounting a fuel supply rail. Tull mills smaller holes at the front and rear of the manifold on each side (total of four), in line with each row of injectors. They then fit a bolt to each hole from the underside which passes through a cylindrical spacer and threads into the two-piece fuel rail. Each rail is really a D-section pipe with one flat side that fits over the O-ringed tops of the four fuel injectors on each side of the manifold. Tull connects the two fuel rails together at the front with high-pressure tubing. Fuel enters at the rear of the two-piece rail on one side, supplying fuel at high pressure to all eight injectors. A regulator maintains a constant pressure in the entire two-piece rail by allowing excess fuel to exit the rail at the rear of the second side and return to the fuel tank through a return fuel line.

It is important to understand that multiple injectors mounted in a single rail that are batch fired *can* actually produce pressure differentials in the rail if the fuel supply is located at one end of the rail and the regulator at the other. The more injectors there are, the worse the potential problem. The physical movement of fuel in such a rail can lead to undesirable resonation effects in the inside of the rail as injectors fire and momentarily produce pressure differentials. This can result in uneven injection of fuel. An alternative is to supply fuel to both sides of the rail with a "Y" fitting.

Factory fuel rails are often a loop configuration in which fuel enters the loop at a single point and flows in two directions to supply fuel to the

A look at Tull Systems' EFI kit, which includes a Moon cross-ram manifold and TWM throttle bodies for a Chevy small-block V-8.

Norwood Autocraft in Dallas converted a Ferrari Testa Rossa with twin turbos. Norwood relocated the injectors to spray into the air-water custom-intercooled EFI manifolds.

This is just one example of how Tull Systems modifies carburetor manifolds for EFI applications, and it also shows injector hold-down methods and connections for fueling.

Tull Systems' injection manifold puts Weber-type throttle bodies on Chevy small-block engines.

injectors. Excess fuel exits at a single point at the opposite end of the loop. Some ECUs batch fire alternate banks of injectors on a V-configuration engine, which lowers the possibility of poor fuel rail distribution. Obviously, sequential injection systems like that from NOS and EFI Technology are protected from the potential pressure problems of batch fire systems. Never build a non-loop rail for more than eight injectors. And *never* build multiple rails with separate regulators and/or separate fuel pumps without constructing some kind of crossover fuel pipe to prevent the possibility of uneven pressure at various injectors.

There are several different systems for holding down fuel injectors in a manifold, and several methods for connecting the fuel supply to the injectors. Injectors may be O-ringed on the base, while the fuel inlet end may be set up with O-rings, hose barb, or inverted flare or another screw-down-type connection. It may be possible to fit a metal collar over the top of the fuel injector, holding it down with two long bolts that thread into holes tapped close to the injector boss on either side. Some Weber-type throttle bodies are already drilled for this. Other hold-downs include a metal plate notched for injectors with square shoulders (one plate might hold down an entire row of injectors), which would usually have bends incorporated that allow it to bolt to the manifold or throttle body. Leave room for the electrical connections.

Besides the O-ringed injector bases, some injectors are designed for brass compression-type connector bosses in which a large brass nut compresses a thin metal sheath that at once holds down the injector and prevents leakage. (See the chapter on the L-Jet EFI Jaguar, in which the TurboGroup Fueler additional injectors are held down with this method.) Injectors that screw in place like spark plugs would be useful but, to my knowledge, do not exist.

Some brave souls have used set screws that push against the side of the injector bases to hold the injectors in place, but this runs the risk that overtightening might damage the sensitive injector internals which require precision tolerances to operate correctly. Injectors that are damaged will probably still work, but no longer flow the correct amount of fuel.

People have used snap-on spring-type fork-like injector hold-down devices that clip around the narrower section of the injector base and are, in turn, bolted to the manifold.

Connecting fuel rails to the injectors may be as simple as using rubber hoses that clamp to hose barbs on type injectors and on the rail itself. O-ringed top injectors are usually designed to push into correctly sized holes machined into a D-section fuel rail with flat bottom; they may also fit

You got the look! Here are some "Weberized" EFI systems with down-draft Weber-style velocity stacks. Weber IDF-type manifolds use throttle bodies cast with electronic injector bosses. Haltech

Dodge-Maxwell runs twelve-throttle-body EFI systems on V-12 Jaguar engines, which use Electromotive control. The engines are available in naturally aspirated and supercharged versions.

A Tull Systems EFI custom fuel rail on 16-injector Chevrolet small-block V-8 engine with twin turbos.

Motorsport Design's injected Porsche flat-six engine uses a four-part fuel rail and custom triple-throat throttle bodies. Rail designers must make sure to eliminate the pressure drop at the ends of the fuel rail; this system, using sequential injection, only fires one injector at a time.

This is a simple two-piece fuel rail on a batch-fire 350ci Chevy engine. Tull Systems

A carb-type V-8 manifold modified for EFI. Note the four-barrel, carb-type throttle body. Tull Systems

inside individual connectors that are held in place with clips that clamp around flanges on the injector top and connector. When drilling holes and reaming for O-rings, measure the diameter of the O-ring (D) and the thickness of the O-ring (d). The hold should be D-(d/4). A 1in ring that is .125in thick requires a hole that is 1-(.125/4). That works out to a .96875in hole. The final fuel connection method uses the inverted-flare threaded devices already mentioned.

Throttle Bodies

To regulate airflow into the engine when converting a four-barrel manifold to EFI, Tull Systems uses a solid-billet Cutler Induction throttle body, which uses the Holley four-barrel carburetor bolt pattern. This throttle-body provides ported vacuum for distributor advance and provides

This is Cartech's custom EFI manifold for Camaros. Note the twin throttle bodies for improved air flow under turbo boost conditions.

This Norwood-Batten engine "stages" two sets of eight injectors on a 4-valve, 4-cam, Chevy Big-block-type engine. Injector staging allows the engine to idle with one set of injectors, which gives good atomization via smaller injectors and a longer pulsewidth. The extra injectors allow the engine to make 1500hp on gasoline at high RPMs.

mounting for a throttle position switch. There are several other outfits that supply throttle bodies, including TWM of Santa Barbara, California, NOS, DFI, and Arizona Speed and Marine. Throttle bodies are available in Holley carburetor bolt patterns, Weber bolt patterns, and GM TPI bolt patterns (high-flow replacement units for TPI throttle bodies).

An alternative to buying a new throttle body is to use a modified carburetor. It may be much cheaper to modify an old carb that is still in good shape than to buy a new throttle body. You'll probably want to remove parts from the carb that are no longer needed since the carb is now only being used to meter air: the choke, booster venturis, and anything else in the way of maximum airflow, plus fuel plumbing, and perhaps even the float chambers. You will have to fabricate some way of attaching a throttle position switch (TPS) to the carb body. With some clever grinding, fabricating, and polishing, painting, or plating, you might even end up with a good-looking unit. Since you no longer have the same low-speed operation considerations as a carb, you are free to choose a carburetor for modification in which the venturi size is optimal for top-end without worrying about hurting low-end operations. A progressive four-barrel or two-barrel throttle body should use mechanically operated secondaries.

When using multiple throttle bodies or a very large throttle-body butterfly area, acceleration enrichment may be a problem. Very small changes in throttle angle will produce large airflow changes. A system producing acceleration enrichment based only on throttle angle could stumble under certain circumstances, even with maximum programmable acceleration enrich-

ment. The DFI electronic control unit now provides transient enrichment based on throttle position *and* rapid manifold pressure changes in order to solve this potential problem. However, many systems have been successfully built with multiple throttle bodies without MAP enrichment.

Fuel Maps

Professional engine builders and tuners have spent a huge amount of time building precise fuel (and spark) maps for various engines. It can be a complex process to build a map from scratch for some engine configurations, particularly if maxi-

This Howell TPI harness allows you to use EFI parts from a salvage yard or new parts to convert carbureted engines to TPI fuel injection on Chevrolet small-block engines. Howell harnesses maintain functionality of all TPI electronics, sensors, and actuators for best fuel efficiency and driveability. Howell

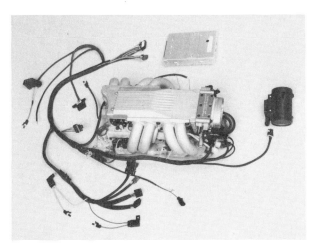

This Howell wiring harness adapts 305, 350, and 454 throttle-body injection engines to older carbureted vehicles. The simplified harness provides full functionality. Howell

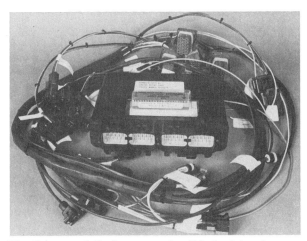

The Street and Performance simplified wiring harness can help when a Chevrolet LT-1 Corvette engine is transplanted. Street and Performance

Howell now provides a kit to let tuners install Holley Pro-Jection 4 throttle body injection using GM TBI wiring and engine management in place of the two-barrel GM throttle body injection for better breathing and power with full emissions compliance. The installation of a Holley Pro-Jection setup on a GM 454ci TBI engine is done with a Howell wiring and adaptor kit. Howell

Typical Vehicle Electrical System

The schematic of a typical vehicle electrical system.

mum power and efficiency are vital and if you don't have access to an exhaust gas analyzer, exhaust gas temperature sensors, and a chassis or engine dyno.

Some people are very good at programming a fuel-spark map for an engine just by driving the vehicle on the streets and working with a PC or other interface to program the system. But since engines will produce best torque within a fairly broad range of air-fuel mixture, it can be difficult or time consuming to optimize both power and efficiency, particularly where it is not feasible to operate in closed loop or at stoichiometric mixtures at partial throttle. Many fuel maps already exist for common engines. Of course, *any* changes from the original engine configuration or even the vehicle configuration could potentially cause a pre-built map to be less than optimal on your vehicle. And an otherwise identical vehicle and engine configuration might not work with the pre-built map if the injectors or fuel pressure are different. But it is still better to start with a good pre-programmed map, if possible. Check around, and see the chapter of this book dealing with the Emtech E6 on a 460ci Ford truck. The E6's Quickmap feature builds a set of fuel maps for you based on five specifications.

Many ECUs have the ability to fire multiple injectors per injector driver, which means that you can potentially use two or more injectors per cylinder. This may actually be cheaper in situations where you need very high flow, since one high-flow injector may cost more than two low-flow injectors which together provide as much or more flow. Some ECUs have the ability to *stage* injectors, providing idle and low-end fueling with one injector per cylinder, and providing wide-open throttle fueling from two or more injectors per

This Kinsler cross ram throttle body/manifold setup for Chevrolet big-block engines is designed to air primary injectors directly at the inlet valve. Note that there are bosses cast into the manifold runners near the fuel rails. These could be machined for additional port injectors if desired. Kinsler

cylinder. This clearly provides far greater dynamic range in the case of a forced induction engine or other motor with greatly differing low- and high-end fuel requirements. The Haltech F3 has the ability to stage injectors based on engine loading such that all loading points beyond a specified manifold pressure receive fuel from both primary and secondary injectors.

It is essential to use injectors that provide a small enough amount of fuel to idle properly without pulse widths much below 1.5-2.0milliseconds (below which the injection events are not precisely repeatable) and still provide adequate high-end fueling without "going static," in which the injectors stay open constantly (which can overheat them) and can no longer meter fuel.

There are a number of aftermarket devices that provide fuel enrichment, usually for stock EFI systems, by staging one or more additional injectors located usually at a single point upstream of the throttle body. This solution can work reasonably well if executed carefully on the right engine with the right intake manifold. The theoretical problems are many, however. You are probably forcing a dry manifold to handle a wet mixture, which can cause distribution problems. And since you are probably providing enrichment for turbo-supercharging, lean cylinders can quick-

Manifold Conversion

Here are step-by-step instructions (following the Tull Systems conversion method) on how to convert your carb manifold to EFI:

1. It is best to remove the old intake manifold and set the new manifold on the engine with throttle body installed in order to check potential injector and fuel rail interference with auto-trans kick-down linkages, distributors, A/C compressors, etc. We used a Holley Pro-Jection-4 four-barrel throttle body and an Accel 1000cfm two-barrel throttle body with a Linkenfelter-built Accel adaptor.

2. Decide what type of fuel rail type of injectors you're using. Most injectors have O-rings on the bottom end that fit into a boss in the manifold. On the injector top, Type-6 injectors are set up for high-pressure rubber hose, while Type-2 injectors have O-ring tops. Type-6 injectors require the fuel rail to be higher up from the manifold, which can some-
continued on next page

The injector boss is set into the manifold while resting on a flat surface so the boss can be marked to be cut properly. (See step 6)

In the Tull installation, the manifold is set upside down and then milled for the injector bosses. (See step 4)

The boss should be cut as marked so it flits into the manifold and sits flush with the inside surface of the runner. (See step 6)

times cause interference problems with throttle linkages, etc., but the rubber hoses also give you the flexibility to *change* the height of the rail depending on the length hose you use, and to locate the rail in various lateral positions due to the hose's ability to flex. EFI builders like Tull Systems typically use D-section aluminum stock to make a two-piece rail for either Type-2 or 6 injectors. Original Equipment fuel rails are often a 1-piece loop design constructed from steel tubing, with an inlet on one end and an outlet for fuel return on the other.

3. Consider the installed height of the injector bosses, and look for interference with anything such as protrusions of the manifold casting, etc. It is possible you will eventually have to relocate throttle or transmission kick-down linkages to clear the fuel injectors and rail once installed.

4. Check the angle of injector squirt in relation to the head port and intake valve. Ideally, the injector should squirt directly at the back side of the valve. OEs have devoted huge amounts of research to injector placement, using deflectors, multiple squirt orifices, various fuel pressures and spray patterns, and so forth. On Chevy mouse motors, the most practical compromise with ideal injector squirt geometry and the limitations of the carb manifold, is to point the injectors straight down. Ivan Tull installs the manifold upside down on a mill-and-drill machine, and sets it dead level. (The carb flange is usually *not* level, to compensate for the fact that most engines are low at the rear, to keep a carb float chamber level.) Tull centers the bottom mill in the port (on our manifolds, the Holley ports were noticeably larger!), and adjusts the mill so the bottom-cut tool circumference is almost even with the outside edge of the manifold port. Beyond that, measurement is not necessary.

5. Bottom mill all eight holes for the injector bosses. Precision tolerances are not necessary. You will be welding or epoxying the bosses in place, and you may want some latitude later. Tull suggests using a bottom cutting tool about .005 larger than the boss.

6. Remove the manifold from the mill and place it on a welding table where you can level it, button-side up. One by one, set each boss in place in the manifold, and support it from the bottom with something flat which puts it at the correct height you have determined for your application. Trace around the boss with a marking pen, remove it from the manifold, and cut it at the tracing. Make sure the boss fits in the manifold and is flush with the inside of the runner. Anything sticking out into the port—including the injector itself!—can hurt air flow. It is possible—and on some engines necessary—to weld the boss in place from the top. It just won't look as good that way unless you are an artist with a TIG welder and a grinder.

7. Weld or epoxy each boss into place, and touch up the finished surface lightly with a die-grinder.

8. Thoroughly clean the finished manifold, removing all traces of metal and welding material. Fit the injectors in place, and mark the rail exactly for milling for upper O-rings or hose barbs (Type-6 injectors). After machining the rail, tap it for the hose barbs, then clean up the inside with a rat's tail file. Clean *all* traces of metal from inside the rail (you can quickly plug and ruin injectors if there is foreign matter in the fuel system.

9. Clamp injector hoses to the rail (most Type-6 injectors already have hoses a few inches long clamped to the injectors. Do *not* use regular screwdriver-type hose clamps. Use special clamps designed for high pressure fuel hose.

continued on next page

The boss should fit flush with the inside surface of the runner because anything sticking out into the port, even the injector, can diminish air flow. You might have to weld the boss in place.

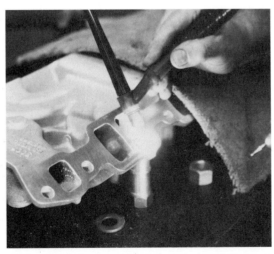

Weld or epoxy the boss into place, being careful to be as neat as possible.

10. In the case of upper O-ring injectors, you will have to fabricate a method of clamping the rail to the engine, which will simultaneously hold down both the injector and rail. Tull has used several systems for this, the simplest being a long bolt which protrudes from the manifold or turbo plenum and threads into the rail. In the case of hose-type injectors, you will only have to fasten the *injector* itself to the manifold. Normally-aspirated engines will tend to hold the injectors in place by vacuum and their own weight (and, in fact, Bosch CIS injector are held in the manifold purely via tight O-rings), but turbo and supercharged engines could literally blow an injector out of the manifold with boost pressure, and must be fastened down with a collar or set-screw.

11. Tap the ends of the fuel rail for connection of fuel supply and return hoses. The fuel regulator is commonly mounted directly on or close to the rail in the return line. Some regulators are set up with O-ring connections. If you are using a batch-fire injection system (all injectors fire at once), you should supply fuel to *both* sections of a two-piece rail with a Y-fitting, to minimize pressure differentials at the injectors farthest from the source—and then Y-together both sections of the rail to a common return/pressure regulator and the other end. This is not as important on sequential-fire injection.

12. Test the fuel rail and injectors for leaks.

13. Install the EFI manifold and the rest of the EFI system (ECU, sensors, fuel supply and return, etc.).

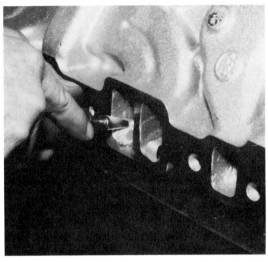

The surface can be touched up with a die-grinder after the boss has been welded into place.

14. Go have fun!

A competent machinist will have an easy time converting a manifold, and a good amateur mechanic can do the job. Ivan Tull does not recommend trying to *drill* holes in the manifold for injector bosses. You can use a ball-mill to clean up the inside of a manifold runner after welding the boss in place. Tull systems will convert a manifold for $400.

---

ly lead to disaster. (However, in turbo applications without intercooling, the hot air from the turbo under boost tends to provide excellent vaporization, which is a somewhat offsetting factor.) The extra injector(s) must pulse at a rate that provides correct fueling, and at the same time provide consistent enrichment to all cylinders.

A trend as of late appears to be adding an entire EFI system to an OE injection engine for fuel enrichment under turbo boost. Bob Norwood, of Norwood Autocraft in Dallas, Texas, applied a Haltech ECU controlling two gigantic alcohol injectors when building his Acura NSX turbo. This provided almost 10lb of boost on an engine with a 10.5:1 compression ratio! Cartech added a Haltech ECU and four additional injectors when building a super-high-output turbo system for a Mazda Miata. In both cases, the Haltech unit is not activated until the engine enters turbo boost, and the Haltech does not use temperature or TPS sensors, since the stock injection system provides cold enrichment, acceleration enrichment, and so on.

Electrical, Wiring Installation

Try to get your ECU manufacturer to supply a schematic and/or a "pin-out" diagram of the EFI electrical system. This will be extremely useful in the case that things don't immediately work right, and you're not sure what's wrong; a schematic and a continuity tester are a godsend when this happens.

All ECUs have the ability to correct injection pulse width for battery electrical voltage variation, which affects the speed at which injectors open. However, most ECUs have a threshold below which they will not start the engine. This is usually around 8volts. At the same time, a low battery and/or inadequate electrical charging system can effectively reduce the maximum injector flow rate due to the slower opening time. The EFI system consumes a certain amount of power that is not required in a non-feedback carburetor, depending on engine speed and injector resistance. Electronic ignition systems require power, as do electric fuel pumps—all of which are in addition to the power requirements of accessories like air conditioning, headlights, wipers, and so forth. You must add up all of the vehicle's electrical requirements under worst conditions and compare them to the output of the charging system. With everything on at night, your battery might be slowly draining. Eventually, the engine would stop. You may have to install a larger alternator as part of the EFI conversion.

High-output ignition systems with high voltages, particularly with wire core plug wires, produce electromagnetic radiation (radio waves) which can interfere with the proper operation of an ECU. Most ECUs require resistor core plug wires and mounting inside the vehicle or in the trunk, away from the heat, moisture, and electrical interference of the engine compartment. Even on the ECUs approved for engine compartments, if at all possible, mount the ECU inside the vehicle. Electronic components do not like heat!

When routing the EFI harness, be sensible about running it away from noisy electrical sources—as well as heat, or sharp or abrasive components, including braided steel hoses which over time can damage wiring by rubbing against it.

Most engine sensors work by varying resistance based on some physical condition of the engine. Beware modifying an EFI wiring harness in any manner that would change the resistance of the sensor on the way to the ECU. For example, suppose you bought a standard wiring harness that cannot reach a coolant temperature sensor without extension. Use heavy gauge wire, and check with the manufacturer of the EFI system regarding the feasibility of re-wiring. In some cases, you may discover any wiring changes void the warranty. In most cases, you can have the manufacturer build a special wiring harness to

your specifications. Always solder wires unless you have access to extremely good quality crimp-on connectors and the right crimping tool.

Fuel pump output is affected by the electrical current available. Most ECUs have built-in fuel pump relays to power an electrical high-pressure pump. You can probably increase the capacity of your pump by running a thick wire directly to the battery and using the ECU's pump wire to trigger a heavy-duty relay (which will itself consume power!). When using more than one fuel pump, do not depend on the ECU to directly energize the fuel pump; use it to trigger a relay.

Give some thought to layout of the system wiring harness before installing the ECU or sensors. It is often helpful to connect the sensors and ECU to the harness, and then drape the wiring in place, getting a feel for what will work the best.

Electronic Control Unit (ECU)

It is essential to provide excellent constant and switched voltage to the electronic control unit itself. Route constant power and ground directly from the battery. Switched power must be connected to a source that is *not turned off during cranking* (or drained to less than 8 or 9volts while cranking). If the ECU provides cranking enrichment, make sure it is triggered by a power source that is only active during cranking, or the system will run rich.

When mounting the ECU (not in the engine compartment!), be aware that the ECU's case is often used as a heat sink. Mount the ECU in a cool place away from the exhaust system and heater where dry, cool air will help to cool it, and where heat can transfer directly from the case into the bulkhead to which it is bolted.

Never mount the ECU on the floor of the vehicle, which can easily become flooded and ruin the ECU's electronics.

Make sure the interface port of the ECU is accessible for programming the system once the ECU is in place.

Injectors are rated for resistance to current flow. Low-resistance injectors draw more power and require heavier duty drivers (see section on selecting injectors). Make sure your ECU has the capability to reliably power the injectors you plan to use. You may discover that it is possible to drive *more* injectors from an ECU if they are high-resistance types.

Ignition System Compatibility

Fuel injection ECUs require electrical signals to determine how fast the engine is turning, and, for sequential injection or spark control, the ability to determine crankshaft position. Many ECUs use a signal from the low-voltage negative side of the coil as a trigger to determine engine speed.

This billet aluminum 4-barrel throttle body bolts directly to most 4-barrel carbureted manifolds, which must also be machined for port fuel injectors. Kinsler

Some may utilize a crank trigger or cam trigger sensor—or all three. If you are using a capacitive discharge ignition (CDI), you must use a special tach signal as a trigger (unless you are not using a spark trigger at all), since the multiple spark capability of a capacitive system can damage your ECU. Most ECUs will work with standard points ignition, GM computer-controlled High Energy Ignition (HEI), or non-computer-controlled HEI, common aftermarket ignitions, and others. However, the ECU may require dip switch settings or factory hard-wiring to properly determine trigger threshold. Check with the manufacturer of the ECU and the ignition, if it's from the aftermarket, for compatibility.

Installing Sensors

You will probably be locating the EFI temperature sensors, an oxygen sensor, and probably a throttle position sensor (TPS), and possibly a crank and/or cam sensor.

Heat soak has been a problem on some air temperature sensors. Try to locate the sensor in such a way that engine or environmental heat does not heat up the body of the sensor, giving a falsely high reading (which will lean out the mixture). Some air temperature sensors are not fast enough to react to the rapid changes in temperature that occur with turbo-supercharged and intercooled induction systems. Haltech recommends that the F3 air temperature sensor be installed in the air inlet, *not* downstream of an intercooler as you'd expect.

Oxygen sensors do not work until they get hot, usually about 600 degrees Fahrenheit. It is essential to locate the sensor as close as possible to the exhaust ports, but in such a way that it sees exhaust from multiple cylinders. You might want to install two oxygen sensors on a V-configuration engine with a toggle switch, if you are concerned about possible variations in exhaust gas oxygen content from cylinder to cylinder. One or two wrong cylinders can cause the ECU to adopt air-fuel strategies that are wrong for all cylinders (see section on sensors). Heated oxygen sensors provide their own heat by internal electrical heating, and can be located farther from the exhaust port, for example in a header collector.

Throttle position sensors come in many varieties. Be careful if you're using an existing OE TPS with an aftermarket ECU. Not all linear variable resistors are the same. Some ECUs, such as the Emtech E6, have the ability to calibrate for different throttle position sensors. Most programmable ECUs have the ability to display what they think the sensor is reading. Check the TPS with closed and open throttle to make sure it's working properly. Many ECUs do not look at the TPS voltage as such, but rather at changes to voltage (delta) on speed-density systems. Therefore, do not automatically assume there is a problem if the sensor's full range is not available to the ECU. It may not matter.

Make sure the TPS turns in the same direction as the throttle shaft, and do not use the TPS as a throttle stop. Make sure that the throttle stop is backed off all the way when you install the TPS so that the TPS does not prevent the throttle

Electrical Requirements for a Haltech System

Component	Amps required
Haltech F3 ECU *	5.8-19.5
Aftermarket electronic ignition (8000rpm)	6-18
Electrical fuel pump	8
A/C Clutch	3-4
Headlamps (2), high beam	13-15
Headlamps (2), low beam	8-9
Heater/Defroster (with A/C high blower)	15-20
Wiper motor	3.5-6.5
Miscellaneous other accessories	up to 80
Total	**62.3-88amps**

* = V-8 port injection, on continuously

Haltech F3, V-8 port injection

	Current draw	
RPM	**14amp injectors**	**2.5amp injectors**
0	0.3	0.3
1000	1.2	3.1
2000	1.8	5.5
3000	2.5	8.3
4000	3.2	10.7
5000	3.9	12.9
6000	5.0	—
Injectors on continuously	5.8	19.5

Data source: Haltech

These Type-6 injectors are mounted on their fuel rail and are ready to go.

from closing all the way should someone back out the throttle stop screw.

ECUs that provide spark control require some kind of engine position sensor. Exact engine position relative to the power stroke for a certain cylinder can only be provided by the camshaft, since a crank sensor has no way of knowing whether a given position represents compression or exhaust stoke on a four-cycle engine. The camshaft tells exact position, but if you are using a flying magnet (versus a toothed gear read optically), the ECU cannot detect and react as quickly to changes in engine speed. Therefore, most ECUs that need to know engine position also require a crank sensor. The DFI unit can use a crank sensor (or electronic distributor), but does not require a cam trigger since it relies on the distributor to send spark to the correct cylinder and fires injectors in batch mode.

The NOS-EFI Technology ECU uses a cam trigger at 45 degrees before top dead center (BTDC) to distinguish compression stroke on number one cylinder, and uses a crank trigger at roughly 15 degrees BTDC for timing sequential injections and spark (after top dead center, or ATDC) using multiple flying magnets. The Electromotive ECU uses a toothed wheel which can be fastened to the crank or cam (different number of teeth) and can instantly tell crank position to a quarter of a degree.

Vacuum/Boost Source

Speed-density EFI systems require very accurate manifold pressure to provide proper fueling. This is *critical* at idle. Some wild-cammed engines are not suitable for speed-density EFI because the idle manifold pressure is unstable. Engines like this should use throttle angle (Alpha-N) EFI control. A problem could occur if you're running multiple throttle bodies, since the vacuum port would only indicate the vacuum of one port, and might fluctuate rapidly at idle, confusing the ECU.

In this case, build a vacuum accumulator of 2ci (cubic inches) volume, with vacuum lines running to all intake runners. The MAP sensor is then referenced to the accumulator. This device will dampen fluctuations and is small enough in volume to react quickly to changes in manifold pressure.

Personal Computer Interface

Most programmable EFI systems are designed to use a laptop computer as a user interface for tuning and monitoring the EFI system. You may find it helpful to have a rudimentary knowledge of the MS-DOS personal computer operating system, although most EFI system user interfaces provide a complete set of commands that will do the job to create and modify fuel maps, and to manage them on floppy or hard disc.

It is vitally important to have a laptop computer so you can program the vehicle while driving. Never attempt to tune and drive at the same time, however. Get a friend to drive the vehicle while you tune. Many expert tuners claim that some road tuning is required even when the raw fuel map was created on a dyno with a gas analyzer. By using one foot on the accelerator, one on the brakes, you can hold various speed-loading points for adjustment.

But remember: It is not safe to drive and tune at the same time. Be smart. Get help!

The Edelbrock Pro-Flo EFI system, and some of the black boxes that modify the actions of the OE computer (such as the Crane Interceptor),

Here's the Edelbrock manifold, converted to EFI applications and ready to be installed on the engine. The first

photo shows the Holley throttle body setup while the second shot uses an Accel system.

have their own user interface, a keypad, and an LCD (liquid crystal display), which means you do not need a PC. However, given the cost of a programmable EFI system, the cost of renting a laptop PC, if you don't own one and can't borrow one, is probably not much of a deterrent to most people; expect it to cost, say, $50-$100 a week.

Most programmable EFI systems support an optional interface module which enables a tuner to vary the air-fuel mixture up to 10 or more percent rich or lean by adjusting a knob on the interface. This allows you to easily change the mixture and instantly note the effects. Once you know what percent change is required at what speed and loading, you can program the change into the computer permanently. Unless you are very experienced, you will find this method easier than trying to tune by altering the raw fuel map—even with the help of an oxygen sensor display! Don't let anyone convince you you don't need the rich-lean module.

I recommend practicing navigating through the menus (screens) of the EFI system PC user interface before attempting to tune the car, and read the software manual several times, memorizing the features and commands—at least to the degree that you can find the exact syntax of the command right away in the manual. Tuning a high-performance vehicle involves a certain amount of risk. Lean mixture or detonation under high power can damage your engine.

Save all your fuel maps so you can recover to an earlier fuel curve if you reach a point where things are not working well on the current map, or if you accidentally erase something. Keep a log of everything you did, and change only one thing at a time.

Chapter 10

Setup and Tuning

Haltech, Emtech, DFI, NOS-EFI Technology, Electromotive and other programmable fuel injection systems permit you to program the basic raw fuel curve for an engine, defining the shape of a series of graphs that plot injector pulse width time as a function of speed and loading (either manifold pressure or throttle position). The graph(s) or matrix looks different in each system, and the resolution is different, but the concept is exactly the same.

A personal computer (PC) runs tuning software that consists of a screen-handling user interface and a communication program which has the ability to communicate with the ECU micro-computer managing spark and/or fuel requirements for the engine. A user can load fueling data (maps) from disc on the PC into the ECU, which can then run the engine, or can download ECU-resident maps into the PC for pos-

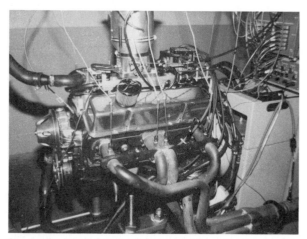

Here's the ideal way to tune an EFI engine: an engine dyno with exhaust gas temperature (EGT) sensors on all exhaust runners, plus a gas analyzer. Haltech tests software with circuitry that emulates EFI hardware. Cutler Induction/Haltech EFI

sible analysis and modification. Each system gives a user the ability to modify fueling maps while the engine is running, making changing to the representation of the map on the PC screen, and then transferring this data to the ECU.

The user is also usually able to make changes to the ECU's map without necessarily saving the change permanently on disc. The map is, in a sense, "saved" in the EEPROM nonvolatile memory of the ECU as soon as the change is uploaded to the ECU. But saving to disc is a separate operation, allowing a user to try changes on the fly without overwriting the fuel map on disc until it is clear that the change should be permanent.

Haltech's environment *displays* 32 or 64 bar graphs of pulse width data (64 is maintained internally) for each thousand-rpm range from zero to 7000rpm (optionally 16,000rpm), which defines a 64 by 8 matrix of pulse width "breakpoints" of load/speed pulsewidth values. For loading/speed points that fall in between the speed and loading breakpoints, the ECU performs a linear interpolation to determine pulse width. A tuner uses PC function keys to move between rpm ranges, and PC left-right arrow keys to move between bar graphs for various engine loading on each rpm range, using up-down arrows to raise and lower individual bars. If the engine is running, the PC instantly transmits the change to the ECU, which loads the data in its internal table, missing one injection event (which will cause the engine to momentarily stumble—and implies you should not make changes under heavy load).

The NOS-EFI Technology system provides a similar graphical environment to the Haltech, except that the pulse width data defines a line graph of injection time versus speed within each *loading* range (throttle angle or manifold absolute pressure), each of which is a separate screen on the PC. A user can define ranges, meaning you are not limited to thousand-rpm ranges—

although the total number of ranges is still the same. If you want finer granularity of adjustment, say, at low rpm, you'll have to sacrifice some resolution elsewhere. The result is the ability to define a non-linear fuel map. When you change pulse width for a particular breakpoint, the change shows up as two dotted line segments on the graph, connecting the new pulse width point with the two adjacent points. Making this change permanent, and transferring it to the ECU are separate operations on older systems; the newest software and mapping interface allows ECU updating on the fly, like the Haltech system. The NOS-EFI Technology ECU works from a matrix of 16 speeds and 16 loading ranges, defining 256 breakpoints. You also have the ability to graph a three-dimensional projection of all data on the computer screen, to get an idea of the overall look of the fueling or spark Map.

The DFI Calmap system displays the entire matrix of base pulse width data on the screen at once, literally as 17 rows and 16 columns of numbers (272 in all). To tune the basic fuel map, you put the PC in "edit" mode, moving between cells in the matrix of numbers with arrow keys, and, once in a particular cell, typing in a new number. The numbers are not actually pulse width, but can be converted to pulse width by multiplying by 0.0627. The DFI system allows you to plot graphs of data to get a feel for the overall look of the fuel curve.

All of the above systems allow a tuner to use a mixture trim device (one or two linear potentiometer knobs) to instantaneously lean or enrich fueling by a percentage determined by the position of the knob(s). This is an invaluable tool in making an instant determination of the effect of fueling changes and the percentage change required when reprogramming the ECU.

Programmable EFI systems all offer the ability to program acceleration enrichment and cold-running enrichment. Some systems allow configuration of fueling corrections for changes in air temperature. Systems like the DFI unit break down cold-running enrichment into cranking enrichment, after-start enrichment, and warmup enrichment. DFI and some other systems provide ignition control, nitrous control, knock sensor ignition retard, and idle speed correction via stepper motor-controlled throttle air bypass. These are all controlled via PC screen menus.

Getting Started

It would be nice to be able to provide a handy formula for programming an ECU off-line that would give excellent results for all load-speed combinations immediately upon startup. It is easy to calculate the volume of a cylinder and therefore the weight of air that enters the cylin-

Haltech (shown here) and Accel/DFI EFI systems both enable the use of a mixture trim device, essential to easy tuning.

der under ideal operating conditions. It is also fairly easy to make a good guess at how long an injector should stay open to spray in an amount of fuel that is a particular fraction of the weight of the air (such as the 14.7:1 stoichiometric or chemically correct air-fuel ratio).

However, there are many factors that go into determining how much air *actually* enters the engine's cylinders under various operating conditions (which is always less than the static displacement of an engine)—except on highly optimized racing engines utilizing ram-effects tuned intake and exhaust systems, or on turbo-supercharged engines, which easily operate at 100 percent or more of static displacement.

A number of factors conspire to prevent a full 100 VE in most normally aspirated street engines. There is always at least a slight pressure drop through a *carburetor*, even at wide-open throttle, due to the need for a restrictive venturi. Carburetors and fuel injection throttle bodies restrict airflow, producing a pressure drop, at partial throttle. Intake ports and valves offer some restriction. The exhaust stroke does not expel all burned gases because some exhaust is trapped in the clearance volume. The exhaust valves and exhaust pipes offer some restriction as well. The camshaft profile of an engine has a huge effect of the VE of an engine at various speeds and loading.

As an engine wears out, its VE decreases—but this may not occur evenly across various speeds and loading ranges or between various cylinders. Even new factory engines vary in VE with perhaps 5 percent very fast (high VE), 15 percent very slow, and the rest somewhere in the middle. Given the varying VE of an engine, the amount of air in the cylinder at any given breakpoint is not perfectly predictable. You can assume that the maximum VE occurs at the point of peak torque (if you know where that is). This will be the point of maximum injection pulse width, with pulse width falling off both above and below this. Maximum power will occur at a higher rpm than peak torque because the engine is making *more* power strokes per time increment, but the power strokes are *less efficient* at speeds above the torque peak, and therefore require less fuel.

Another complicating factor in designing a fuel curve is that even if you know how much air is entering the cylinders at a given time, it is not necessarily clear what air-fuel *mixture* is optimal. Most hot rodders want the maximum power possible at wide-open throttle, using the least possible fuel to accomplish this (lean best torque). But under some circumstances, it may be desirable to run at *rich* best torque (or even richer) in order to design in a safety factor to help prevent detonation with bad gas. (This safety strategy used on certain injected 5.0 liter Mustangs allows you to improve power by *leaning* out injection at wide-open throttle!).

And what about throttle response versus efficiency at part throttle? Are you willing to sacrifice some idle quality for fuel economy or reduced emissions? Does the overlap of your cam dilute the idle mixture such that you need a particularly rich mixture for an acceptable idle? These kinds of questions complicate tuning even further.

Additionally, there's the real-world performance of the circuitry that activates the injectors, and the physical response of the injectors themselves which can vary from injector to injector.

Manually Building a Startup Map

Given the complexity of designing a theoretically correct fuel map, most tuners don't even try. If possible, they use a pre-existing map from a similar vehicle or engine. Otherwise, they build a "startup" map designed purely to be rich enough to get the vehicle running and warmed up. This is made easier by the fact that warmed-up fuel-injected engines will run with mixtures as rich as 6.0:1 on up to lean mixtures near 22.0:1, and even cold engines are fairly flexible about air-fuel mixtures that will run the motor.

With the engine running, ideally on a dyno, tuners adjust the engine at each breakpoint combination of speed and load, and, using test equipment and a mixture trim module, set ignition timing and injection pulse width to achieve low emissions, best torque (lean or rich), or a specific air-fuel mixture—or some combination of all three. Then they road test the vehicle and fine-tune it under actual driving conditions, also fine-tuning the enrichment maps.

If your ECU has closed-loop capability, and is running in a speed-throttle position range in which closed-loop operation is activated, your ECU may be able to tell you what the mixture *would* have been if you were running open-loop–based on what amount of mixture correction was required to achieve a stoichiometric air-fuel mixture. You can then make corrections to the raw fuel map based on this information.

If you happen to have a volumetric efficiency chart for your engine, it should be possible to build a fairly good theoretical map in advance. Plan to run 12.5:1 mixture under wide-open throttle, perhaps as high as 13.5:1 on mild street engines that are not turbocharged. Under very high vacuum, run 15.5:1 or 16.0:1 (or even fuel cut on deceleration!). Mild-cammed engines with tuned runners and little overlap should idle at 14.7:1. Big-cammed engines will not idle well at stoichiometric mixtures, needing 13.0-13.5:1 mixtures to idle as smoothly as possible.

Build in *smooth* increases in mixture as the engine increases in speed toward best torque and as loading increases. Remember that injectors are not accurate below about 1.7milliseconds (a millisecond is 0.001 of a second). In addition, most injection systems will not open the injectors more than 16milliseconds under any conditions. Also remember that the amount of time available for injection is determined by the speed of the engine. At some point, the injectors are static, that is, open all the time, and you have lost control of fuel flow in relation to engine fuel requirement changes while in this realm. Since this would most likely occur under conditions of high loading at high speed, lean mixtures could lead to disastrously lean mixtures. Check to make sure that the injection pulse width is *less* than 56,000 divided by rpm. If so, you're OK, the injectors will not be static.

If you don't have a VE chart, but know the

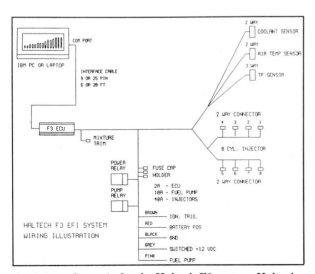

A wiring schematic for the Haltech F3 system. Haltech

peak torque speed for the engine, assume 80 percent VE for a street engine at peak torque, 90 to 100 percent for racing engines, and 100 percent or more for supercharged engines.

First, compute the weight of air in the cylinders. Convert displacement to displacement at volumetric efficiency (80-100 percent). Divide displacement in cubic inches by cubic inches per cubic foot (1,728), which gives you engine displacement in cubic feet. Multiple this by pounds of moist air per cubic foot (.07651) at standard temperature and pressure, which gives you pounds of air that enter the engine per two revolutions. Divide this by the number of cylinders to get air weight per power stroke at each cylinder (injector!). Divide this figure by the target air-fuel ratio to get pounds of fuel per power stroke. Divide this number by the number of injections per power stroke (usually one for sequential injection, two for batch-fire port injection), which gives you the weight of fuel per injection. Compute the pounds of fuel injected per millisecond of injector pulse by dividing the pounds per hour of fuel flow by 3,600,000.

And, finally, divide the weight of fuel per injection by the weight of fuel per millisecond of injector pulse to get the number of milliseconds of pulsewidth to set calibration. Here's an example:

454ci engine * .9 VE = 408.6ci air drawn into engine at peak torque

408.6 / 1728 = 0.236458333cu ft air drawn into engine

0.236458333 * .07651 (pounds per cubic foot air) = 0.018091427lb air entering engine per two revs

0.018091427 / 8 = 0.002261428 (pounds per power stroke at each cylinder)

0.002261428 / 12.5 (target air-fuel ratio, peak torque) = .000180914

.000180914 / 2 = .000090457 (pounds fuel per injection, batch fire)

30lb/hr injectors / 3,600,000 = .000008333 = pounds fuel per millisecond

.000090457 / .000008333 = 10.85 ms pulsewidth at peak torque with 30lb injectors on 454ci engine at 90 percent VE.

Remember, most EFI regulators vary fuel pressure to keep it constant in relation to manifold pressure. If necessary, convert fuel volume to weight (using formulas in the injector selection section). Convert fuel flow in weight per hour to flow per second by dividing by 3,600. For example, 24lb per hour divided by 3,600 equals 0.0066667lb per second.

Now, divide the fuel flow in weight per time by the fuel weight calculated to achieve the desired mixture. This will tell you the fraction of a second you need to open an injector in order to inject the right amount of fuel. Injectors do not open instantly, but assume this is figured into the pulsed flow rate. Convert this time to thousandths of a second, if necessary, always rounding upward. Don't forget to divide this in two if your injection system uses *two* batch fires per power stroke. Perform the necessary math if you are using fewer throttle-body injectors. Make sure the pulse width is less than the lesser of 16milliseconds or 56,000 divided by rpm.

Maybe you don't want to mess with theoretical mixtures. Given the flexibility of engines to run with widely varying air-fuel mixtures, Haltech simply recommends building a startup map by setting light-load bars for all rpm ranges to 2.5milliseconds, sloping pulse width smoothly upward to 7.5milliseconds in the higher manifold

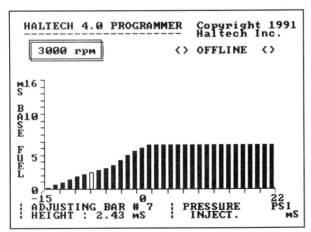

Printscreens of Haltech system fuel map showing typical pulsewidth difference for vacuum-pressure breakpoints over two RPM ranges. The hollow bar is what's currently being modified, while an arrow points at the

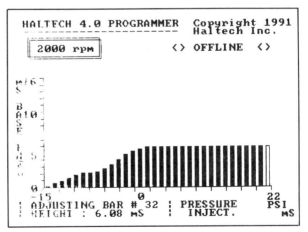

bar currently fueling the engine if it's available on the current screen. The graph plots injection pulsewidth within a certain RPM range as a function of engine loading. Haltech

pressure or wider throttle angle bars.

Most EFI system software gives you the ability to set multiple speed-load points at once, and to modify multiple points by a given percentage or to a given slope. You should not have to manually set all 256 or 512 breakpoints in the startup map.

Haltech recommends setting acceleration enrichment to 35 percent, enrichment sustain to 20 percent before starting. Virtually all EFI systems provide a default set of other enrichment maps that are usable to start the motor.

Startup and Tuning

Before starting, always make sure all sensors are making sense. This means using the PC's interface to look at what the ECU thinks sensors are reading. It may immediately be possible to pick out some sensor data as indicating a short or open circuit or bad sensor. You should make sure the throttle position sensor is properly calibrated, if necessary rotating it such that it reads correctly at idle and wide-open throttle (see chapter 9 on installation do's and don'ts).

ECU's that estimate engine load based on throttle position may need a fairly steep increase in pulse width at light loads, particularly on systems with large throttle areas in which there is a large change in airflow for a small throttle angle change. Check out the maps displayed in this book to see what some real fuel maps look like.

Now start the engine with a mixture trim adjustment device connected to the ECU, if at all possible. The immediate goal is to get the engine to idle reasonably well so that it will warm up. If possible, do not modify the cold-running enrichment until you have had a chance to get right the base raw fuel map with the engine warm. If necessary, use the mixture trim knob to lean or

enrich the mixture while the engine is warming up, but try not to change the maps yet because you won't know if the problem is with the base fuel map or the cold-running enrichment map. The engine should start with no more than five to

---

Startup Maps

Startup maps are basically generic fuel curves designed to approximate actual requirements of a similar engine well enough so the engine can be started and run so it can be fine-tuned via computer. The engine displacement is less important than the cam specs of an engine. In other words, a mild-cammed 350ci Chevrolet small-block is closer in fuel requirements to a mild-cammed Chevy 400ci small-block than two 350s are to each other—if one is mild cammed and the other is wild cammed.

The following is a list of startup maps for Haltech's F3 and F7 ECUs.

Unit Type	MAP name on Disc	Engine Application
All F3/F7	STD4	Most 4-cyl. engines
All F3/F7	STD6	Most 6-cyl.
All F3/F7	STD8	Most 8-cyl.
F3	STD12	Most 12-cyl.
F3	MOD4	Highly modified 4-cyl.
F3	MOD6	Highly modified 6-cyl.
F3	MOD8	Highly modified 8-cyl.
F3	TURBO4	Most turbocharged 4-cyl.
F3	TURBO6	Most turbocharged 6-cyl.
F3	TURBO8	Most turbocharged 8-cyl.
F7 (10000rpm+)	MC4	High-RPM 4-cyl.

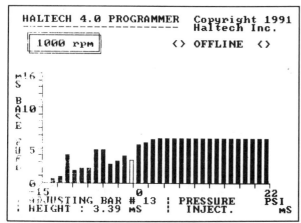

These printscreens show incorrect fuel mapping. The VE changes as a function of load are smooth and directly correlated to throttle opening at a given RPM, and never vary wildly up and down. Similarly, the second

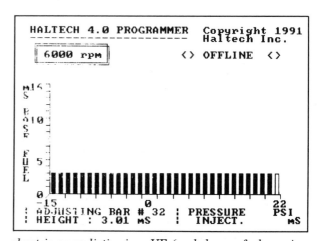

chart is unrealistic since VE (and, hence, fuel requirements) does change with throttle opening and engine speed. Haltech

ten seconds of cranking. If there is a problem go to chapter 11, the troubleshooting section of this book, or to the appropriate section of the EFI system manual.

If the engine starts but dies, try enriching the mixture with the trim knob. You might have to observe the breakpoint under which the engine was being fueled when it died, increasing the pulse width until the engine starts and runs slightly rich (some black smoke will come from the exhaust).

With the engine at operating temperature as shown in the EFI system's "Engine Display Data," it is time to tune the car under light loads (stopped). If you have an exhaust gas analyzer, use it to try for a stoichiometric mixture on a mild engine (bigger cams need more fuel to idle acceptably). Turn the mixture trim knob from rich to lean at a certain rpm, noting which direction makes the engine run better. Make a note of the increase percentage, multiply the pulsewidth at the speed-loading point by the percent of change, then let the engine return to idle and increase or decrease the pulse width by the correct amount, returning the mixture trim to the zero position.

Remember that ECUs determine fueling for speed-loading points between the actual breakpoints in the fueling matrix by an interpolation based on the points to either side. Haltech points out that an rpm of 2200 is fueled 80 percent by the 2000rpm range Map, 20 percent by the 3000rpm Map.

If the engine backfires through the intake, the mixture is lean. Adjust the mixture trim and note where the engine is running on the PC's monitor screen showing the raw fuel map, and raise the correct breakpoint(s) and those immediately around it until the engine will take increased throttle smoothly and rev properly without backfire.

It is far more preferable to run too rich than too lean when beginning the tuning process. Work from rich to lean for safety at higher speeds and loading points. According to Corky Bell at CarTech, if you are very careful not to damage the engine, working lean to rich can result in improved fuel economy.

The ideal method for tuning is to put the engine or vehicle on a dynamometer, setting the power, speed, and loading at each element of the fueling matrix (map) for best power, economy, or lowest emissions.

According to an EFI Technology spokesperson, "The basic principle of mapping is to run the engine at as many of the table breakpoints as possible and determine the optimum fuel and spark for each point. The data is then input into the table to create the new map."

It may not be desirable or practical to run at all the breakpoints within the limits of the fueling matrix. Just because some elements of the map were not accessible on a dyno does not mean the engine will not see these on the road. A tuner should complete all areas of the map with plausible data for best performance, and should road test the vehicle as completely as possible. As a final check, load the completed map into the ECU if not already there, and verify that some of the breakpoints are correct. And finally, do an exhaustive road test.

That's the ideal way to do it. But most people

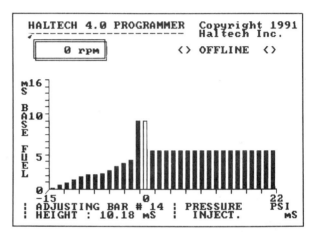

This printscreen shows an adjustment to aid F3 starting. Zero load at zero RPM can only occur during cranking. F3, with no cranking enrichment, may require a very rich mixture at high manifold pressure to start easily. Haltech

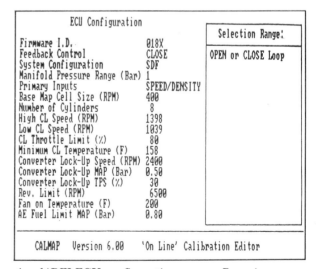

Accel/DFI ECU configuration screen. By using arrow keys and the space bar, tuners can configure basic engine information used to compute injection pulsewidth, ignition timing, and other factors. Accel/DFI

don't have the $1,000-plus that it takes for several days of dyno time with an expert consultant. Many good tuners don't even have a gas analyzer, relying instead on exhaust gas temperature, and oxygen sensor, or simply some "seat of the pants" expertise, plus a stop watch and a spark plug wrench. For road tuning, you'll need two people and a private test facility to do this safely.

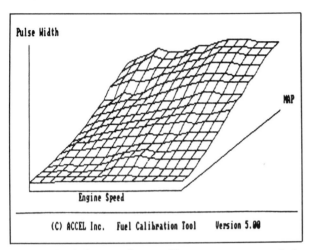

Accel/DFI Calmap software allows a tuner to graph the entire base fuel map to get a "big picture" look at the entire fuel curve. Pulsewidth (the vertical scale) increases as a function of manifold absolute pressure (depth scale), and to a lesser extent, with RPM (horizontal scale).

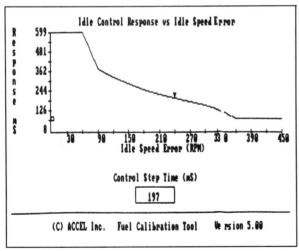

Accel Calmap software allows very sophisticated programming of all functions. Idle control functions are shown here. Two maps allow target idle to change with engine temperature, and regulate system response to idle speed error as a function of the degree of error. The final graph tells the system how many "steps" the IAC stepper motor should make as a function of stall rate. Accel/DFI

Go for a drive. Watch the PC screen that is monitoring where the engine is operating on the fuel matrix. (Usually the graph bar or breakpoint is highlighted somehow by the PC so you can easily tell which data breakpoint is currently fueling the engine.) If the engine coughs and dies, notice which bar the engine was on when it went lean, and enrich this element of the fuel map and the elements in the direction of heavier loading while maintaining the same overall curve *using the mixture trim,* if you have one.

If the engine coughs (meaning it's too lean), then runs well, adjust only the area around the problem spot, leaving the rest of the matrix alone. An engine running rich will be very slow to respond to throttle inputs and may blow black smoke as you begin to load it. Try leaning it out with the mixture trim. Then follow the above method for map adjustment, *lowering* the pulse width rather than raising it.

Once the engine accelerates smoothly, adjust part- and wide-open throttle settings. Observe the current map element that is fueling, and adjust only that area. The mixture trim is helpful in determining what action to take at a trouble spot. Accelerate at a steady engine loading in a higher gear, perhaps with partial braking. Then observe the current area of the fuel map while adjusting the mixture trim for best running conditions.

Many EFI systems allow you to log engine data to a disc file on the personal computer. Using the Datalog, you should be able to review the range and map elements that were current, along with the percent of mixture trim that worked. Use this information to make adjustments to the base fuel map. Unless you are an expert tuner, always start rich and tune down to leaner mixtures in small steps—lean mixtures can cause detonation and engine damage.

It may be possible and helpful initially to tune all rpm or all loading ranges at once, eventually concentrating on a single range. The general shape of various ranges will be the same, with the most fuel needed at the RPM of peak torque. But some EFI systems allow you to automatically rough in all ranges when you do one. Cruise at the intervals suggested by the various graphs which will show pulse width plotted against intervals of rpm or pulse width plotted against increments of load. Tune to maintain rapid throttle input between shifts while you are making other adjustments to maintain smooth, even running conditions.

Adjust acceleration enrichment. Haltech suggests a 35 percent increase and 20 percent sustain. Adjust the increase upward if there is an instant bog, and add to the sustain if there is a slightly delayed bog. If you reach 100 percent increase and the engine still lean-coughs, the base fuel map is too lean somewhere, or the engine data configuration is wrong, or the ECU hardware is wrong for your application. As noted earlier, engines with very large throttle area (such as one throttle blade per cylinder) will greatly increase manifold pressure with a slight turn in throttle angle. One hundred percent enrichment may not be enough in some circumstances. The DFI system's 6.0 Calmap software allows you to provide acceleration enrichment on throttle angle changes *and/or acceleration* enrichment based on manifold pressure changes.

Adjust wide-open-throttle fueling. If you don't have a gas analyzer and/or dyno, try using a stopwatch to time acceleration runs, adjusting fueling for maximum acceleration and power. If necessary, check the spark plugs after hard acceleration. Shut off the engine at full load (making sure you don't lock the steering) and immediately check the plugs. Overly light or white plugs indicate a lean mixture, while dark, "sooty" plugs imply too rich a mixture. When things are right, normal plugs should be light brown in color *immediately* after a hard run.

When you have adjusted the engine for normal temperature running and acceleration, it is time to adjust cold-running enrichment, cranking enrichment, after-start enrichment—whatever is available to provide enrichment when the engine is cold or being cranked. Different ECUs offer various ways of providing this enrichment, but the key is to let the engine cold-soak over night and to work quickly while it is warming up to achieve good cold running. Some systems, like DFI's Calmap-based ECU, allow specific *cranking* enrichment. Haltech's does not, but you can program a very high pulse width at zero rpm at very low manifold vacuum which approximates a cranking enrichment. Some modifiers have rigged devices that simulate a "spark trigger," causing the ECU to trigger injections before cranking, providing a priming dose of fuel. Haltech's F7 throttle position system offers built-in priming.

There are many additional programming features on some injection systems, including, most importantly, ignition spark timing. The spark timing map plots spark advance against loading and rpm. The major advantage of this feature, over traditional advance via centrifugal weights and a vacuum diaphragm, is that any advance is possible under any conditions and need not be related to advance at adjacent map breakpoints. Additional advance is possible for cold running or when an air conditioner is running.

Spark retard is easy based on the data from a knock-sensing microphone or under conditions of nitrous injection, as well as under the positive manifold pressure created by turbo-supercharger boost. The best method for mapping spark advance is exactly like that for fuel mapping—on a dyno. But the road-tuning methods already mentioned can be used to set spark advance as well as fueling. A good place to start is with the specifications on the stock centrifugal and vacuum advances.

Other features you may need to set are idle speed control, in which the ECU uses a stepper-motor-driven idle air control (IAC) module to

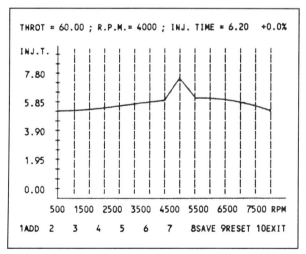

The EFI Technology main display shows air, water, and oil temperature in degrees Celsius; manifold pressure in inches of mercury (Hg); battery voltage; injection phasing in degrees ATDC; status of the rich-lean control; and more. Software systems from leading manufacturers have main menus the display for tuners lists of system parameters that can be modified by the tuner. EFI Technology

An EFI Technology graph of 50 percent throttle position, showing injection pulsewidth as a function of RPM. The modifications to the system beginning at 4000rpm have been programmed in by the tuner, and can be loaded into the ECU to alter performance. EFI Technology

allow air to by-pass the throttle blade, providing idle speed stabilization. The DFI system allows you to set target speeds for various operating temperatures, as well as thresholds for operation, plus strategies to use the IAC to prevent stalling on sudden throttle closing.

You may have the opportunity to program conditions under which the system will use an oxygen sensor to operate in closed-loop (feedback mode), adjusting air-fuel for cleanest emissions.

The DFI and Electromotive systems allow you to program torque converter lockup conditions, turn on cooling fans, set rev limits (using ignition and/or fuel cut), and fuel cut on deceleration and up to several stages of fuel enrichment via injection for nitrous injection. Follow your instruction manual, or pay an expert to tune up your system, perhaps allowing you to watch.

Without expensive measuring and diagnostic equipment, fuel mapping involves trial and error, and experience and intuition are invaluable. If you are careful, patient, and above all, methodical—logging what you do, changing one parameter at a time, getting help when you need a second person, and following thoughtful safety practices—you can achieve excellent results.

F3 Menus

The Haltech F3 main menu and sub-menu enable users to pick tuning and setup functions. Menu-driven functionality means users with no personal computer knowledge can understand and use the PC to tune in vehicles by manipulating graphs and filling in the blanks.

The main menu includes the following:

X: Range 1, 0rpm
F1: Range 2, 1000rpm
F2: Range 3, 2000rpm
F3: Range 4, 3000rpm
F4: Range 5, 4000rpm
F5: Range 6, 5000rpm
F6: Range 7, 6000rpm
F7: Range 8, 7000rpm
C: Current position
W: Warm-up characteristics
S: Store vehicle information to disk
L: Load vehicle information from disk
E: Erase vehicle information from disk
    The sub-menu covers the following information:
R: All ranges: Unique <> The same
B: The number of bars: Normal <> Doubled
O: Haltech: Online <> Offline

S: Stage injectors: No <> Yes
U: Units: KPa <> PSI <> inHg
—: Setup—use <I> Identification to set up engine
I: Identification—display/set engine characteristics
T: Throttle accelerator pump—set amount
E: Engine data—shows current engine data
D: Datalog—saves engine date
H: Help—how to move

Haltech's Datalog feature lets a tuner log engine data as a series of "snapshots." The Datalog menu permits a tuner to view, store, load, print, erase, and go automatic with the Datalog.

A Datalog listing will provide a tuner with the following information: engine speed (RPM), pressure (PSI), engine temperature, throttle (percentage open), air temperature, trim (percentage), injectors (ms), range number, bar number and time. An example of a Datalog printout is as follows:

Speed	Pres.	Eng T	Throt	Air T	Trim	Inject	Range	Bar #	Time
3400	0	187	92	127	1	5.76	4	14	33:24:23
3400	0	187	92	127	1	5.76	4	14	33:24:34
3600	0	187	92	127	1	5.76	5	14	33:24:45
3600	0	187	92	127	1	5.76	5	14	33:24:56
3600	0	190	92	127	1	5.76	5	14	33:24:67

Chapter 11

Troubleshooting

All EFI systems are ultimately controlled by a computer which, as we've already discussed, is called an electronic control unit. *ECUs very seldom fail.*

Automotive ECUs are extremely rugged, built to withstand the harsh automotive environment of vibration, heat and cold, high humidity, electrical interference, and other factors, and still perform with the precision required to calculate engine fueling, spark, and other management tasks in millisecond time frames.

The ECU must perform perfectly on a minus 10 degrees Fahrenheit morning in Buffalo, as well as a baking south Texas summer afternoon just after a thunderstorm in 100 percent humidity. It must perform perfectly in a four-wheel-drive vehicle, jouncing and vibrating through extremely rough off-road conditions. Automotive engineers rarely put the ECU in the engine compartment, preferring to locate it inside the vehicle or trunk where the environment is kinder to electronic components. Why tempt fate any more than you have to?

It is possible to design an ECU that will withstand the incredibly harsh engine compartment environment in which underhood temperatures can reach hundreds of degrees, where the electromagnetic and radio interference close to high-voltage ignition components can induce killing voltage in normal nearby wiring, and where vibration can shake apart sensitive electronic components—not to mention mechanical parts.

Mil-spec equipment, designed in some cases to withstand the electromagnetic pulse of a nuclear blast, is shielded from radio interference by the enclosure, and protected from humidity and vibration by a bath of hardened plastic sludge that is literally poured into the enclosure, completely surrounding components by plastic.

Mil-spec cabling and harnesses utilize failsafe connectors and attachment systems. Such systems are too expensive when the simple option exists to put sensitive components out of harm's way inside the vehicle. On race cars and nuclear re-entry vehicles, you go mil-spec. There are one or two "hardened" automotive ECUs available in the aftermarket, such as the race unit from EFI Technology and NOS, which sells for roughly $8,000. All electronic control units are very rugged, but it is only common sense when designing an EFI system to mount your ECU and wiring so the ECU stays happy.

Assuming the engine itself is healthy, in most cases the problem with an EFI system is not with the computer but with the data it is receiving from its sensors—or with some related electrical or physical air-fuel system problem. Low fuel pressure, clogged injectors, defective sensors, leaky vacuum hoses or fittings, and electrical system shorts or incorrect wiring can drive you crazy when trying to troubleshoot an EFI system, either upon initial startup or later on. It is important to go about troubleshooting in a methodical way, checking one thing at a time, substituting one part at a time, then moving on to the next step. If you accurately follow a troubleshooting algorithm, it is inevitable that you will isolate the problem.

It is important to realize that troubleshooting a modern computerized EFI system is a little like playing chess with a hidden opponent. The computer itself, with its own bag of tricks, will be doing its best to analyze or work around or compensate for perceived problems. Of course, the ECU's view of the world is completely through the sensors. A problem like a small vacuum leak can fool the ECU into assuming a lean condition exists, causing it to erroneously enrich the mixture. *One bad injector, either too rich or too lean, can throw off the average air-fuel mixture as perceived by the computer based on *one* sensor measuring exhaust gas oxygen coming from all cylinders.

Incorrect fuel pressure will result in the

wrong amount of fuel squirting from working injectors. This will show up immediately in open-loop systems such as the Haltech F3. However, it may be compensated for by the ECU at idle or cruise during closed-loop operation, only to show up disastrously at full throttle—which is still almost always open-loop (predetermined injection pulse width). A bad EGR valve can cause the ECU to believe the mixture is lean. A plugged fuel filter may only show up during very heavy loading or high rpm, or *intermittently* at other times, causing a closed-loop computer to constantly chase correct mixtures. Many computers maintain internal lists of correction factors designed to compensate for changes in engine VE due to aging or other factors.

Modern ECUs also make use of tactics that cause them to disregard suspect sensors under certain circumstances. The computer may outsmart itself in attempting to correct for unusual circumstances, possibly making things worse. When the computer attempts to compensate for an inaccurately perceived lean condition by enriching the mixture at idle, the engine may run roughly and produce a "rotten egg" smell at the exhaust.

Throttle position sensors out of adjustment or broken can cause the engine to stumble at certain throttle positions or on sudden acceleration.

If the EFI system incorporates knock sensing, ECU strategies to prevent engine damage by knocking may mask other problems. Bad gas, plugged injectors, new platinum spark plugs, or oil introduced into the mixture by turbochargers or positive crankcase ventilation (PCV) systems can all cause pinging or detonation. Since the ECU may retard timing to prevent detonation,

the problem may be masked. What the user sees is lack of power.

In virtually all cases, EFI problems can be traced to the computer somehow getting inaccurate data, or some other physical problem outside the ECU.

Troubleshooting Chart
Trouble: Engine will not start
Possibilities:

Injectors are not operating because:
    ECU is not receiving 12volt switched power.
    ECU is not receiving 12volt constant power.
    Insufficient ground.
    Ignition system not compatible with ECU.
    Bad ECU.
Check: *Connections, fuses, relays, plug wires.*
    ECU is not receiving an rpm signal from the ignition system.
Check: *Wiring for proper connection, ignition compatibility, ignition system operation.*
    Voltage drops below 9 volts during cranking.
Check: *Battery voltage, connections.*

Injectors are operating but:
    Fuel mixture is too lean.
    Fuel mixture is too rich (spark plugs will be wet with fuel).
Check: *Plugs, and adjust fuel delivery bars as required.*
Injectors do not have proper fuel pressure.
Check: *Pump operation, fuel rail pressure.*
Engine is not receiving ignition spark.
Engine ignition timing is incorrect.
Check: *Ignition system function, and timing.*
Algorithm:
1. Check for spark; if spark exists, go to 2.

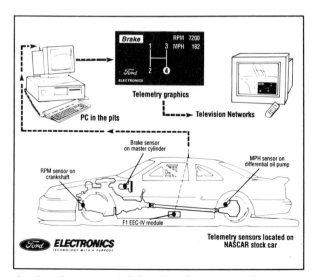

Ford's Formula 1 telemetry system (used on F1 cars and NASCAR racers) is a more sophisticated version of

the data-logging capability found on many aftermarket electronic control units (EEC-IV engine control). Ford

1.1 Disconnect EFI tachometer wire from ignition system; if still no spark, repair ignition; otherwise go to 1.2.

1.2 (Electrical problem in EFI system) Disconnect ECU; if spark, substitute spare tested ECU and recheck; otherwise go to 1.3.

1.3 (Bad EFI wiring harness) Check EFI wiring harness.

2. Check fuel pump—with ignition on, pump should audibly run a few seconds, then stop. If pump runs, go to 3; otherwise go to 2.1

2.1 (Bad fuel pump or electrical problem in ECU) Check switched and continuous power to ECU, all grounds. If bad, fix; otherwise go to 2.15.

2.15 Check pump fuse and all other fuses. If blown, go to 2.3; otherwise go to 2.2.

2.2 (Fuse OK) Check pump power and ground for several seconds after activating ignition. If power OK, replace fuel pump; otherwise check wiring harness and if good, substitute replacement ECU.

2.3 (Fuse blown) Replace the fuse (make sure it's the correct rated fuse!). If fuse again blows, go to 2.4

2.4 (Fuse blows again) Check wiring harness, repair if necessary; otherwise go to 2.5.

2.5 Disconnect fuel pump, injectors, and other sensor connectors from the ECU and try new fuse. If the fuse blows again, substitute new ECU; otherwise go to 2.6.

2.6 Reconnect EFI components one by one until the fuse blows, and then replace the faulty component.

3. (Fuel pump runs, engine will not start) Check fuel flow direction at pressure regulator and pump. If correct, check fuel pressure at the regulator inlet for ten seconds after turning system on. If pressure is OK, go to 4; if pressure is low or there is no pressure, go to 3.2; otherwise go to 3.1.

3.1 (High pressure) Check return line for blockage. If OK, replace regulator.

3.2 (Low pressure) Clamp off return line, then retry. If high pressure, replace regulator; otherwise go to 3.3.

3.3 Check supply line from pump to injectors and regulator and fix if blocked (blocked fuel filter, pinched hose, blocked fuel feed screen at tank, low fuel, and so on). If OK, replace fuel pump.

4. (Pressure in fuel rail OK) With ignition on, crank engine with coil wire disconnected. Fuel should pulse in 0.01 second squirts from one or more injectors (may be able to tell by listening for clicking from the injectors). If fuel pulsing is OK, EFI system is OK (replace coil wire, check ignition timing, firing order of the plugs, *check battery voltage to the ECU during cranking* [should be above 9volts], and so forth); if no fuel pulsing, go to 4.1; if continuous fuel flow from one or more injectors, go to 5.

4.1 (No fuel pulsing) Reconnect coil wire and check for valid tach signal to ECU. If tach signal OK, check power to injectors with a test light (plus side of battery injector switched ground wires (colored) and if bad, replace ECU; otherwise go to 4.2.

4.2 (No tach signal) Check wiring harness and connectors/pins to all components, then check ECU. Check ignition components that generate the tach signal.

5. (Continuous fuel from one or more injectors) Disconnect electrical connections on injectors, recheck for spray. If no injector sprays, check wiring harness, connections, and ECU; otherwise go to replace damaged injector(s).

Trouble: Engine starts, then dies
Possibilities:
Tach source problem.
Sensor problems.
Intake air leaks.
Check: *Sensors, tach signal source, integrity of intake system.*
Algorithm:

6. Check critical engine connections (tach lead to tach source (coil/tach driver), lead to coolant temperature sensor, ground connection, MAP/MAF sensors, and so on). Correct problem if required; otherwise go to 6.1.

6.1 Check resistance of tach-to-ECU circuit. If required, replace any wiring/connectors; otherwise go to 6.2.

6.2 Check other sensors for legitimate electrical values based on known physical conditions (temperature vs. legitimate coolant sensor resistance, air pressure in manifold vs. MAP signal, and so forth). Replace sensors if bad; otherwise go to 6.3.

6.3 Check for major air leaks in intake system (throttle body, runners, vacuum hoses and ports, and so on).

6.4 Check for other ignition problem such as bad ballast resistor.

Trouble: Difficult cold start, poor operation when cold
Possibilities:
Bad coolant temperature sensor.
Warmup map needs more enrichment at lower temperatures.
Zero-rpm map needs more duration on cranking bars.
Cranking primer needs more duration.
Check: *Coolant sensor, maps for proper adjustments.*
Algorithm:

7. Disconnect coolant temperature sensor, check resistance of the sensor to ground (need chart of

resistance per degrees temperature) with ohmmeter (in the case of thermistor-type sensor). Verify that Zener diode-type sensor is good or substitute known good sensor. If bad, replace sensor and retry running; otherwise go to 7.1.

7.1 (Good coolant sensor) If the engine is not hard to start, adjust the prime fuel injection pulse width under warm conditions; otherwise go to 7.2.

7.2 Verify operation of startup enrichment devices (extra injector or injectors, thermo-time switch, fast idle equipment, and so on). If bad, replace; otherwise go to 7.3.

7.3 (Incorrect startup enrichment on programmable system) Reprogram the warmup enrichment percentage(s), verifying that the values are correct when the system is again cold (which may take some time).

Trouble: Difficult hot start
Possibilities:

> *Engine flooded.*
> *Air temperature sensor (if installed) is heat soaking.*
> *Fuel lines are heat soaking.*
> *Fuel pump problem.*

Check: Air temperature sensor mounting location, fuel line routing. (Move away from engine/exhaust heat, if possible.)

7.4 Engine flooded (use "clear flood" mode if it exists).

7.5 Low battery voltage (below 8.5 volts) when cranking. Try starting with additional voltage or by powering the ECU with a separate battery.

7.6 Unusual fuel pump condition (vapor-locked, overheated motor, and so forth).

Driveability improvement to engine that runs

8. Verify correct prime engine sensors (MAP, MAF, tach signal, and others). Replace if bad; otherwise go to 8.1.

8.1 Check fuel pressure setting during running conditions with gauge connected to fuel rail.

8.2 Check for air and vacuum leaks.

8.3 Check injectors for correct operation. Injectors should match flow at all duty cycles as closely as possible (for racing, have injectors individually cleaned and matched by experts such as New Age in Fort Worth, Texas).

Fuel economy improvement for engine that runs
Possibilities:

> *TPS poorly calibrated.*
> *Wrong air-fuel mixture.*
> *Acceleration enrichment problem.*
> *Leaky injectors.*
> *Other engine problem.*

Check: TPS, mixture, acceleration enrichment maps, injector balance test.

Algorithm:

9. Check TPS for calibration (incorrect setting could cause undue acceleration enrichment).

9.1 Check air-fuel mixture at idle and cruise (14.7:1 is correct stoichiometric; smooth, lean idle is best). Check content of exhaust gases for carbon monoxide (CO), hydrocarbons (HC), and so forth.

9.2 Check acceleration enrichment percentage and sustain. Back off the enrichment until the vehicle begins to bog slightly, then enrich slightly. Adjust sustain according to manufacturer's recommendations, then try backing off until vehicle bogs, and enrich slightly again. Poor economy is probably not due to faulty acceleration enrichment if driveability is good. Black fuel smoke under heavy acceleration is a good indicator that acceleration enrichment is excessive.

9.25 Check for leaky injector(s).

9.3 (EFI system good) Check distributor curve, engine timing, vacuum advance, and other functions.

Trouble: Engine runs rich
Possibilities:
ECU adjustments set too high.
TPS calibrated incorrectly.
Leaky injector(s).
Excessive fuel pressure.
Nonfunctional temperature sensor.
Bad ECU.

Trouble: Engine runs lean
Possibilities:
ECU adjustments set too low.
TPS bad or incorrectly adjusted.
Low fuel pressure.
Low switched or continuous power to ECU.
Bad ECU.

Trouble: Engine revs to an rpm and develops a misfire
Possibilities:
Incompatible ignition system.
Check: Tach signal on engine data page.
Fuel mixture changes drastically from one rpm range to the next.
Fuel mixture is too rich.
Fuel mixture is too lean.
Check: Fuel delivery maps for proper adjustments.

Engine is running out of fuel
Check: Fuel pressure.

Trouble: Fuel pump does not operate
Possibilities:

ECU is not receiving power or ground.
Fuel pump relay is not operating.
Pump is not receiving power or ground.
Check: *Connections, relays.*

Trouble: Tach reading is incorrect
Possibilities:

Number of cylinders or other data entered incorrectly to ECU.
Incompatible ignition type.
Check: *ID page, ignition compatibility chart.*

Trouble: Slow throttle response
Possibilities:

Fuel delivery maps too rich.
Ignition timing retarded.
Check: *Fuel maps, ignition timing.*

Trouble: Engine coughs between shifts
Possibilities:

High-rpm light throttle areas of maps too rich.
High-rpm light throttle areas of maps too lean.
Accelerator pump values too rich.
Accelerator pump values too lean.
Check: *Accelerator pump maps, fuel delivery maps.*

Trouble: Engine coughs under rapid throttle movement

Accelerator pump enrichment too lean.
Accelerator pump enrichment extremely rich.
Fuel maps too lean at part throttle.
Ignition timing retarded.
Check: *Accelerator pump maps, fuel maps, ignition timing.*

Trouble: Engine misfires under hard acceleration
Possibilities:

Fuel maps too lean.
Fuel maps too rich.
Improper fuel pressure.
Ignition system failing.
Battery voltage falling.
Check: *Fuel maps, fuel pressure ignition system, battery voltage.*

Trouble: Engine misfires under cornering
Possibilities:

Improper fuel pressure.
Fuel pickup problems.
Check: *Fuel pressure.*

Trouble: Engine performance will not repeat from one test to the next
Possibilities:

Fuel pickup/pressure problems. Ignition tach signal problem.
Fuel maps adjusted erratically.

Engine warmup map adjusted erratically.
Poor or erratic manifold vacuum signal (speed-density units).
Battery voltage fluctuating.
Check: *Fuel pressure, tach signal on engine data page, fuel maps for proper adjustment, vacuum signal, battery voltage.*

Trouble: Engine surges under light cruise conditions
Possibilities:

Fuel mixtures too rich.
Fuel cut on deceleration feature is on.
Check: *Fuel maps, fuel cut problem.*

Trouble: Engine lacks performance/power
Possibilities:

Full-throttle settings are too rich (black smoke from exhaust).
Full-throttle settings are too lean (high exhaust gas temperatures).
Check: *Fuel maps.*

Trouble: Poor or erratic idle
Possibilities:

Throttle plates are not synchronized (multiple butterfly systems).
Fuel maps adjusted erratically in idle area.
Poor manifold vacuum signal.
Check: *Throttle synchronization, fuel maps, manifold vacuum.*

Troubleshooting Sensors

This section is written based on data furnished by Sutton Engineering of Evanston, Illinois.

Car companies have been working hard to increase the self-diagnostic capabilities of original-equipment electronic fuel injection engine management systems, but these systems can still seem inscrutable when you have no idea what's wrong.

Sutton Engineering reports that according to General Motors, 80 percent of driveability problems don't report a trouble code in the computer. Intermittent problems, such as loss of ECU ground or a bad sensor, may just not show up in the diagnostics trouble codes. The bottom line is, when something is wrong, don't blame the computer. The problem is much more likely to be that the computer is not receiving good data from the sensors. How do we look at this data to decide if there is a sensor problem?

You will need either a scan tool or a digital multimeter (in some cases, two nails and a wire jumper will cause the Check Engine light to flash out trouble codes!). According to Sutton, the fol-

Scan Tool

- Easy to access trouble codes
- Easy to check temperature sensors
- Good at finding intermittent wiring problems (wiggle test)
- Monitors events while driving
- Records readings changes while driving for later playback (readings every 1.25 seconds)
- Usually can't measure pulse width
- Can show command issued by ECU, but can't show if execute

Fluke 88 digital multimeter

- Tests same sensors as scan tool with more effort
- Tests not influenced by wiring or ECM problems
- Tests sensors scan tool cannot test (IAC, cam, and crank position)
- Tests injector pulse width and resistance
- Tests traditional electrical components (alt., regulator, starter, coil, plug wires)
- Finds bad connections & high-resistance circuits
- Recording/averaging feature lets you find average or maximum reading without having to watch meter

---

lowing list summarizes the pros and cons of the two diagnostic devices.

Some systems require an analog multimeter, or a digital multimeter (DMM) with analog simulation like the Fluke 88 so you can see trouble codes spelled out as pulses. The scan tool's ability to function while you drive is nice, but it reflects what the ECU *thinks* is happening, not necessarily what is actually occurring. The Fluke measures pulse width at the injector rather than assuming actual pulse width by analyzing the situation at the ECU—which can point out a bad injector driver. It can also be used to compare PROM chips.

Exhaust Gas Oxygen Sensor

Let's start with the oxygen sensor because many factory ECUs believe this sensor before any other. A functioning O_2 sensor offers a good snapshot of how the engine is running (although it too, can be fooled). According to Sutton, it is a good idea to routinely replace the sensor before proceeding, since it's relatively inexpensive and, if known to be good, is a valuable aid in diagnosing other problems, such as other bad sensors. The O_2 sensor is used in feedback mode by the ECU to trim air-fuel mixture, and thus directly affects injector on-time.

The voltage range fed by the sensor to the ECU is 0.1 to 0.9volt, with 0.5 being the stoichiometric or theoretically ideal mixture. The sensor must be heated to 600 degrees Fahrenheit to work (and may have supplemental electrical heating to bring it up to temperature within ten or twenty seconds of start). The oxygen sensor bounces from rich to lean every few seconds by design, but it is possible to check these oscillations with a scan tool or digital multimeter (DMM). The sensor voltage should jump from rich to lean every few seconds. If this doesn't happen, or if the sensor voltage stays in the 0.3 to 0.6volt range, or stays lean, the sensor is bad.

Some DMMs have an averaging feature that allows you to read the idle mixture, also telling the maximum high and maximum low, giving you some idea of the sensor condition. A scan tool lets you look at the block learn counts which will tell you if the ECM is drastically altering the air-fuel mixture. As an example, the Sutton Buick GN should read 128 as the normal block learn count; above 138, the ECU is interpreting sensor data to imply lean running, and will add fuel, while below 118, the reverse is true.

The oxygen sensor must remain connected to the ECU and in normal closed-loop operation during measurement. You can scrape insulation off the sensor wire, or possibly make use of a breakout box connected between the sensor and wiring to connect the meter. Sutton warns not to try using an analog multimeter, which can damage the sensor by drawing too much current. If it is a two-wire oxygen sensor you can disregard the ground wire, according to Lucas. They offer single-wire sensors that work fine in place of the two-wire variety, leaving the ground wire disconnected. Check a shop manual for the wire function in multiple-wire sensors. (Some Chrysler oxygen sensors use *four* wires!)

Since low voltage corresponds to a lean mixture, failing sensors very seldom erroneously indicate a rich condition. According to Sutton, sometimes the sensor will intermittently quit, which shows up as rich running, with the check light occasionally coming on. This could show up in an ECU trouble code, indicating that the O_2 sensor seemed to be staying lean too long (voltage went below 0.5 and stayed there for a long time).

Oxygen sensors usually last for 10,000 to 40,000 or more miles. Sutton suggests that some sensors are much better quality, recommending Bosch or Lucas if you don't want to pay the money for an OEM unit.

They also recommend an eight-step procedure

Temperature Sensor Resistance

GM and Chrysler			Ford	
Temperature (degrees F.)	Resistance (ohms)		Temperature (degrees F.)	Resistance (ohms)
210	185		248	1,180
160	450		230	1,550
100	1,800		212	2,070
70	3,400		194	2,800
40	7,500		176	3,840
20	13,500		158	5,370
0	25,000		140	7,700
-40	100,700		122	10,970
			104	16,150
			86	24,270
			68	37,300
			50	58,750

Note: At 210 degrees Fahrenheit, the GM and Chrysler systems should be producing stoichiometric mixtures (14.7:1); at -40 degrees F., they should be producing 1.5:1.

---

for checking for possible wiring problems between the O_2 sensor and the ECU:

1. Disconnect the O_2 sensor connector.

2. Tap into the sensor wire with a nail or similar object.

3. Leave a meter hooked up to the sensor.

4. Hold the nail in one hand while touching the positive battery terminal with the other (safe with battery voltages).

5. The ECU will see a high voltage; interpret this as a rich condition, and lean out the mixture, causing the motor to stumble, possibly die.

6. The meter connected to the O_2 sensor will indicate voltage dropping to 0.1volts or below.

7. Switching your hand to the minus or negative battery terminal should cause the ECU to enrich things considerably, indicating 0.8volts or above on the meter.

8. When you drive the system lean, a new sensor will indicate below 0.1volts, while an old tired sensor may not go below 0.2volt; the reverse is true at the rich end of the scale.

To verify a bad ECU causing a problem with closed-loop mode, or a bad oxygen sensor circuit, Sutton suggests connecting a scan tool to the ALDL and with the ignition on, engine off, disconnect the sensor lead, and ground the lead. The scan tool should indicate 0.2volt or below.

If you have a DMM, with engine off and ignition on, check the voltage at the ECU lead, which should be 0.3volt or below. Verify that the ECU is *very well grounded!*

Temperature Sensors

When an EFI engine is cold, before the oxygen sensor reaches operating temperature, the ECU must rely on temperature and other sensors to get the engine running. Indeed, basic fuel injection pulse width is computed based on engine speed and manifold pressure or mass airflow, corrected for temperature. The oxygen sensor is important for tuning or trimming the basic injection pulse width, but the key word is *trim*. The ECU logic allows it to go only so far in making oxygen sensor corrections. A bad temperature sensor can result in a situation in which the car is running rich, and the ECU *knows* it is rich (it is, in fact, storing a trouble code that says the mixture is rich), yet it cannot correct sufficiently.

Suspect a bad temperature sensor in this case, but before hauling out the diagnostic tools, first check to make sure that a low coolant level isn't causing the temperature sensor to read inaccurately.

You can test a thermistor-type coolant temperature sensor by checking the resistance across the two leads (one usually being a ground routed to the ECU which often supplies its own ground to sensitive sensors) with the connector removed using a DMM (a scan tool makes it much easier if the sensor is hidden in some inaccessible place). The coolant temperature sensor is usually located on the intake manifold, sometimes on the water pump or head. Check for corrosion on the leads; anything affecting resistance through the sensor wiring would change the sensor reading. Compare resistance to the nearby chart, then verify the figures with a known good thermometer:

The MAT (manifold air temperature) and IAT (inlet air temperature) sensors, if fitted, can be tested the same way. Look for these sensors in the manifold or air cleaner ducting. If the car cold-soaks overnight, all temperature sensors should read the same. When reconnecting the sensors, make sure the connectors are seated correctly, and that none of the connector pins push out of the connector (some can!). Electronics supply houses sell conductive chemicals that help to prevent corrosion on connectors.

Mass Airflow Sensors

There are two kinds of MAF sensors, those that output varying direct current (DC) voltage like most sensors, and those that output a varying frequency. For varying frequency, a Fluke 88 or scan tool is required. Sutton Engineering claims that MAF failures usually begin with intermittent symptoms that are followed by total failure. The company says: "For example, you're driving down the highway and feel a momentary loss of power, usually accompanied by the Service Engine light flashing on and off. If it does fail completely, the light will stay on, though the car should still be drivable."

Sutton suggests that tapping on the MAF with the engine running may indicate a failing MAF if the engine stumbles. "If the engine is running rich or lean and disconnecting the MAF helps, it's no good."

Sutton sells jumper wires you can hook to the MAF and read voltage with a DMM. MAFs usually have three wires: ground, 12volts in, and sensor output. You can hook the DMM to the ground and sensor output, which yields about 2.5volts on the Buick GN used by Sutton. Switching to DC volt frequency allows you to look for big frequency changes in response to small changes in engine speed. You can blow through the MAF with something like a hair dryer, tapping the MAF to see if it's affected. Road testing is possible with the scan tool or DMM with Sutton extended test leads.

A scan tool will read grams per second of air, which should be 4-7 at idle on the Buick, the complete range varying from 3-150grams per second. A failed MAF will show up on the scan tool as the default output by the ECU. DMMs show frequency variance from 32-150hertz. The idea is to look for no output or suspiciously rated output. Remember, the scan tool displays what the ECU thinks is happening at the sensor rather than what is actually happening.

Sutton Engineering measured the following on their test Buick:

Mass Air Flow Sensor Testing Valves

MAF output	DC volts	Hertz
Idle	2.599(avg.)	45
5psi boost (2nd gear)	2.613	118
10psi boost (2nd gear)	2.620	125
17psi boost (2nd gear)	2.635	142

MAP and BP Sensors

The MAP (manifold absolute pressure) sensor outputs a value based on absolute pressure, not relative to the altitude the vehicle happens to be at right now. Before diagnosing the MAP sensor, check the hose feeding the sensor for any leaks. Like the MAF, MAP sensors come in two breeds, those that output varying voltage (GM) and those that output a square wave 5volts DC that varies in frequency (Ford), requiring a DMM that can measure frequency in hertz. Sutton suggests that since it is hard to get documentation on what the output of a MAF should be, measure a known good vehicle first and then compare it to the one in question.

Chapter 12

Project Car–1970 Dodge Challenger 383

What does it take to change a 1970 Dodge Challenger 383 big-block from a dinosaur into a creature of the 1990s? Perhaps some good modern tires and wheels, some suspension gimmicks, hardened valve seats in the heads, things like that. And maybe a fuel system upgrade?

Possibly the single most important great leap forward in American automotive engineering since Chrysler built the 1970 Challenger 383 is the application of fuel injection to V-8 motors. Fuel injection directly led to greatly improved emissions and economy—while maintaining or improving the power output of modern V-8s. Injection improved driveability by broadening and increasing an engine's torque curve, improved efficiency by allowing higher compression ratios on modern pump gas, and eliminated the need for certain emissions control strategies such as retarded ignition timing and low compression, which also improved power.

Since electronic fuel injection (EFI) requires a computer for calculating injection pulse width, the onboard computer makes it feasible not only to compute and time sequential injection pulses, but also to apply computer control to spark

advance, and to dynamically coordinate injection control with ignition and emissions control devices such as EGR. All these systems work together on a millisecond-to-millisecond basis—yielding clean power with good economy. It's a win-win situation. This is what you get when you buy a modern performance car like a 1992 Mustang GT or a Corvette.

It is very possible to retrofit electronic fuel injection and computer-controlled spark advance—even emissions control—to older carbureted cars. There are two problems, however: the cost, and the complexity.

Holley Throttle-Body Injection

Holley's Pro-Jection is designed to be an affordable injection system that is simple to

Author's 1970 Dodge Challenger 383. The engine originally used a 2-barrel carburetor. A past owner had switched to an Edelbrock Streetmaster single-plane manifold and Carter AFB four-barrel carb. The first EFI conversion was a Holley Pro-Jection 2 throttle body system with throttle position load-sensing.

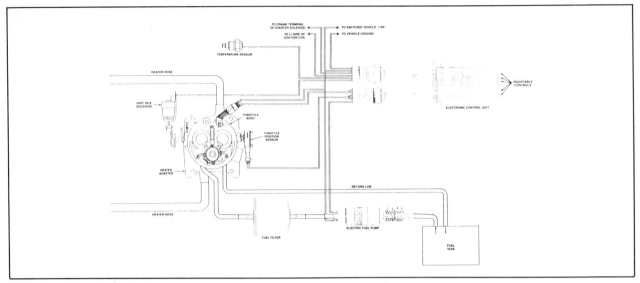

A *Pro-Jection fuel injection system diagram. The throt-tle body installs virtually as easily as a carburetor. The installer must then mount the temperature sensor, fuel pump, and ECU. Holley EFI replaces the four-barrel carb. The installer must mount a sensor and connect*

wires, fuel lines, and vacuum hoses. The ECU mounts inside the car. A high-pressure electric pump mounts at the fuel tank and a fuel return line is required. The Pro-Jection fuel regulator is integral with the injector mod-ule on the throttle body.

understand and tune. It is designed to replace the four-barrel carburetor on older V-8s. Holley began with a single-point injection throttle body with two injectors that had been developed as an OE replacement part for certain late-model vehicles, and made it part of a kit which also includes a computer, wiring, a standard sensor or two, and some miscellaneous mounting adapters. The Pro-Jection 2 is simple and inexpensive.

Naturally, there are tradeoffs.

An installer paying the half a grand or so for a Pro-Jection 2 system could expect some advan-tages compared to a carburetor. First, there is no float bowl, so that hard acceleration and corner-ing on harsh terrain cannot impact the operation of the fuel system as it can with a carb. Second, fuel delivery is very precise and infinitely vari-able because the Pro-Jection provides fuel in mul-tiple bursts or pulses that can be timed in incre-ments of less than 0.001 second. Since the Pro-Jection system does not use separate and overlap-ping fluid-air systems as a carburetor does for idle, mid-range, top-end, transient enrichment (accelerator pump), and cold-start operations, a properly tuned system would tend to conform more perfectly to an ideal air-fuel curve, yielding more power and economy compared to a carb.

A third advantage is that the Pro-Jection sys-tem allows adjustable enrichment for cold start-ing and includes a fast-idle solenoid. And the sys-tem can be tuned via a set of screwdriver-adjustable dashpots while the vehicle moves down the street or rolls on a dyno—obviously an

advantage compared to the repeated disassembly that may be required when making jet changes on a carburetor. Also, being a pulsed fuel injection system, the Pro-Jection is not subject to mixture problems resulting from reversion pulses flowing backward through a carburetor, particularly in a wild-cammed engine with a single-plane mani-fold, which results in the carb overenriching the mixture by adding fuel to the air twice as it reverses direction through the venturi(s).

Another benefit of Pro-Jection is that since the system instantly cuts fuel delivery when you turn off the key, dieseling cannot occur as it might with a carb. Vapor lock is much less likely as well under the 12-20psi Pro-Jection fuel pres-sure, compared to the *reduced* pressure of a mechanical vacuum pump *sucking* fuel forward to the engine.

And finally, hot air percolation, in which gasoline boils and overflows the float bowl(s) in a carb in hot weather—additionally pressurized by the action of vapor pressure in fuel lines—is not possible with the Pro-Jection system.

On the other hand, one of the tradeoffs of the simple and affordable Pro-Jection is that fuel is injected from only two injectors at one place—at the two-barrel throttle body. Compared to supply-ing fuel from individual injectors at every intake port, throttle-body injection's ability to deliver equal fuel and air to every cylinder is subject to any limitations and design flaws of the intake manifold, which must handle a wet mixture. Gasoline tends to fall out of suspension in the intake manifold air during cold starting, or sudden throttle openings that rapidly change manifold pressure. It then "tears" off the surface of the manifold unpredictably, in sheets of liquid that interfere with equal distribution to individual cylinders. There is simply no way to guarantee equal distribution with single-point fueling. In addition, high air velocity is required to keep fuel suspended in the air at low rpm. This means that the Pro-Jection cannot use the radical dry manifolds of port fuel injection, which provide great high-end breathing while relying on port injection to put fuel directly into the swirling dry air at the intake valve at low speed for equal distribution and consequent good idle.

A second drawback is that the Pro-Jection system cannot control ignition spark advance or other emissions control devices. Third, Pro-Jection estimates air mass entering the engine based on throttle position and rpm, with no provision for measuring actual mass airflow (MAF) or manifold absolute pressure (MAP), which means it is not able to compensate for varying amounts of air entering the engine at equal rpm and throttle position based on, say, the action of a blow-through turbocharger. There is also no provision to raise fuel pressure (a relatively low 15psi) to compensate for pressure changes.

Obviously, the Pro-Jection cannot time fuel injection for individual cylinders as in sequential port fuel injection, a tactic to improve emissions, power, and fuel economy. And there was no provision for closed-loop operation in the Pro-Jection system featured in this book (although Holley now offers an add-on module that can be connected to the Pro-Jection for closed-loop operation). The system cannot read changes in air-fuel mixture from an exhaust gas oxygen sensor and tune the engine on-the-fly as it runs. This affects mostly emissions at idle and economy at steady cruise. Actually, it is doubtful that closed-loop would work well with the cam on this 383 Dodge Challenger, which has a fair amount of overlap and thus requires a fairly rich mixture to idle well—more like 13.0:1 to 14.0:1, rather than the 14.7:1 affected by closed-loop control.

As a footnote, all current closed-loop systems use oxygen sensors that change voltage rapidly at 14.7, but have virtually no ability to discriminate between mixtures much more than a half point away. Systems like the DFI are able to deduce open-loop mixtures specified by base fuel maps while operating in closed-loop mode by observing what adjustments were required to drive the mixture to stoichiometric. The latest Electromotive software on the TEC units allows a tuner to build a table of target air-fuel mixtures that can be applied as adjustments to the base fuel maps. Electromotive is somewhat secretive about the ECU strategy used to achieve this, but it is logical to assume that the algorithm involves testing

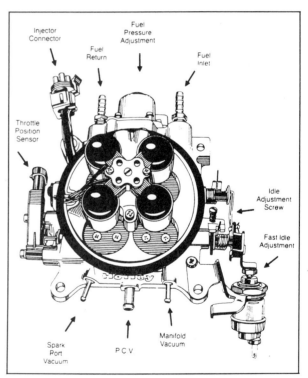

Holley throttle body connections; these include fuel supply and return, two vacuum, one ported vacuum, plus electrical connections for TPS, injectors, and fast idle. A fuel return line pressure over 10psi while the engine is running indicates that the tubing diameter may be too small, or that there may be too many bends in line, or that there is a restriction in the return line of fuel tank. The fast idle solenoid adjustment (lower right) causes the engine to run faster when cold. Holley

The five tuning dashpots on the ECU allow adjustment of fueling while driving.

Holley fuel pump's efficiency must be assured by providing properly-sized fuel lines. Performance can be improved with thick wiring directly to battery and a user-installed relay activated by the Pro-Jection module.

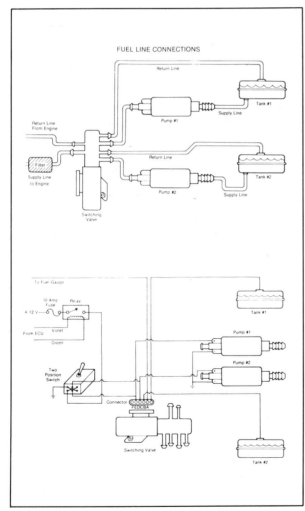

Pro-Jection connections for fuel and electrical hookups. To increase voltage to fuel pump, one optional fuel pump wiring approach is to wire the relay (upper left) directly to the fuel pump rather than going through the connector. Holley

what enrichments or enleanments are required to affect the mixture near stoichiometric, extrapolating to regions beyond the range of the stock EGO sensor in a linear fashion.

Installing the Holley System

When I first began to work on this 1970 Challenger, it was running an ancient Carter AFB carburetor on an Edelbrock Streetmaster 383 manifold. The car was running the stock compression ratio (9:1), but ran a fairly hot aftermarket auto transmission camshaft from Competition Cams. The "L" code on the car told me that the vehicle had originally been built as a 290hp two-barrel 383. Clearly, someone had made the conversion to four-barrel power *long* ago because the AFB carb was so old and worn that it was impossible to eliminate an annoying flat-spot when accelerating off idle. This resulted from excessive slop in the accelerator pump linkage (causing pump activation to lag slightly behind throttle blade opening). Once I installed a new AFB, that problem was eliminated.

With a fresh paint job and a brand-new interior, plus a newly rebuilt engine, new air-conditioning compressor, and a host of other details like a new wiper switch and door handles, I later set about to install the Pro-Jection on the Challenger. Although the Pro-Jection 2 is a two-barrel throttle body, it will not fit on a stock two-barrel manifold. The system bolts to an adapter plate made to bolt on a four-barrel manifold, and is workable on most small- and medium-displacement American V-8s, flowing up to roughly 675cfm. For engines with displacements of 400ci and up, a Pro-Jection 4, which flows 900cfm is necessary—or two Pro-Jection 2 systems on a dual quad manifold.

It's easy to install the Holley system. You begin by designing a way to return fuel to the gas tank. Like virtually all injection systems, the Holley system must provide constant pressure to the injectors, regardless of the engine fuel requirements. This is done by providing a fuel loop that pumps pressurized gasoline from the tank to a pressure regulator in the engine compartment, and then back to the tank. The regulator, integral to the throttle body in the Pro-Jection, pinches off return flow to the degree required to maintain a preset pressure in the fuel supply line. The amount of excess fuel returning to the tank varies, depending on engine fuel consumption. A lot of fuel is returning at idle; very little is returning as if the engine fuel consumption approaches the capacity of the fuel pump under high-rpm heavy loading.

Next, I removed the fuel filler neck pipe, cleaned it carefully, and welded on a fitting to attach the returning fuel line. An alternative

Small Block Test Data

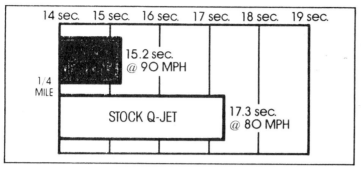

14 sec. 15 sec. 16 sec. 17 sec. 18 sec. 19 sec.

1/4 MILE

15.2 sec. @ 90 MPH

STOCK Q-JET

17.3 sec. @ 80 MPH

Average quarter mile E.T. of a 1979 Chevy 350 CID Z-28 with a Holley 300-38 manifold and headers vs. stock.

Big Block Test Data

37 More Ft. Lbs. of Torque Over Stock[†]

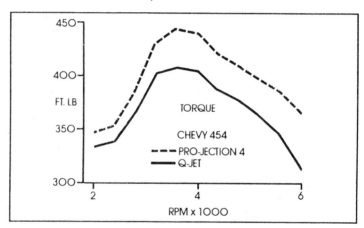

450

400

FT. LB

350

300

TORQUE

CHEVY 454

- - - PRO-JECTION 4
—— Q-JET

2   4   6

RPM x 1000

55 More Horsepower Over Stock[†]

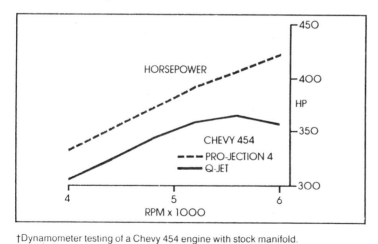

450

HORSEPOWER

400

HP

350

CHEVY 454

- - - PRO-JECTION 4
—— Q-JET

300

4   5   6

RPM x 1000

†Dynamometer testing of a Chevy 454 engine with stock manifold.

The top chart shows that on the strip, Pro-Jection and headers knocked off 2.1 seconds of E.T. in the quarter-mile on a 1979 350 Z-28 with Q-Jet. The dyno results on a 454 Chevrolet (middle and bottom graphs) show Pro-Jection 4 made 55 more horsepower than Q-Jet, and an extra 37lb-ft of torque. Holley

return might be to remove the sending unit for attachment of a return fitting. Obviously, you can't simply drill a hole in the tank. If it is necessary to remove the tank for drilling or welding, you should have it worked on by a fuel tank specialist. Ideally, returning fuel should exit at the bottom of the tank. OE EFI tanks usually contain a reservoir of fuel (a tank within a tank) to guard against power loss at very low fuel levels on turns

and hills, and the return line exits into the reservoir.

An empty fuel tank, inevitably loaded with fuel vapor, is incredibly explosive!

The next step is to mount the fuel pump in a safe, low spot near the fuel tank, preferably where it will be primed by gravity rather than the reverse. Holley suggests mounting the fuel pump no higher than the top of the tank, and locating the pump at the bottom of a fuel line loop so that the pump will always have liquid fuel to pump when it first starts.

When you turn on the key, the computer will *momentarily* activate the pump to pressurize the injectors. If fuel is not immediately available to the pump, the engine may be very hard to start. Naturally, on an old dog like the 1970 Challenger, you'll want to remove the mechanical fuel pump from the engine, and blank off the hole in the block with a plate (available at most speed shops).

I removed the old carburetor next, and mounted the Holley adapter plate and throttle body, connecting the fuel supply line and a return line I had already installed and connected to the return fitting on the filler neck. Chrysler cars with automatic transmissions use a mechanical kick-down linkage and may require an adapter to attach the linkage to the Pro-Jection. This is not included in the Pro-Jection kit. I got one at Super Shops (Holley builds a Mopar adapter, but doesn't include it in the standard kit). The linkage on the Challenger, having already been doctored in the conversion to the Carter AFB four-barrel, required some fudging to get it just right.

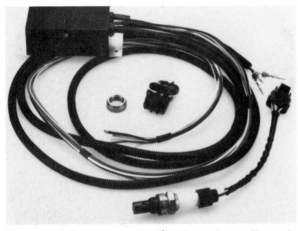

The closed loop conversion kit shown here allows the Pro-Jection unit to utilize oxygen sensor data to meet emissions standards. Under idle and light cruise, the computer tunes for a 14.7-1 air-fuel ratio using O_2 sensor to see results of combustion.

Aftermarket fuel injection computers, other than incredibly expensive mil-spec racing units like EFI Technology's Competition unit, tend to work better in a friendly environment, away from lots of heat and electrical interference—which means inside the car or in the trunk. I mounted the Pro-Jection computer on the console ahead of the shifter, and fed the wiring harness through an existing hole in the firewall to connect to the throttle body, the new EFI coolant temperature sensor unit (which I'd mounted in a 1/8in fitting in the water pump), and the fuel pump. That left several wires that needed to be connected to constant positive 12volts, switched positive 12volts, and negative 12volt coil or tach-drive voltage.

Startup time.

Since the fuel pump only runs a second or two, it's a good idea to jumper the fuel pump to positive voltage on the battery in order to fill the fuel system with gas, and then to listen carefully when you turn on the key to make sure that it is operating. With the fuel pump working, I verified that the dashpots on the computer were at the correct position specified by Holley for initial startup, then cranked and *watched* the injectors

Starting with the single-plane Edelbrock manifold, the first step was to convert it to two-barrel induction, although stock two-barrel carb manifolds will not work with the huge 650cfm two-barrel Holley throttle body. An option that can be added is a Holley heated spacer that fits under the throttle body to improve cold running performance in cold climates. The spacer even has hose connections that can be attached to heater lines.

with the air cleaner removed from the throttle body. It was easy to see the big throttle-body injectors spraying fuel, and in a few seconds the engine came to life.

I immediately went to work on the idle mixture dashpot, hunting for the position that would give the smoothest idle. Disconcertingly, this occurred at a point as lean as it would go. Consulting the manual, I decided that perhaps the throttle position switch—a linear potentiometer mounted on the throttle shaft on the side of the throttle body—might not be calibrated correctly. Since the computer determines engine loading directly from throttle position and rpm, it is essential that the switch read the right voltage. Using a digital resistance meter and some jumpers, I was able to watch the resistance of the switch change as I opened the throttle.

Bingo! The switch was reading too high with the throttle closed. Loosening the switch, I was able to rotate it until the meter showed the correct voltage for a closed throttle. Starting the engine, the idle mixture dashpot now yielded the best mixture farther up the scale, as it should.

Holley's installation manual lists procedures for tuning the mid-range and high-end power, which basically involves tuning for best mixture at 3000rpm unloaded in neutral, then using a stopwatch to time acceleration runs at wide-open throttle (WOT) until the Pro-Jection is set up for best power, as indicated by the stopwatch. Pro-Jection 4 units have one extra pot for tuning high-end power.

Out on the highway, I noticed an interesting thing. Although the car *felt* as if it had better low-end torque, what was missing was the sudden burst of power under hard acceleration that you get with a four-barrel as the secondaries open up under WOT.

The Pro-Jection system was a vast improvement over the carburetor on the Challenger. It started quickly in all types of weather, provided fast idle when cold, and was free of the hot-weather starting problems encountered by the AFB in the heat of a south Texas summer. Throttle response was good under all conditions as well. The system had no way of compensating for the air-conditioning compressor coming on-line, but I might easily have rigged a relay to trigger the cold-start solenoid to remedy the situation.

Haltech and Tull Systems Multi-Port Injection

In the meantime, I got access to a Haltech ECU that could control multiple port injectors on a V-8. I decided to convert to the Haltech, just for laughs. It turned out this was extremely easy, given that I had already made the conversions for the Holley TBI. I already had a fuel return line. I

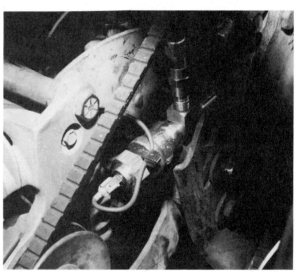

With the throttle body mounted (first photo), it was necessary to install a coolant temperature sensor (second photo). There were no suitable locations without drilling into the water pump. It was also necessary to switch to a 180-degrees thermostat from the 160 on the engine so that the engine would run warm enough for the Holley to discontinue warm-up enrichment. Due to the Chrysler mechanical kickdown linkage, the throttle linkage on the Dodge required a special Holley linkage part available at Super Shops.

already had a mounting port for a coolant temperature sensor. It turned out to be possible to use the Holley throttle body to meter air—and the throttle position switch on the throttle body is compatible with the Haltech. The injector-regulator-fuel fittings assembly is a one-piece unit that bolts to the main section of the Holley throttle body with three Allen screws. I removed it and fabricated an aluminum plate to cover the hole.

The single-plane Edelbrock manifold on the Challenger uses runners that are perfectly in line with each other. Tull Systems milled holes for injector bosses from the underside of the manifold (once I'd removed it from the car!), and welded the injector bosses in place from the bottom, grinding the excess boss material away so as not to interfere with airflow.

Tull Systems installed type 6 O-ringed Lucas disc fuel injectors in the bosses that were fitted for hoses on the fuel input side, constructing a D-section fuel rail with hose barbs to supply fuel.

The biggest problem had to do with the fact that 1970 vintage Chrysler cars used a mechanical kick-down linkage that was originally connected to the carb linkage, and later, with small adaptations, to the Holley throttle body. Unfortunately, the injector assembly and fuel rail were exactly where a linkage support had bolted to the intake manifold. When I got the manifold back from Tull, I discovered it was possible to move the kick-down linkage outboard of the left bank of injectors by cutting the linkage support in two pieces and welding it back together with the addition of some some mild steel bracketing. I also cut the linkage itself and inserted a 3/4in inward off-

Unused fuel returns to the tanks via a hose connection (lower left) welded to the filler neck. The filler neck was easily removed from the tank. Other fuel-return line connections can sometimes be made easily into the tank level sender plate. Otherwise, you'll have to remove the tank and have an expert weld a return connection which releases fuel at the bottom of the tank.

set so it could properly connect to the Holley throttle body.

It was an easy matter to connect the fuel lines to the new fuel rail (using 900psi hose at $0.33 an inch!). I used a 39psi pressure-referenced regulator I had taken from an L-Jetronic injection system, and I robbed the Bosch fuel pump I'd used in an original XKE turbo-EFI system featured in another chapter of this book, installing it inline in the return side of the Challenger's fuel rail. The fuel pump was necessary since the Pro-Jection pump is not designed to produce the high pressure required to provide stable fuel pressure to eight batch-fire port injectors.

Wiring the Haltech ECU is simple, and programming is discussed in other sections of this book. Haltech provides a nice, rich set of base fuel maps for a modified V-8, a good starting point for a car like the Challenger. Although this engine is not *really* radical, given the hotter cam, the headers, and the large-port intake, this seemed like a good place to start since it is always preferable to begin rich and work lean when programming.

I had to install an air temperature sensor for the Haltech ECU in the air cleaner inlet. (This is better than using a port hole in an intake manifold runner, which can heat-soak the sensor and lean out the mixture as the ECU tries to correct for hotter intake air than actually exists.)

Finally, I had to build a connector to adapt the Holley throttle position sensor connector to the foreign Haltech wiring harness. I located the Haltech F3 ECU inside the car on the side of the transmission hump, near where the Pro-Jection system had been. I removed the Holley wiring harness and equipment and set it aside. It would be easy in the future to replace the Holley throttle body with something else, and use the whole Holley system on some other project.

There is a wonderful crispness to multi-port injection that is properly set up, given that the injectors are spraying fuel at high pressure directly at intake valves only an inch or two away on a setup like that of the Challenger. The Haltech ECU offers the finest resolution of any unit, basically providing a 512 element matrix of speed-load breakpoints that defines the engine fuel map. Obviously this provides greater flexibility than the Pro-Jection system, which defines the base fuel map with three control knobs and a default internal table.

Is multi-port injection worth it?

It is interesting to consider that I *could* have used the Haltech unit to control the two big Holley injectors if the Holley fuel curve seemed inadequate. I would have had great flexibility to build a very precise fuel map with the Haltech. The advantage of the Holley system is that it is easy and inexpensive, and a lot better than a carburetor. Clearly, a properly tuned Pro-Jection system would outperform a poorly tuned Haltech port-injected system. Gasoline-fueled engines can be reasonably forgiving about mixture, with a fairly wide margin in air-fuel ratio separating lean best torque and rich best torque.

The fairest thing to say about whether it's worth it depends on what you are asking the simpler Pro-Jection system to do. How good is the manifold you're using for wet mixtures? How smooth and consistent is the volumetric efficiency of the engine as power rises? How peaky is the engine in its torque curve? How high is the compression? How important is fuel consumption? Do you have the equipment and/or patience required to take advantage of the programmable port EFI system's flexibility?

If you have a radical manifold on a peaky engine with a lot of compression, it is important to have the flexibility to build an oddly shaped fuel curve, and then you'd clearly want a programmable port EFI system.

But on many engines, considering only peak power at wide-open throttle, the Pro-Jection is right up there with the best of them. Of course, it will clearly not have the wonderful low- to mid-range broad torque range of a tuned multi-port injection system with long runners. But that's a different story. And of course, when you've got 383ci, you'll always have torque.

In the end, the author decided to convert to multi-port injection. Tull Systems mounted the injectors in the Edelbrock manifold. An injector block-off plate was fabricated for the Holley throttle body in conversion to multiport injection. For now, the Holley throttle body—minus the injectors—works fine. The biggest problem was dealing with kickdown linkage problems resulting from interference with the left bank of injectors (which are at the top of this photo).

Chapter 13

Project Car–L-Jetronic XKE Jaguar with Rajay Turbo

This E-type Jaguar 4.2 liter was born in 1969, fighting for breath through twin Stromberg emissions carburetors, the slowest of the entire XKE line—having lost its lovely triple SU carburetor induction system to the battle against smog in North American cities.

Jaguar no longer advertised horsepower in 1969, but clearly this car had less than 265hp. It had also put on a few pounds since 1961: 150 or so. Although Jaguar claimed 265hp in the XKE, experts say a really "on" engine might measure 220hp at the crankshaft.

In 1975, you probably could have bought this 1969 XKE used for $1,600; by 1982, the year I acquired the car, the price was up to $5,000. And although the car appeared dull and looked a little beat-up, it was never poorly restored.

By the late 1980s, when top V-12 XKEs sold for prices approaching six figures, and even Series II E-type roadsters brought half that, no

one in their right mind would have hot rodded one—they're too valuable to modify, which is why you'll never see another one like this.

But in the early 1980s, V-8 conversion kits, particularly using the compact 302 Ford, were still popular for hot rodders who wanted to give an XKE more of an edge. Lots of people were attacking Jaguars with hacksaws and hammers. I was willing to give this car some help, but it had to stay Jaguar, engine and all.

The 4.2 liter XK engine always was a machine with great potential. Like the Offenhauser four that dominated Indy 500 Championship Automobile Racing Team (CART) racing for many years, the twin-cam Jaguar six-cylinder engine has decades of development behind it, with roots going back before World War II. The block was produced in 2.4, 3.4, 3.8, and 4.2 liter versions (and even an experimental twelve-cylinder version that was basically two sixes siamesed together). It predated the flathead 5.3 liter V-12 engine used in the final Series III XKEs from 1971 to 1975. The 4.2 XK engine utilizes Weslake hemispherical combustion chambers in an aluminum head, twin overhead cams, large ports, multiple carburetors, and a tough seven-bearing crankshaft with castle-nut rods above a 9qt cast-aluminum oil pan.

The car seemed to beg for turbocharging: the limited-slip rear end would handle up to 600hp; the semi-gradual buildup of turbo boost is reasonably forgiving on the clutch; the XK crankshaft and bearings are very strong and can easily handle large power increases; and the hemispherical combustion chambers resist detonation very effectively.

The project began in northern California in 1982 and continued for eight years. The world didn't know as much about turbocharging in those days; even factory turbos were not always successful. I'd heard rumors of a turbocharged XKE or two, but that was all it was—rumors. The

The Bosch L-Jetronic-injected turbocharged XKE Jaguar.

project required extensive research and experimentation, from reading Society of Automotive Engineers (SAE) papers on turbocharging, to fabricating parts and tuning and road testing. Over the years, the car has seen six different carburetion and fueling systems, various fuel pump and fuel regulator combinations, two turbo manifolds, and several turbine housings and wastegates. There have been some stunning failures involving cracked pistons and broken rings—and ultimate successes as well.

The project began with a complete stripdown to bare metal and a new Midnight Blue lacquer paint job, a new interior, and a complete engine rebuild. That was when I first tore off the emissions carburetors and bizarre wraparound intake manifold that runs part-throttle intake air through an extra couple feet of heated runners on its way into the engine. I bolted on a triple carb setup from a Series I XKE. I equipped the engine with 8:1 compression cast-aluminum pistons designed for 4.2 liter engines in Jaguar four-door sedans (stock 9:1 XKE pistons are unsuitable for high-power turbocharging). I painted the motor Ford Red from top to bottom like the Detroit diesel truck motor I had admired on a 12,000lb super-modified pulling tractor. I siamesed together two cast-iron Jag headers into a turbo flange, bolted on the Rajay turbo, pressurized the carburetor float bowls, and re-jetted the carbs.

More complicated was how to route the boost air from the turbo's compressor around the cross-flow head to the carbs, and where to route the exhaust from the turbine—all in a very tight engine compartment.

And what to do with all the extra heat.

In retrospect, the major problem turned out to be the original blow-through carburetor turbocharging system. As a first step toward higher performance, I had replaced the twin Strombergs with triple SUs, which are *constant-velocity* carburetors, based on the following principal: As engine speed increases, liquid fuel flows more readily than air, meaning that, uncorrected, a standard carb would run increasingly rich at higher engine speeds. Constant-velocity carbs effectively change the size of the venturi with a sliding airfoil which enlarges the venturi as manifold pressure decreases. This keeps air flowing through the venturi at a constant speed, which means only minor air correction is needed—easily handled with a tapered needle that gradually withdraws from the main jet as the constant-velocity slide opens.

Turbocharging at medium to high levels of boost requires highly enriched fuel mixtures to produce maximum power and to prevent detonation. Alternate jet needles with a richer taper helped but did not cure the problem, and given

The Bosch L-Jetronic-injected turbocharged XKE Jaguar used 1979 Jaguar EFI from a Jag sedan. The EFI was adapted with a spacer plate and slight frame modifications to fit in XKE. A Bosch velocity air meter was relocated to the left side of the motor, upstream of the single turbo.

the fact that SUs were not designed for forced induction, the selection of jet needles was extremely limited.

It did not seem feasible to modify the jet needles in the same sense that you might drill main jets to enrich the mixture. And once the constant-velocity slides were open wide the air velocity *would* increase, which would tend to enrich the mixture. However, this was not predictable and not always repeatable, given the wide variety of air pressures possible on either side of the throttles, combined with various possible throttle positions. Trying to keep the SU running well under low to medium throttle and yet achieve high performance under boost was nearly impossible. To add insult to injury, the turbocharger on the E-type, blowing through the triple SU carbs, had a tendency to bang open the constant-velocity slides under heavy boost with great force, sometimes causing them to stick.

In the meantime, companies like BAE and Spearco were achieving excellent results with turbocharging fuel-injected motors like the Datsun Z-car with its Bosch L-Jetronic injection, or the Volkswagen water-cooled fours with the K-Jetronic. Fuel injection seemed to offer possibilities. What's more, Jaguar had switched to Bosch L-Jet injection around 1978 on the same basic 4.2 liter engine used in the E-type. Perhaps it was possible to convert over to EFI and make the system work with turbocharging...

As luck would have it, I was able to buy a nearly complete 1979 Bosch L-Jet fuel injection system from a California company that converted Jaguar sedans to American V-8 power. What was missing was the fuel injection wiring harness, a self-contained loom that connects together all the fuel injection components and the computer, and has only a handful of outside connections for tach/coil (engine speed), continuous power, switched power, starter voltage, and so on. I was unsure at the time whether custom-building a wiring loom (I had the Bosch schematic!) could cause problems if the resistance of wires was not precisely correct, given that the analog computer controlled injection pulse width via sensor voltages. So I decided to buy a complete Jag wiring harness from a Jaguar salvage yard, which cost nearly as much as all the rest of the injection system.

The stock Jaguar injectors are Bosch pintle designs that flow 214cc per minute. To convert this to horsepower potential, multiply by 0.1902044, which means the stock injectors can make at least 250hp without enrichment at standard pressure (2.5 bar). Since fuel pressure on the L-Jet system is referenced to manifold pressure and should rise with boost from 38 to 53psi at 15psi boost, horsepower potential is actually some 20 percent greater, probably in the neighborhood of 300 (without enrichment).

I removed the old Jaguar intake manifold and carburetor system and tried out the EFI manifold. Several problems occurred. First, the space frame that surrounded the E-type engine was in the way of the EFI plenum. Second, the plenum, if located outward with a spacer plate to miss a longitudinal space frame rail, would interfere with a different section of the frame. And third, the plenum interfered slightly with the firewall. I solved these problems by building a 1in-thick aluminum spacer that located the manifold directly outward so the EFI runners passed over the rail and located the plenum just outside the rail. I slightly modified the diagonal frame rail so that the plenum would miss it, and reshaped the firewall sheet metal slightly.

The manifold would now fit, but another problem showed up. The manifold was built to bolt on with studs and nuts since the curvature of the runners and the thick spacer meant you could not get bolts through the manifold flange and spacer plate. But studs would not work either, since the manifold did not have the clearance to slide straight onto long studs.

The answer was to fit the studs into the spacer and manifold flange, lower the assembly into place, screw in the studs with vice grips or double jam nuts, and then fit the nuts. Not an operation you'd want to do very often. (And, by the way, not necessary if you were willing to remove the twin-cam head!)

With the inlet manifold mounted, it was a simple matter to plumb the turbocharger compressor outlet into the EFI throttle body. I relocated the EFI air meter to the left side of the car to be *upstream* of the turbocharger (a velocity air meter must be *upstream* of the turbo to avoid being damaged by the surging action of the turbocharger's output. A mass air meter, on the other hand, should be *downstream* of the turbo to correctly measure air density after compression heats the air (and after the intercooler, if there is one).

Since the 1979 Bosch L-Jet unit used a velocity meter and had to be upstream of the turbo—a problem, given space constraints—I solved the problem, first by *removing* the car's heater, later by fabricating a curving air path between the air meter and the turbo compressor inlet (not ideal from a performance point of view, but it got the heater back on line for top-down driving on cool

A modified Jaguar (Lucas) distributor provided spark advance under vacuum and retard under turbo boost to prevent detonation.

The car's earliest turbo engine used no add-on fuel enrichment under boost other than the air meter's sensing-based fueling. Later the author added enrichment via the cold start injector.

northern California winter days). By carefully routing the EFI wiring harness, it was possible to make the harness connection to the air meter and still connect the harness to the EFI engine sensors and injectors on the right side of the block.

The original L-Jetronic system connected to an electronic distributor, but the XKE did not use one of those; the points–coil negative side turned out to provide a fine engine-speed trigger voltage for the L-Jet computer.

The stock EFI electronic control unit is located in the trunk of the 1979 Jag sedans, out of harsh weather, far from engine electromagnetic interference (EMI) in the engine compartment. The harness I acquired was easily long enough to reach the XKE trunk, requiring only large holes in the firewall and rear trunk bulkhead.

I replaced the Jag electric fuel pump (low-pressure) with the Bosch high-pressure EFI unit, attaching the new pump directly to the L-Jet ECU's pump electrical connection. (The unit is designed to activate the pump for a couple of seconds upon ignition, run the pump during cranking and while the engine is running, and then shut off the pump in case of an accident—when the engine stops or via inertia switch if the engine is not dead.)

Since the L-Jet system (like all electronic-pulsed EFI systems) requires a fuel return line, I had to plumb in an extra line so that excess fuel exiting the regulator would have a way to return to the fuel tank. XKEs have a bolt-on metal plate and gasket on top of the fuel tank which locates the fuel tank sender and fuel suction line; it was a simple matter to remove it, drill and tap it for fuel return. (If I had wanted to get fancy, I could have constructed a small tank within the main fuel tank so that the returning fuel would enter the auxiliary tank—from which fuel would be drawn for the engine—and so that violent maneuvers and steep hills with low fuel would not cause the pump to starve. The XKE already incorporates a deep depression in the bottom of the tank, so I concluded this was not necessary.)

For an EFI fuel filter, I used an inline unit from a Datsun Z-car with stock L-Jetronic injection, locating the filter below the fuel rail in the engine compartment.

Mistakenly, I did not use the oxygen sensor that came with the EFI system, since the exhaust manifold did not have a place for one. Very early L-Jet systems did not use one, and later systems will work fine without one (assuming you don't ground the O_2 sensor wire). However, an oxygen sensor permits the ECU to achieve good, smooth idle (with a stock cam) and excellent cruise fuel economy by closed-loop feedback tuning (correlating the results of mixture trim to EFI pulse width, making corrections).

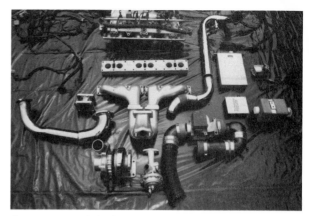

Components of the L-Jet, Miller-Woods injected Jaguar engine with Rajay turbo. Note the manifold adaptor plate that relocated the entire manifold outward by approximately 1in so the plenum cleared the XKE space frame fore-aft rail. The compressor-out pipe has twin add-on injectors.

I wired the EFI harness' full-time ECU power connection to the battery and its switched power to the key behind the dashboard (for which there was plenty of harness length).

With everything connected, I tried to start the vehicle. No dice—a little stumble, then nothing. I began checking electrical connections everywhere, speculating about whether the coil was a legitimate engine speed indication. Finally, I pulled all the injectors out of the manifold, plumbed everything back together, and again cranked the engine.

Pffffuuuuuufff!!! Injectors batch-fired a huge burst of fuel twice per power stroke. The system was working, but something was wrong.

Eventually I discovered that one tiny connector in a six-wire plug to the air meter was pushed out of place, causing a radical increase in injection pulse width and immediately flooding the engine. With this fixed, the engine fired right up, and ran great.

Great until I *drove* it, that is, whereupon there was a big, ugly flat-spot on warmup. It ran fine at operating temperature. The car had the wrong thermostat for EFI (too low a temperature), and a bad coolant temperature sensor. (Remember, sensor problems, vacuum leaks, and so on, are the biggest causes of EFI problems. See the chapter on sensors. When it came time for a high-speed pass, it was rapidly clear that the car was leaning out at boost above 5psi. My initial solution was to wire the seventh (cold-start) injector to operate above 2psi boost. The cold-start injector is a binary, nonpulsed device (either off or constantly on) designed to shoot a continuous stream of pure fuel at the throttle plate when the engine is cranking and very cold. It is controlled by a thermo-time switch and a cranking sensor. It was possible to wire it up with relays so it could still perform its cold-start function and also provide enrichment under boost. Given that the fuel regulator would be increasing fuel pressure as boost rose, the extra injector would tend to increase fueling as engine requirements rose, but it was still a very crude method of fueling. The cold-start-type enrichment helped a lot, but I decided there were probably still one or two lean

The Jaguar uses two additional injectors controlled by a Miller-Woods TurboGroup Fueler for fuel enrichment under turbo boost conditions.

cylinders; when boost began to get serious, the enrichment was not making it evenly to all cylinders.

Later I bought a Miller-Woods TurboGroup Fueler, an add-on computer that pulses one or two extra injectors under boost to provide accurate enrichment in response to engine speed (via negative coil connection) and manifold pressure (via hose barb in the compressor-out plumbing and hose running to the auxiliary computer which was located under the dashboard). Installation instructions said to silver-solder or MIG weld the two injector bosses into the inlet air plumbing *upstream* of the throttle body by at least 9-12in. T-fittings and EFI pressure hose made it a simple matter to tap into the high-pressure fuel line upstream of the regular fuel rail. It was a simple matter to tap into the negative side of the coil for engine speed and power, exactly the same as for the main L-Jet ECU connections.

There was a dramatic increase in performance with the extra injectors, enabling boost to increase from intermittent 8 or 9psi, to 15psi (which illustrates the importance of a good, rich mixture under high boost).

When you punch it, power comes on with the incredible rush of an old Kawasaki 500 two-stroke three-cylinder superbike on a full-throttle roll-on. When turbo boost comes on, the TurboGroup Fueler computer from Miller-Woods activates and times the pulses of two extra injectors located upstream of the throttle body. Exhaust gases sweep smoothly through headers into twin J-pipes and into the 301E Rajay turbo with 0.6 turbine housing. You can alter the activation pressure of the stand-alone wastegate with an in-dash dial-a-boost mechanically controlling the secondary port on a Turbonetics Deltagate which permits access to varying boost from 5psi to blow-up.

Chapter 14

Project Vehicle–Cadillac 530ci-Powered GMC Motorhome

Cadillac Speed-Density EFI

Some time ago, enterprising motorhome fanatics in Los Angeles discovered that you could replace the 455 GMC (basically a 455ci Oldsmobile engine) in vintage GMC motorhomes with a 500ci Cadillac block, actually saving weight over the original engine. The 500ci block, a bored and stroked Cadillac 429/472 engine available since 1970, had optional port EFI in 1975 and 1976, its last years of production, and in either case easily bolted to the GMC automatic transmission (basically a Turbo 400 modified for front-wheel-drive applications).

The owner of this vehicle had driven his 1977 GMC Class One motorhome for many years with the original 455 engine, but when it finally needed a rebuild, he decided to convert to the fuel-injected Cadillac. The solution was to buy the complete engine with fuel injection system and contract to have it installed.

Like many OEM fuel injection systems, the Cadillac EFI system is pretty much self-contained: the system has its own wiring harness, sensors, and control unit that are independent of the vehicle's main electrical and ignition system, except for connections for continuous 12volt power, tach signal, starter voltage, switched power, and so on. The Cadillac system is a speed-density type that deduces engine operating conditions from a MAP sensor and engine rpm (coil or tach driver signal), looking up injection pulse width data in a table in computer memory, making additional enrichment adjustments for altitude, engine temperature, and air temperature.

In place of the GM Quadrajet four-barrel carburetor, the Cadillac injection has a huge two-barrel throttle body with a thermostatically controlled air by-pass valve designed to deliver fast idle when cold.

To install the EFI Cadillac motorhome system, it was first necessary to install a high-pressure EFI fuel pump downstream of the stock

A twin-turbo 530ci Cadillac engine powers this 1977 GMC motorhome. The engine first used Cadillac EFI, and later was fitted with Haltech EFI control.

tank-mounted fuel pump, and make arrangements for a fuel return line to the tank(s). The installers put a Cadillac EFI high-pressure fuel pump near the engine at the front of the vehicle on a bulkhead behind the left front wheel, and were able to tap into the fuel filler neck. This location was chosen so that excess fuel exiting the injector fuel rail via the pressure regulator could return to the fuel tank (although with multiple fuel tanks, this is more complicated than it would be on a one-fuel-tank vehicle). With the new high-pressure pump and fuel return installed, it was

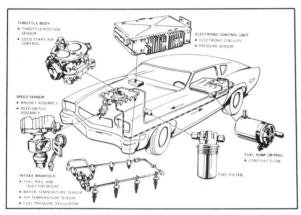

Elements of 1975-76 Cadillac 500ci engine's EFI system. The GM motorhome adapted easily to Cadillac powerplant with Cadillac Speed-Density EFI. The later, twin-turbo version used Haltech programmable EFI. The Haltech speed-density control EFI system was an easy replacement for Cadillac system, and left the door open for an easy return to stock, if desired. In the project vehicle, the throttle body and fuel rails were from Bendix, and Cadillac designed the two-barrel manifold setup for port injectors. Cadillac

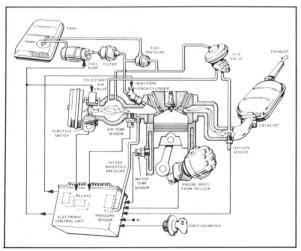

A Bendix EFI schematic. Bendix convinced Cadillac that America was ready for EFI in 1975. Cadillac

possible to plumb hoses to the fuel rail loop on top of the Cadillac V-8 intake manifold for fuel supply and return.

The Cadillac ECU fit nicely under the passenger seat, allowing the installers to route the *stock* Cadillac EFI wiring harness to the injectors and sensors on the engine in the motorhome—basically integrating the routing of the EFI wiring harness with the existing 455 harness, and wrapping the combined harness in electrical tape. The installers also had to provide switched and constant battery power to the Cadillac ECU, and to connect the ECU's fuel pump control wire to the fuel pump. All other connections between the ECU and the EFI components were integral to the stock EFI wiring harness (sensors, injectors, distributor tach drive for engine speed sensing, and so forth) and virtually self-contained.

The biggest challenges resulted from the Cadillac engine swap, rather than the fact that the new engine was injected instead of carbureted. Installers had to reconcile existing engine accessories to the new engine, which required some new GM brackets and some custom fabricated brackets. It was also necessary—but trivial—to connect a host of vacuum-driven accessory hoses to the new engine.

Turbocharging

After troubleshooting the Cadillac motorhome, and driving over Donner Pass in the Sierra Nevadas at 7,000-plus feet on the way from San Francisco to Idaho, the owner decided that he needed more power. We discussed options, finally deciding to proceed with building a stroked and turbocharged Cadillac motor for the motorhome. Since the Cadillac ECU could not deliver the additional fueling needed for the bigger engine under boost without extensive reprogramming (which was out of the question on the analog ECU), and since we were also concerned about the ability of additional injector controllers to provide adequate fuel distribution from a single-point injection system under the extreme loads of a boosted motorhome, the way to go was clearly aftermarket programmable fuel injection. The goal became a system that could pass the Federal Test Procedure (FTP) for exhaust emissions—although we expected this would be a piece of cake on a 1977 motorhome which, since it would not have been emissions-tested when new, would probably require before and after comparison testing to demonstrate that the EFI turbo engine kept emissions within 10 percent of original specs.

Haltech EFI with Twin Turbos

The Haltech EFI system went on without problems once we replaced the Cadillac EFI sensors with the Haltech-supplied sensors; a bolt-in swap allowed easy return to the stock EFI system if necessary. We fabricated a metal plate that bolted to the Cadillac throttle body, and enabled the Haltech throttle position sensor (TPS) to bolt to it and ride on the Cadillac throttle shaft. The stock injectors (GM part number 1181247, for a '76 Cadillac Eldorado 500ci), were sufficient to provide fuel for 8-10psi of turbo boost at roughly 50lb system fuel pressure.

Haltech supplies the F3 ECU with several startup fuel maps. When configuring the system, we started with a map designed for a generic V-8 turbo. The map was clearly more appropriate for a 350 Chevy than a stroked Cadillac motor almost 50 percent larger in displacement. We ended up increasing the injection pulse width *massively* to get a good air-fuel mixture at all rpm and loading points from idle on up to 21lb of boost.

It is absolutely essential that the Haltech get over 8 to 9volts from the battery in order to start and run well—as we learned the hard way when we used batteries that had not been charged enough, and suffered additional voltage drop during cranking. Fortunately the GM motorhome has circuitry to put two or even three batteries on-line for emergency situations, which enabled us to get the engine running.

The weather was warm at initial startup, so the warmup enrichment programming (percentage increases) were initially guesses, based on the Haltech manual. We used the mixture trim control as we tuned the Haltech to achieve instantaneous plus or minus enrichment or enleanment up to 10 percent, which was useful upon initial startup to get the engine running, and then later for tuning. We left the warmup enrichment map at the default values that came with the V-8 turbo map as shipped from Haltech. The Haltech has a time-dependent warmup function, activated when the ECU first starts the engine, which provides 10 percent additional enrichment for the first 256 fuel injections (about 15 seconds at 600rpm, considering two injections per power stroke). Initial startup occurred at 85 degrees Fahrenheit, but a few days later, when the weather turned colder, we were able to correctly program warmup enrichment.

We started the engine, experimenting with the mixture trim control to search for the best mixtures, then used a laptop computer to incorporate the changes into the fueling map in memory, backing off the trim as we went. We used this technique at all rpm ranges, and then began programming increased fueling for heavier loading, which meant taking the vehicle for a drive. We were always careful not to make map changes under heavy loads, since the Haltech misses one

Here's the stock Cadillac 500ci EFI engine in the GM motorhome. The author spent four weeks lying on top of the engine in the motorhome while developing the turbo-EFI system, and he plans to stick with backpacking next time. A laptop personal computer made it easy to program the Haltech injection using a Haltech Gas Analyzer to instantly determine the air-fuel mixture.

or more injections when the ECU's internal map is being updated, which means there is a momentary miss that could be harmful under heavy loading. Haltech recommends using the mixture trim to test mixture changes under load, then backing off power to make changes to the map. John Milledge, Haltech's technical director, worked the laptop PC in the final stages of tune, with a high-speed UEGO gas analyzer hooked up to the O_2 sensor port just upstream of the right turbo. With the analyzer in place, tuning was easy.

Since this was a motorhome—not a race car—that had to be able to run on whatever quality gasoline was available in an emergency, the plan called for a knock sensor which would protect the engine from damaging detonation while helping fuel economy by allowing us to run full-spark advance under normal conditions, while retarding advance under boost. The J&S knock sensor includes a computer that can be programmed to retard *all* cylinders when knocking is detected, or just the cylinder(s) that begins knocking—which is nice, given that various cylinders run hotter or cooler than others and are more susceptible to knocking.

The J&S system can also be adjusted for sensitivity. The system we used had the optional LED display that indicates the degree of retard, and can also display the air-fuel ratio based on exhaust gas oxygen detected by an O_2 sensor—which we had installed just upstream of the right

This is the Cadillac stroker 530ci motor with forced induction. The Haltech injection used stock throttle body with the Haltech TPS sensor, and used stock fuel injectors.

turbo. We dealt directly with John Pizutto, the owner and chief engineer at J&S, who was very helpful. Knock sensors like this may not be glamorous, but they get the job done.

The Cadillac (Rochester) fuel injectors were relatively new, but it turned out that a couple were running a little lean (which can fool closed-loop air-fuel sensing equipment or gas analyzers such that *all* injectors end up too rich). We replaced the bad injectors, but since the OEM spec injectors are a fifteen-year-old design, we switched to an entire set of new Lucas disc injectors which are much more modern and produce better spray patterns and have better dynamic range than the old-style injectors. With the system in place and in excellent tune, we were finally ready to take on the EPA and the California Air Resources Board (CARB).

The EFI Cadillac motorhome with Haltech injection and turbocharging achieved the goals of providing low emissions, good idle and low-end torque, and greatly enhanced horsepower and torque under boost. This would not have been possible with carburetion.

Chapter 15

Injecting the Chevrolet Small-Block V-8

When a customer approaches Ivan Tull regarding a potential Chevrolet/GM-engined EFI project, they'll often want to know exactly what performance advantages they can expect from fuel injection. Tull is very experienced building turbocharged and supercharged small-block Chevy motors with port EFI. But before he can answer the question, Tull has to ask the customer a number of questions of his own.

In the first place, Tull wants to know what application the customer has in mind for the Chevy engine, and what the engine configuration currently looks like. He'll want to know if the engine will be used for street or drag racing, whether appearance is important, and what are the cost constraints. Tull will want to know why the customer is interested in converting to EFI. If it's for gas mileage improvement to save money, he will not recommend converting to EFI. Although EFI can double the gas mileage on badly done carbureted vehicles, the Tull Systems conversion will cost a minimum of $3,000. Assuming a 10-12 mile per gallon (mpg) increase, it would take 20,000-30,000 miles of driving just to break even. Of course, if a customer wants to increase mileage for ecological reasons, that's another story.

A customer looking for EFI because it's the "hot new thing" will probably want an exotic-looking system, which Tull can provide, perhaps offering one of the TWM Weber-type throttle-body setups on a cross-ram Weber bolt-pattern manifold. Such a system is not cheap but offers exotic looks and *tremendous* flow capacity.

A downdraft Weber-type EFI system costs $3,600, a cross-ram system $4,000-$4,200 due to the cost of the cross-ram manifold. Individual runner manifolds are impossible to beat in

The 1955 Chevy now runs a later-model 350ci engine with twin turbos and Haltech injection. The original Tull Systems EFI system used a cross-ram manifold and twin Weber-type throttle bodies. It was easily converted for turbocharging by replacing air filters with

turbo plenums and mounting twin turbos of custom small-block Chevrolet turbo exhaust manifolds. The engine reprogramming job was also easy; all that was required was simply filling in some additional bar graphs on a lap top PC via the arrow keys.

torque, although the idle is not as good as a single throttle-body system. (Tull has lately taken to machining balance passages in some multiple throttle-body manifolds.) Throttle bodies of 45mm and above will flow plenty of air for any small-block Chevy motor, while eight individual runners flow a massive 1800cfm with quad 45mm TWM throttle bodies, with two butterflies per throttle body. The intake ports should always be matched to the heads, says Tull, and the heads should be ported—something that usually yields *dramatic* power increases and is too often ignored by hot rodders.

If a customer is looking for better mileage and power, where cost is a consideration, Tull will recommend converting a four-barrel manifold for

Haltech-based EFI systems use Weber-type manifolds and throttle bodies with Weber-type bolt patterns with built-in injector bosses. The Tull Systems bolt-on port injection system uses Cutler Induction four-barrel throttle body on a modified carb-type manifold. A Haltech ECU controls port injectors via a lap top PC. Tull Systems

port fuel injection, and bolting on a Tull Systems four-barrel throttle body which is machined from billet aluminum and has a Holley carb bolt pattern. Tull converts single-plane aluminum manifolds for port injection by milling and welding the inlet runners to accept bosses to hold injectors such that they point straight at the intake valves. Tull then adds a D-section fuel rail that is O-ringed and clamped to the injectors. Without machining, a Chevy port EFI conversion costs roughly $2,800.

If the motor is stock, and always will be, Tull claims it is hard to beat the GM TPI system, which works well up to 4600rpm. If the motor is not stock and/or you need power above 4600rpm, the stock TPI computer and manifold will have to be modified with larger runners (available from Arizona Speed and Marine, TPIS, Accel, and others), and an aftermarket ECU, *or* a modified PROM that is matched to the engine modifications. If the engine is modified further, you may need yet another PROM. Tull says that stock TPI manifolds negate the effect of better heads. On the other hand, with the Moon cross-ram manifold, the heads become the flow bottleneck.

As I've mentioned more than once, Tull calls turbos and EFI the "last, best speed secret" for the small-block Chevy. "You can buy a crate HO Chevy motor setup for 345hp for $3,000" that's entirely suitable for turbocharging, says Tull. "Turbocharging and EFI will cost less and provide more power than a naturally aspirated race motor designed for equal output, which can cost $10,000 in parts alone."

According to Tull, the most spectacular gains in torque (25 percent!) will occur when the current configuration is a huge single four-barrel carb on a single-plane manifold. Such a setup

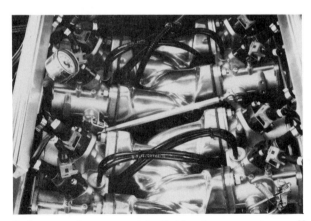

Balance tubes connect individual runners to small plenum which provides stable manifold pressure to Haltech MAP sensor. TWM throttle bodies mount on any Weber-type intake manifold, mount one or two injectors per runner.

Tull Systems is partial to forced induction on Chevrolet engines. The Moon cross-ram manifolds offer an exotic look but serious performance is due to equal length tuned runners.

(assuming the rest of the engine is balanced properly for the carb and manifold) will perform well at 6000rpm and above, and the addition of port fuel injection will greatly increase the torque due to the poor performance of a large carb and single-plane manifold at handling wet mixtures at low velocities at lower and mid-range rpm. On the other hand, Tull says, it's hard to beat a small 4V carburetor system on a good manifold when the goal is good low- and mid-range street performance. Horsepower increase with EFI may only be 5 percent. Torque and mileage will improve, and consistent and precise mixtures will allow higher compression ratios without detonation.

The '55 Chevy pictured in this chapter uses a medium-compression 350ci Chevy small-block. Any vehicle older than 1965 did not have emissions controls required by law—some earlier California cars required a positive crankcase ventilation (PCV) system in place of the old road-draft venting of crankcase fumes—and can, therefore, be highly modified with no concern for legality. Tull modified the fuel tank's sending unit to accept a fuel return, and installed a fuel return line. A high-pressure fuel pump replaced the old mechanical fuel pump, and a block-off plate sealed up the block where it had been. TWM Weber DCOE bolt-pattern throttle bodies bolted to the cross-ram manifold without modifications, and Tull constructed a two-piece fuel rail from D-section aluminum, ready to accept O-ringed injectors. The pressure regulator connects to the outlet end of one side of the rail, the pressurized inlet fuel line to the other, with a crossover hose connecting the two rails.

After mapping the fuel curve for the first iteration of the '55 hot rod, preprogramming for turbocharging basically meant changing the flat segment of the loading bars higher than atmospheric pressure (a range that a naturally aspirated

A 16-injector EFI system is capable of more than 1000hp on a Chevrolet engine like this. One set of smaller injectors provides excellent idle via a long, fine spray pattern, while larger auxiliary injectors kick in for high-end power under turbo boost. Tull Systems

engine could never see) to the correct slope for turbocharging. Tull removed the K & N air cleaners from the throttle bodies, and fabricated plenums from intercooler end-tanks to pressurize the throttle bodies. The turbos bolted to cast Chevy small-block turbo exhaust manifolds. (That's the great thing about small-block Chevys—whatever you want, somebody makes it!) The rest was muffler shop-type parts, piecing together constant-radius tubing to feed air from the two compressors to the throttle-body plenums.

The great thing about this car is that it's real. Go to San Antonio on a warm summer evening, and you may find the owner of a really clean, red '55 Chevy motorvatin' down Interstate 35. Takin' it to the streets—no hangar queen here!

This car is real.

Just don't try to catch it.

Chapter 16

Project Car–Turbo Lotus Europa with DFI Injection and Nitrous Power

DFI's bread and butter is injecting small- and big-block Chevrolets; they supply everything from injection parts to turn-key systems complete with everything from injectors to high-output tuned port induction manifolds.

To that end, DFI, a subsidiary of Accel Engine Management Systems of Farmington Hills, Michigan, builds a very sophisticated programmable ECU. When it came time to play around with a DFI unit, what I had available was a Lotus Europa: four cylinders, 1,300lb, mid-engine, fiberglass body, British. It was quick and nimble, but there's always room for improvement, right?

The point is, what interesting things can a DFI injection computer do for an engine, and what is it like to program it?

The original Lotus Europas were built in England in the late sixties, but used a French motor. It was a Renault 1.6 liter four of wedge-head design that output 78hp. A special version was built for the Europa with 10.5 compression,

The author's Lotus Europa with Renault Fuego EFI-turbo motor, DFI engine management control, and NOS nitrous injection. Turbo plumbing by Latham Race Cars, Austin, Texas.

still a wedge head which used a standard Solex carburetor on a combined intake and exhaust manifold on the left side of the block. In their day, people developed plenty of hot rod parts for the Renault engine, and some really pumped Weberized motors output 125hp or so. Some later Europas were available with a Ford twin-cam four of 1.5 liters, but they are very scarce by now, and very expensive, and therefore not suitable to swap into lower class Europas. The twin-cam made probably 115hp in stock form. Some people have tried Ford Cortina engines—which are much more common than the twin-cam (and have the same transmission bolt pattern)—in ordinary Europas, but these are not very interesting engines. The last Europas rolled out of the factory in 1974.

The engine on this Europa smoked badly and looked *ugly,* right down to its aftermarket Weber carburetor, which still worked but appeared to be in critical condition like everything else. Rebuild time...

Unfortunately, Lotus parts are ridiculously expensive. A set of the unique Europa-Renault high-compression pistons is something like $800. Other parts costs are nearly as extreme.

I discovered that Renault aluminum-block engines similar to those used in the Lotus had continued in production into the eighties in other vehicles, gaining such amenities as hemispherical heads, overhead cams, fuel injection, and turbocharging. Renault had spent years evolving the little four-cylinder motor into something much better. Renault has done a lot of high- tech racing, and has built some real terror turbo motors. The 1.6 engine was virtually modular. For example, the 1980s turbo Fuego motors used 1.6 liter hemi-head pushrod motors (spark plugs sticking out of the valve covers like the original Chrysler Hemi and all!), with Bosch L-Jet EFI and Airesearch T-3 turbos that made 125hp or so at 10-12psi of boost. They had identical bellhousing bolt patterns, and bosses for Lotus-style motor mounts.

I bought a Turbo Fuego motor, complete, at a junkyard for around $300 and set about figuring how to fit it in the Lotus—and how to rebuild and modify the engine for some serious pumping. Through some good luck and a newspaper ad I'd placed looking for a turbo Renault engine, I came across an outfit that was of critical importance in doing the project right. The French Revolution in Austin, Texas, specializes in orphaned French cars, that is, cars imported for sale in America, and then abandoned when their builders quit the US market. Owner Pat Whale and mechanic Jonathan Burnett knew all the nitty-gritty details of the evolution and lineage on Renault engines. The plan was to install the injected Fuego motor, upgrade it and its turbo-injection system where required to make a lot more boost and power (from 10 to 15–20psi), while adding a very mild port nitrous kit which would receive fueling via the fuel injectors rather than gasoline ports or spray bars or anything. About the least nitrous you can port inject is 10hp per cylinder, so we decided to start with 40hp nitrous jetting.

The DFI electronic fuel injection controller, harness, and sensors had all the features I needed to handle sophisticated raw fueling, idle speed control, nitrous fueling and enrichment, spark timing, and so forth.

The rebuild began with a complete tear-down at French Revolution. If you're building a turbo motor, it's nice to start with a block designed to stand up to turbocharging. During the rebuild, French Revolution installed new moly rings, new gaskets, bearings, and so on, and handled the machining. Besides a performance valve job, Burnett converted the head to use a rear water pump instead of the front water pump used on Fuegos. This sort of thing might normally be a nightmare except that the head contains vestiges of both front and rear pump mounting bosses and water passages. The conversion meant aluminum welding to close a passage on one end of the block, grinding *open* a passage on the other end, building and fitting a blank-off plate on the front of the engine, and fitting a rear water pump to the back.

Another tricky part was when it became clear that we needed the larger clutch assembly used on the Turbo Fuego motor instead of the wimpy unit used on the Lotus. The Fuego flywheel has a set of optical teeth behind the ring-gear starter teeth for use by the stock electronic ignition as a crank trigger. The teeth interfered with the Lotus bellhousing, and had to be machined off. Burnett also built a custom throw-out bearing combining parts from the Lotus and Fuego units and some light machining.

The stock Lotus did not have any crank

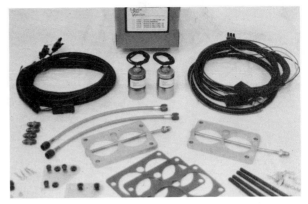

Accel/DFI offers integrated EFI-nitrous products for GM TPI. ECU and solenoids optionally provide three levels of nitrous power under computer control. The ECU lengthens injector pulsewidth for nitrous fueling. Accel/DFI

The cross-ram Fuego motor bolts to the Lotus transaxle in place of the original S2 wedge-head Lotus/Renault motor. The high-compression wedge head motor made about 70hp, while the stock Fuego engine was rated closer to 110hp. The author targeted 200hp with improved efficiency, larger injectors, higher boost, and 40hp port nitrous setup.

141

The finished EFI-turbo motor with Accel injection used Accel Laser II coil driver and super coil. Note the nitrous solenoid controlling port nitrous injection (lower right).

damper or pulley on the front of the block, and instead drove the water pump and distributor using a special cam that protruded from the *rear* of the block with an overdrive pulley. The Lotus cam will fit in the Fuego block, but the geometry is all wrong for the hemi-head valvetrain. A cam exists that will work, but it did not have the combination of high lift and good high-rpm duration but very little overlap, which is the right way to go for a turbo. We ended up amputating the pulley-driving tailshaft from the Lotus cam, machining it and the rear of the Fuego cam to fit together in a press fit, and finally pinning the two pieces together. The Renault does not need a crank damper for engine balance, but we were able to machine a very small front pulley that cleared the rear Lotus firewall and the shifter mechanism (which is a real bear), and can now be used in the future to drive an air-conditioning compressor. It also made a great place to mount flying magnets for a crank-triggered ignition setup via the DFI electronic control unit.

With the body removed for restoration and painting, I installed the finished motor in the Lotus frame for testing. I decided it made sense to test the motor by starting and running it with a carburetor, to make sure everything was working right without introducing the complexity of a ground-up programming effort of all parameters. French Revolution had a loaner carb manifold for the hemi-head motor, and I had an almost new Weber DGAV carb with the right jetting for the wedge-head motor. Since the Fuego distributor had no provision for centrifugal or vacuum advance—this being provided electronically via an optical crank trigger and electronic ignition controller—I borrowed an older but compatible points distributor from French Revolution.

The engine started immediately and ran well

with excellent oil pressure. I eliminated an oil leak at the sending unit, set the timing with a strobe light, and ran the motor for ten minutes at varying speeds to make sure everything was OK.

Time for fuel injection.

Installing the New Fuel Injection

The next step was to do a mock-up installation of all injection and turbocharging components while access was easy with the body off the car. This was mainly a plumbing issue: routing turbo oiling lines, routing the injection wiring harness and sensors, locating the intercooler in the new engine compartment, plumbing it to the turbo and injection manifold with 2.25in steel tubing and silicone hoses, and routing heater hose connections (including to the center section of the turbo where I'd replaced the Fuego T-3 center section with a later-model liquid-cooled T-3 center section, which would help the turbo run cooler).

The Europa engine compartment is large, with space to fit a fiberglass luggage compartment box behind the engine, over the transaxle. However, because the front of the car has some space for luggage, I decided to eliminate the rear luggage box, instead locating the Fuego intercooler in its place just under the fiberglass engine cover, and fabricating a hole through which the stock intercooler fan could suck air from below the intercooler. Engine clearance with the body turned out to be more of a problem than I'd first thought when examining the generous engine compartment space. The EFI intake manifold and turbocharger exhaust manifold projected outward from the block much farther than carb and standard exhaust manifolds.

Consequently, it became clear that the body would not lower into place on the frame with these items in place. Fine, they'll have to be removed to remove and replace the body. But how often are you going to remove the body? Maybe never again. It appeared that Renault had provided very restrictive plumbing from the compressor to the intercooler, a fault I eliminated in this installation. With the less restrictive turbo plumbing and exhaust system, and with the ability to reprogram the fueling and ignition, it would be possible to increase the turbo boost by tightening the threaded actuator rod on the wastegate to increase spring pressure in the wastegate diaphragm, keeping the wastegate closed to higher levels of boost.

The turbocharger oil return had to be rerouted to clear the Lotus frame, while the oil supply line, originally a metal pipe with short rubber hose connections at either end, was replaced with a flexible braided steel line. The stock plumbing that routed compressed air to the intercooler and into the engine was all wrong in the engine's new home. So Jeff Latham of Latham Race Cars in Austin, Texas, a craftsman who can do anything with metal tubing—from building a complete race car chassis (for example, the front and rear frames for the Perkins M2) to building custom headers for *anything*—constructed all-new turbo piping out of mandrel-bent and straight mild-steel tubing using silicon/bronze inert gas welding rod. At the same time, Latham built a straight-through exhaust pipe dumping from the turbocharger straight out the rear of the car with no muffler.

Latham welded an EGO (exhaust gas oxygen) sensor boss to the exhaust pipe immediately behind the turbo so that the DFI fuel injection system would be able to operate happily in closed-loop mode, setting its own air-fuel mixture at idle and light to medium cruise conditions.

The stock Europa gas tank was a mess inside, and after attempting to clean and coat it with motorcycle tank treatment chemicals, I finally cut one side of the tank open and completely sandblasted the tank, inside and out, welded the tank closed (after welding in new fittings for fuel supply, return, and vapor emissions purging), and then coated the inside of the tank.

Now it was time to replace the body and fuel tank around the engine, which was easy with the help of one or two strong assistants, with the manifolds off the engine.

Time to install the EFI.

The DFI injection unit is a batch fire nonsequential system, and with Calmap 6.0 firmware, includes the ability to provide spark advance. I set the engine at 6 degrees BTDC on the number one cylinder, and adjusted the crank trigger so that it was centered on the magnet. The injection system fires all injectors together once per engine revolution, twice per intake stroke for good, even distribution to all cylinders.

The DFI wiring harness I was using was actually a modified V-8 harness, with two injector connections removed from each of the two sides of the vee harness. The injector harness unplugs from the main section of the harness, so it was an easy matter to remove the harness cover and do some minor rewiring to clean it up for appearance's sake and for ergonomics in working in what would now be a fairly crowded engine compartment. I wanted the air temperature sender downstream of the intercooler for accurate air temperature, but it was wired closely with the coolant sensor which on this engine is now on the front water pump block-off plate. More rewiring was needed, but was not difficult.

Normally, DFI would have supplied a custom harness for a weird application like this, but due to time constraints, I had decided to use a GM V-

8 harness. Actually, it worked out just fine, and will probably be cleaned up further for the most sanitary installation. Some ECU manufacturers void the warranty on the harness if you modify it; however, anyone who knows how to use a soldering iron can modify a harness by shortening or lengthening wires with no trouble. Remember to make good, hot solder joints, never use crimp-on connectors unless you really know what you're doing and have the right tools, and cover everything properly with heat-shrink tubing, tape, and/or flexible cable wraps (also called zip ties). Those cable ties made of plastic that pull through themselves to tighten are great for fastening a wiring harness to almost anything.

DFI provides an idle air control (IAC) stepper motor and adapter plate which allows air to bypass the throttle body for fast idle in cold conditions or to stabilize idle at a particular speed. DFI's Calmap software is very sophisticated,

The author decided to run the motor with a Weber carb prior to replacing the fiberglass body on Lotus Europa. The new Weber carb used jetting identical to that on the original engine's carb, meaning the new engine could be run at a known good state of tune to check for leaks and problems rather than having to immediately tune the engine with a completely new fuel system.

allowing you to specify speeds for IAC control activation, as well as specifying how fast and to what degree the ECU and IAC will react to changes in idle speed—a useful feature that allows you to deal with stalling under sudden rapid throttle closing.

I plumbed the IAC into the pipe from the air cleaner to the compressor inlet, which provides clean, cool by-pass air. I located the air cleaner on this Lotus to the front right of the engine, behind what amounts to a fiberglass "body gusset," next to the battery behind the passenger seat. It is a diesel Mercedes inline-type unit with ducting connections on the inlet and outlet sides, so that you can duct cool outside air into it (in this case, from in front of the engine cover), and duct outlet air to a turbocharger. Since the piping is located near the hole through which all wiring passes through the firewall separating the engine from the passenger compartment, the wiring harness connection for the IAC was in easy proximity. I routed the DFI wiring harness (two main cables) through a hole cut in the fiberglass with a hole saw, close to the stock wiring harness.

With the manifolds and turbo in place, oil fitting connected, turbo coolant lines in place, and new gaskets locating the EFI intake, the end was in sight.

I located the high-pressure fuel pump below the fuel tank where it will always self-prime, grounded it to the frame, and connected it to the fuel pump relay wire from the DFI electronic control unit. I installed a pressure gauge in the stock EFI fuel rail so it would be clear if the fuel pressure was correct. I connected the fuel return line from the pressure regulator to the tank connection, and jumpered 12volt positive current to the large lead on the Bosch fuel pump. The pump came to life and began pushing fuel through the rail and back to the tank. With no idle reference vacuum to lower fuel pressure, the gauge showed 39psi, exactly what it should be.

With the battery disconnected, I connected

the crank trigger connector, the three-wire connector for the heated O_2 sensor, the temperature sensors, and the MAP sensor, which I held in place near the intake manifold with cable wraps, using a short hose to reference pressure to it from the manifold.

The throttle position sensor turned out to be a challenge. The three-wire Bosch TPS, designed for an air-metered EFI L-Jetronic system, seemed to only supply continuity on either idle position or full throttle, and since the DFI ECU likes to see continuously changing voltage as the throttle opens, it didn't appear possible to use the Bosch sensor. DFI normally supplies GM throttle position sensors, which are triggered by a "crank arm" on the side of the sensor.

It would have been difficult and time consuming to construct an elegant way to interface this TPS to the stock Weber throttle body on the Fuego engine; on the other hand, it was easy to use the sensor Haltech supplies with their EFI system, which is allegedly a Ford OE sensor from a Ranger. With the sensor bolted to a fabricated plate on the side of the throttle body, with the ECU powered up, and a laptop PC showing a log of engine sensor, the new sensor's range was zero percent to over 70 percent, or about 19 percent to 99 percent, which seemed reasonable. I adjusted

The programmable DFI ECU controls the Turbo Fuego motor in Lotus, replacing the engine's original L-Jetronic ECU. This enables computer-controlled ignition timing, fueling for higher levels of boost and VE increases due to less restrictive induction and exhaust systems, and injection fueling for nitrous control. DFI's Calmap software sets nitrous injection parameters including throttle position threshold, time delay, RPM, fuel enrichment, and ignition retard.

The modified Weber throttle body now uses Ford-type TPS as supplied by Haltech.

it to the 19-99 percent range. Clearly this is not the whole range, but the ECU only looks at the *delta* for acceleration enrichment, and the throttle position is programmable for the position that will allow activation of nitrous. It seemed reasonable that this sensor would work OK. I'd find out.

It was now time to power up the DFI electronic control unit, and do some reconfiguration with a laptop DOS-type personal computer.

First power up the PC, then load the Calmap software according to the DFI manual. A series of menu screens will route you through programming steps. In this case, it was necessary to change certain engine parameters before even attempting to start the vehicle. These include manifold pressure range of the MAP sensor (1, 2, or 3 bar), number of cylinders, trigger rpm for closed-loop operation, parameters for torque converter lockup (if applicable), rev limit, and fan on temperature—that sort of thing. You must also specify the firmware identification of your ECU (which allows the one version of Calmap PC software to configure and tune several different DFI ECUs).

Reviewing the base fuel map, I decided that it appeared plausible for initial startup, and indeed, the engine fired up, and after a few initial coughs, ran well—too well, in fact. The engine seemed to want to run too fast, which clearly indicated some kind of manifold air leak. Only there *was* no air leak. Well, eventually it turned out there was a hose fitting from the manifold open to the atmosphere in a location that could not be seen or felt with the manifold on the engine. With the manifold off, this was a good time to check the condition of the injector bottom-side O-rings. I replaced the O-rings as a matter of course. The engine now ran great, with an apparent tendency to run hotter than you'd expect. Eventually, it became clear that routing the turbo coolant out of the heater inlet hose and back into the other was not the hot

The DFI Idle Air Control (IAC) allows air from the air cleaner to bypass the throttle plate under control of the ECU.

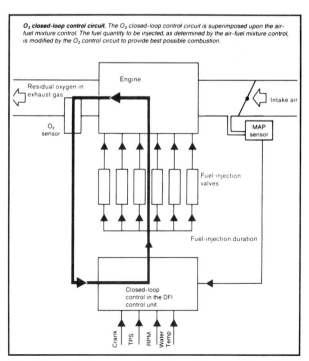

The Europa/Fuego uses DFI closed loop mode with O$_2$ sensor at idle and light cruise to trim mixture. Bosch

The NOS crank trigger detects magnetic bolts in the front pulley. (The Europa version of Renault motor does not use the front pulley.)

ticket—except, well, it *was* the hot ticket. The cool ticket was to route the hot coolant from the turbo directly back to the hot side of the radiator for immediate cooling.

Looking at the stock injector capacity at 2.5 bar (40psi) fuel pressure, the Bosch injector (part number 0280150125) rated at 188cc per minute. Each injector maxed out at roughly 36hp per cylinder (188cc per minute * 0.1902044), which translates to roughly 143hp in a four-cylinder.

However, assuming the fuel pump could provide the flow at 54psi, with 15psi boost pressure referenced to the fuel pressure regulator, injector capacity would increase the maximum injector flow rate from 188 to 221cc per minute, which would make 42hp per cylinder, or 168hp total. (This is calculated applying formulas from an earlier chapter.)

If the goal were to produce 200hp, we would have to raise injector capacity to 262cc per minute, which would mean raising system pressure to 76psi.

To solve the equation, we'll use the following:

SQR (New Pressure / Old Pressure) * Old Statflow = New Statflow.
Inserting what we know:
SQR (New Pressure / 39) * 188 = 262.
Divide both sides by 188:
SQR (New Pressure / 39) = 1.393617.
Square both sides:
New Pressure / 39 = 1.942168.
Multiple both sides by 39: New Pressure = 75.744.

We just built a new formula. Given that we know how much horsepower we need to make, we can apply actuator equation formulas to rapidly derive the injector flow rate needed to make this horsepower. We can then calculate the new fuel pressure required to raise our injector flow rate to the required level.

New Pressure = (New Statflow / Old Statflow)^2 * Old Pressure.

A fuel pressure of 75psi (about as high as you'd want to go!) will make 200hp through the current injectors, which will provide fueling for forty nitrous horsepower on top of 160 turbocharged horsepower.

OK, new fuel pump would be needed. Tuning the DFI system is covered generically in chapter 10 on setup and tuning. The thing to understand its that to tune the DFI, you must set base pulse width for speed and loading breakpoints in the base fuel matrix of 272 numbers. You change breakpoints by running in edit mode and literally typing in new numbers. For some reason, possibly having to do with avoiding floating point math in the 68HC11 microprocessor, the numbers in the matrix are not pulse width, but rather pulse width divided by 0.0627.

This tuning task will be substantially easier with a gas analyzer and/or mixture trim control,

The Lotus Europa went from having six gauges to having ten in its turbo-nitrous version. The car uses top-quality gauges to monitor things such as turbo boost (top) and exhaust gas temperature (bottom). The car also has an engine oil gauge and uses two fuel gauges, one for the tank level and the other for fuel rail pressure. These VDO gauges are from United Speedometer.

Traditional nitrous system provides both nitrous and enrichment fuel as shown in this Chevrolet V-8 system. Newer systems like that on the Europa use the fuel injectors to provide additional fuel for nitrous.

which is a DFI option, and which has separate trim knobs for idle and wide-open throttle mixture. You may be able to use the screen display in closed-loop mode which shows what the mixture *would* have been if not for closed-loop mixture adjustments.

You will be setting a number of functions: cranking pulse width; after-start enrichment; warmup enrichment; possibly idle speed versus coolant temperature; idle speed control response versus idle speed error; idle control limits versus throttle position; air temperature corrections; ignition timing versus engine speed and load; additional pulse width versus acceleration; acceleration temperature correction; closed-loop speed ranges; nitrous oxide control (including ignition retard versus speed, nitrous activation versus throttle angle, nitrous delay time, nitrous speed threshold, percent nitrous fuel enrichment, and percent nitrous correction versus engine speed); and a few other parameters.

This might sound intimidating. DFI gives the tuner tremendous flexibility in tailoring the ECU to individual needs. However, there is no reason in most cases why, for example, a user would have to change the default air temperature correction table. Not all tables require modification from default values.

DFI points out that providing nitrous fueling via injectors avoids wall wetting and distribution problems associated with traditional methods of nitrous fueling. Fuel injectors provide fuel particle size in the range of 150 microns. The nitrous itself can be considered a gas, therefore this nitrous fueling method maintains the dry flow characteristics of the intake manifold. DFI suggests that by using an enrichment factor that is multiplicative (a percentage), a better air-fuel ratio is maintained when the nitrous is introduced. DFI's literature makes the additional point discussed earlier that there is a limit to fuel flow through injectors at a given pressure, which occurs when the injectors are constantly open.

At this point you lose control of fueling and if the mixture goes lean under turbocharging and nitrous, you can very quickly turn the engine into a paperweight. An injector should never run static for this reason—as well as the fact that injectors can overheat and quit or permanently change flow rate if run static. If you decide to change injectors or raise the fuel pressure on an already-programmed system, DFI software allows you to shift the entire fuel curve up or down by that percentage.

The way to tune a complex system like the Lotus, is to get the low-load base fuel map right, followed by acceleration enrichment, then high loading, high-rpm running, then cold-running enrichment, and finally nitrous enrichment.

Remember, start conservative and work toward "hairy edge" tuning—which means work from rich to lean, from ignition retarded toward advanced, unless you are very experienced.

How do you compute an initial nitrous enrichment factor for an engine? You have to know how much power your nitrous is set up to produce, and then make some assumptions about what percentage this will be of the power the engine was producing *without* nitrous when the nitrous comes in. Assume you know how much power the engine makes at maximum torque, and the maximum torque rpm. What percentage of this will the nitrous be? In our case with the Lotus, assume it made 100hp at 3200rpm, and that this was max torque. Since nitrous provides 40 additional horsepower, total nitrous fueling at this rpm and power would be 40 percent. DFI can provide up to 32 percent fuel enrichment, plus an additional correction versus engine speed of up to 10 percent. Placing a 40hp nitrous kit on this engine is nearing the limit.

DFI's electronic control unit has the ability to stage nitrous using two different-sized nitrous solenoids: You bring in the smaller nitrous valve, switch to the larger valve (killing the smaller valve), finally bringing in both, something like a three-way light bulb with two filaments. I didn't try using staged nitrous, figuring this is something you'd want on a drag race car, which the Lotus is not.

At this time, the DFI ECU is not using a knock sensor. The car will always use high-octane gas and has no need for the protection of a knock sensor, given the fact that it will only be operated by drivers familiar with high-output racing-type engines.

There is no question that trying to duplicate the running environment of this Lotus without fuel injection would be difficult or impossible. EFI provides excellent driveability under normal conditions, safe operation via excellent distribution and programmable fuel enrichment and ignition retard under high levels of boost, and additional retard and fuel enrichment for nitrous operation.

You *might* be able to do it all with carburetion, but why would you want to?

Chapter 17

Project Car–Triple-Turbo Jag XKE with Staged Injection and Nitrous Power

In its first iteration, this 1969 Jaguar XKE breathed through triple SU carburetors that were pressurized by a single Rajay 300 series turbocharger. The second-generation car used Bosch L-Jetronic EFI with the Rajay, using the cold-start injector for enrichment under turbo boost (see Chapter 13). In the final stage of its previous life, the car had an add-on TurboGroup Fueler controller that pulsed two additional injectors for more precise enrichment and just flat-out more fuel. The life story of that car is featured in another chapter of this book.

When it came time to consider more modifications, in the end, I had a number of goals:

1. Programmable ECU: to eliminate the

The author's three-turbo, twelve-injector, six-port nitrous, 3x2-throttle body Jaguar XKE. The fueling system has run with both Haltech and NOS EFI control. The enormous Cartech Intercooler (far right) is tilted slightly forward for radiator air flow. TWM throttle bodies have over-and-under injectors, a total of twelve of them on a twin-cam, six-cylinder engine. A Bosch fuel pump located on the bulkhead in the trunk's spare tire compartment, provides plenty of fuel for up to 800hp. Note the triple turbo "Heiney Manifold" by Latham Race Cars, Austin, Texas.

"Kluge" aspect of running two computers to do what should really be done by one, and to once and for all eliminate any fuel starvation problems by providing port fuel enrichment under turbo boost, rather than at a single point with additional injectors.

2. Bigger fuel pump to make sure the injectors always had enough fuel pressure under the most extreme conditions.

3. More power.

4. No turbo lag at all—which meant nitrous combined with turbocharging, an excellent combination in which the nitrous provides great low-end torque and power, the turbo great high-rpm power.

5. An exotic look.

6. More efficient engine compartment, which eliminated certain space considerations of the earlier system that made it hard to service certain engine parts.

7. Intercooling.

8. Programmable ignition advance as opposed to the earlier generation vacuum advance-boost retard distributor, which protected the engine but was not an ideal ignition advance curve.

9. Clean emissions.

10. Reliability. This had to be a street-driven car.

11. Have it end up as something very different from anything else.

12. Eliminate intake restrictions in the L-Jet air meter and the complex plumbing that enabled the air meter to fit in place upstream of the turbo, while retaining the stock heater.

13. Electronic boost control instead of the mechanical dial-a-boost used in the earlier generation car.

14. Eliminate the water injection system, if at all possible.

These are all reasonable goals.

The initial idea was to install a Haltech F3 injection system on the car as it was. This would have met many of my goals, but not all. It would have been simple to remove the Jaguar L-Jet ECU along with its wiring and its air meter and other sensors, and install the Haltech on the single-throttle-body Jaguar injection manifold with its single turbo. With a larger fuel pump and perhaps a regulator change, goals 1, 2, 3, 6, 9, 10, 12, and 14 would be under control.

The next idea was to use nitrous oxide injection. I began to wonder if there might be some way to provide fueling via the staged feature of Haltech injection, which could control two injectors per cylinder, using the fueling from the second set of injectors only for the nitrous.

However, this meant there had to be a way to mount two injectors per cylinder. I discovered that TWM was making DCOE Weber-type throttle bodies with two injectors per intake port. Of course, that means you needed a Weber-type manifold. TWM, it turned out, could provide that too.

By this time, the project began to look pretty radical. From this point on, the design goal became "take it to the limit." This would involve: twin turbos with liquid cooling, custom-fabricated turbo exhaust manifold, twelve injectors, one throttle per cylinder, port nitrous, speed-density injection with nitrous capability, crank-triggered ignition, and *more* than two turbos—try three!

The first big challenge was building a good turbo exhaust manifold that could hold three turbos. Turbo Power of northern California supplied three T-2 AiResearch turbochargers, the kind used on the 1.5 liter Nissan 200SX Turbo or the Buick Skyhawk. After building 0.5in thick header flanges and turbocharger exhaust in-and-out flanges, I removed the old turbo manifold and spent hours playing with the three turbos. (*And managed to drop* one of the turbos on the car's red paint!)

Jeff Latham of Latham Race Cars added his formidable ability to conceptualize anything made of metal tubing to the three-turbo exhaust manifold design effort. You couldn't do it with standard header tubing; there didn't seem to be a way to get excellent exhaust flow. Log manifold? Not! But finally, using tight-radius black steel *pipe*, mounting the turbos in a transverse position, it turned out there was a way. Latham went to work with a band saw and a TIG welder, building the manifold.

When it was finished, with all surfaces ground smooth and ready for high temperature coating (HPC), we took a look and began laughing. The design was beautiful, the flow smooth, poetry in black steel. But somehow, the thing had the look of three babies' butts mooning you. So we dubbed it the "Heiney Manifold."

Latham built a triple exhaust system that

After the initial start-up with the Haltech ECU and original points distributor, the author installed a modified Jaguar electronic distributor which contains an aluminum disc containing a fly magnet cam-speed trigger used to time NOS sequential fuel injection.

bolted to the three turbos, and constructed a three-into-one compressor-out pipe that crossed over to the right side of the engine to plumb into the Weber manifold. The original idea was to build an air-to water intercooler on the right side of the engine, in which a large C-shaped pipe connected all three turbos and plumbed into a plenum outboard of the liquid intercooler which was outboard of the Weber manifold.

Tull Systems' turbocharging and EFI specialists assembled the turbo system, designed a linkage for the triple two-barrel throttle bodies, provided oiling for the turbos and liquid cooling, and in general got the system ready to start. This included removal of the oil pan and drilling for additional oil return. Tull Systems bent a custom steel pipe oiling system for the turbos, and constructed a two-into-six coolant block that routed cooling water to all three turbos and back into the cooling system.

Cartech now took over, and owner Corky Bell offered some convincing statistics regarding the possibility of 90 percent maximum efficiency in air-to-air intercooling versus 80 percent max in air-to-water. He also designed a way to construct a custom intercooler that mounted in front of the Jag radiator. The trick was to get the compressed air to and from it. Cartech ended up reversing the compressor-out pipe, while Tull systems re-indexed the compressors and wastegates for a slightly different orientation. Cartech then notched the top of the Jag radiator, lowered the whole thing about an inch, and constructed a gigantic intercooler obtained from Thermal Transfer Systems' (in the Dallas-Fort Worth area) intercooler cores. The intercooler was set at such an angle that there was room for air to rush around the sides to provide full engine cooling by the radiator.

Cartech fabricated an inlet on the Tull Systems plenum outboard of the throttle bodies, and plumbed intercooler-out air into it. The design looked good, and more important, would *function*. The final touch was a Cartech heat shield, which kept exhaust manifold heat away from the compressor-out pipe.

In the meantime, Tull Systems had installed 288cc Lucas disc injectors *(twelve!)* and installed a high-volume, high-pressure Bosch fuel pump to replace the stock Jaguar unit. I decided to fire up the car using the points distributor (with vacuum advance-boost retard), using a Haltech F3, set up for staged operation of twelve injectors.

In the meantime, I had removed the distributor and modified another Jaguar electronic distributor to include a flying magnet cam trigger in order to run an NOS Competition sequential fuel injection system. This is a top-of-the-line race system designed in cooperation with EFI Technology. Systems like this are used on cost-is-no-object, Indy 500-type race cars, competition offshore boats, and other all-out vehicles in which flexibility and reliability are vital. The ECUs are designed with mil-spec wiring and enclosures, and are made to be absolutely bulletproof. EFI has added programming to not only activate nitrous and nitrous fueling via the port injectors, but also to *pulse* a nitrous solenoid rapidly like an injector to provide *proportional* nitrous flow.

Nitrous can come on very gradually, or in a scorching sudden blast. The ECU provides spark timing, with the cam trigger operating 45 degrees BTDC (before top dead center) as a reference for compression stroke number one cylinder for *sequential* injection (the only US aftermarket ECU to provide this capability at the time this book was written). Crank triggers provide crank position six times per revolution. Using magnetic bolts, by removing the crank damper, it was possible to drill and tap holes with which to mount the six flying magnets next to a pulley groove in the damper.

When using cam and crank triggers to provide spark timing, it is necessary to coordinate the position of the distributor, the cam trigger *in* the distributor, the rotor-flying magnet in the distributor, the crank trigger, and the flying magnets on the crank. It is a simple matter to offset the first crank magnet 15 degrees from TDC, separated from the others in 60 degree intervals. Next, you adjust the crank trigger exactly over the timing pointer at TDC. The trick with the distributor is that there is a slot that holds the cam trigger, with 45 degrees of movement possible. Rotating the distributor will no longer affect ignition timing, but the trick here is that the rotor, on average, must be centered over number one cylinder when spark occurs so that all degrees of timing advance and retard provide a narrow gap for the spark to jump when generated by the ECU, coil driver, and coil.

Accel Performance Products recommends a procedure for indexing this type of distributor using a strobe light and a clear distributor cap, and that's fine if you have something common like a small-block Chevy. But no clear cap is available for the XKE. Compute the mid-position between most and least spark advance. Put the engine at this position on compression stroke number one cylinder (either with a degree wheel, via marking degree already on the flywheel or

A Tull Systems-built twelve-injector fuel rail. Fuel enters at one end of one rail, travels through high pressure braided steel hose to the other rail and regulator. This setup would be questionable due to possible pressure differentials along a very long rail with twelve injectors on batch-fire injection systems. Still, it is all right for sequential injection. Note the NOS nitrous solenoid and Lucas port injectors.

The Jaguar project required extensive fabrication for hood clearance of turbo plumbing, including removal of sheet metal from the cold air tunnel to the heater/blower inlet.

damper, or by measuring the distance from TDC to some marked BTDC position.

For example, suppose 10 degrees BTDC is 1in from TDC, and you are trying to locate 21 degrees BTDC. The equation would read:

21 / 10 * 1(in) = 2.1in from TDC

Or, suppose 10 degrees is 3/4in from TDC. It would read:

21 / 10 * 0.75 = 1.575in

It is not critical to get the cam trigger position *perfect* on the NOS electronic control unit, since the cam trigger is a general reference indicating compression stroke, not a marker of engine position. But it should be within 10 degrees of 45 degrees BTDC, according to EFI Technology. With the engine at this position, point the rotor in a convenient direction for organizing plug wires and such. (Remove the distributor, if necessary, to index the distributor drive gear.) The Jaguar distributor can only point in two directions since it engages a slot in a driven gear, not the crankshaft or camshaft itself. Install the distributor cap, plug the timing plug wire (usually the number one plug) into an appropriate hole in the cap, and center it over the rotor. Now move the engine to 45 degrees BTDC, observe the position of the flying magnet, and adjust the trigger so that it is exactly above the magnet. That's it.

It turned out that on the initial installation, I had the flying magnet in the cam-trigger installed with magnetic polarity wrong, which set the timing off by 60 degrees, preventing the engine from starting.

I decided to start the XKE with a Haltech ECU, to get things sorted out and working correctly before moving the Haltech to another project vehicle featured in the book, a 1970 383 Dodge Challenger. We turned the key on the XKE at Tull Systems, and *it fired up immediately!* One nice thing about the Haltech F3 was that Ivan Tull had already had a working map we could use from a Jaguar 4.2 liter engine he'd modified with a similar TWM induction system. This vehicle had different-sized injectors, but the map could be adapted simply with Haltech's new Delta feature which changes entire map ranges or segments of ranges, or even *all* ranges by a percentage.

Naturally, we'd have to map in the loading bars above atmospheric pressure, but Tull has plenty of experience with Haltech-controlled turbo engines, and I had already set up the Haltech twin-turbo Cadillac motorhome engine featured earlier in this book. After getting the vehicle running nicely with the Haltech, it would be a relatively simple matter to switch over to the DFI unit and map the fueling pulse width the same as the Haltech—with the exception that the Haltech could stage in the second set of injectors at a programmable loading point, whereas the NOS unit would fire all injectors all the time. But it would be a matter of some easy calculations to adapt the programming of one ECU to the other, assuming both ECUs used peak and hold or equivalent saturated circuitry to open injectors at the same rate. In any case, it would be a good place to start.

Installing the NOS system is pretty straightforward. The GM throttle position sensor is a little different from the shaft-mounted TPS used by Haltech, but not a problem on the TWM throttle body (which has a special boss for the TPS). The

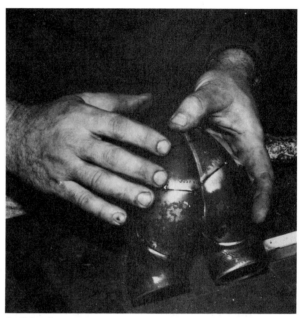

Jeff Latham constructs triple turbo exhaust manifold from tight-radius black-steel weld bends.

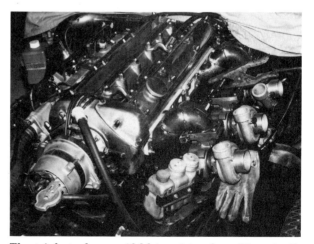

The triple turbo manifold is set in place. Note the L-Jetronic EFI manifold on the passenger side (on the left in this photo) prior to installation of the TWM induction system.

NOS system recently gained the capability to run in closed-loop mode with an O_2 sensor, so we welded three EGO sensor bosses in the exhaust system, each ijust downstream from a turbo. All wiring harness connections are unique, so it is impossible to confuse what goes to what. One nice thing about the NOS Competition ECU is that it is set up to provide diagnostics via a Check Engine-type light located somewhere within the driver's vision. If there is an ECU-detected sensor failure, for example, the light will flash out a trouble code.

The NOS unit is actually designed for racing use, so it doesn't normally do "frivolous" things like stabilize idle via IAC, or control knock sensor (in racing, the engine is expecting good race fuel,

Inequality for All: EFI Technologies' Individual Cylinder Engine Management

What is a V-8 engine, really? Eight single-cylinder engines hooked up in a line, doing their best to work together. Not identical engines, however. This is why the most sophisticated aftermarket engine management systems, like the Race System from EFI Technologies, offer not only sequential injection, but individual cylinder calibration of injector open time (pulse width), injection start time (phasing), and spark timing. Such systems produce higher output cleaner power on otherwise identical engines.

Good fuel atomization is critical to efficient combustion, and really good atomization will produce more power for a given amount of fuel. Engines are run at richer than stoichiometric (chemically ideal) air-fuel mixtures at peak torque/power in order to increase the odds that every molecule of air that makes it's way into the engine finds some fuel to burn. Excellent atomization makes sure that there are fewer localized "islands" of air in the air-fuel mixture without fuel, reducing the need for richer overall air-fuel mixtures. A really well-mixed homogeneous air-fuel mixture produces higher flame speed during the burn event, which implies more horsepower and less required ignition timing. If injectors spray on a runner wall or against a closed intake valve, fuel will pool and run into the engine in droplets. Injectors should aim at the back of the valves with minimum contact with port walls, and fire precisely in sequence at the correct time.

Variations in the intake system, cylinder head, and exhaust system, even with equal-length runners, cause air flow to resonate slightly differently for different cylinders, resulting in slightly varying volumetric efficiency. "Even with identical header length," says EFI Technologies' President Graham Western," some exhaust tubes are more forgiving than others. On true racing engines, fuel pulsewidth trim of 1 to 2 percent correction is required to eliminate mixture variations due to this slight breathing differential."

While batch injection (all injectors firing at once) is reasonably efficient on lower rpm multi-cylinder engines with little pulsing in the intake, on high-rpm wildly pulsing competition motors, sequential phasing is more effective, particularly at peak torque where tuned intake and exhaust systems are most efficient. On racing engines, where charge density of atomization can be improved by taking advantage of the intercooling high heat of vaporization by injecting further upstream, spraying at the wrong time can result in fuel being blown back out the stacks or directly through into the exhaust system on valve overlap, producing distribution problems or wasted fuel and high emissions. In order to eliminate standoff distribution problems, it is critical to inject fuel when the intake valve is open so that fuel does not hit the closed valve and bounce back along with the decelerating, bouncing air column. On a plenum-stack turbo engine with compressed air entry at one end, depending on the resonant frequency, standoff fuel can be blown to the stacks furthest away. Individual cylinder pulsewidth or injection phasing adjustment can correct for distribution problems related to resonant differences in the air flow to each cylinder (particularly when the injectors are open a lot)—realizing as much as eight percent more power. According to Western, 60-70 percent injector duty cycle usually makes best power. Larger injectors get all fuel in while the valve is open, but the tradeoff with short injection time is poorer vaporization and cooling.

Western says you always see power increases over batch fire injection at mid-to-high range torque, typical being a Mickey Thompson six-cylinder truck which tested at 280hp with batch-fire injection, picking up 20lb-ft of torque at peak torque and 12-16hp at peak power with EFI Technologies' sequential injection. A 700hp racing engine might make up to five percent more horsepower due to general phasing correctness.

Individual spark trim is usually associated with detonation-limited engines. Retarding timing on just the offending cylinders (typically 2-3 degrees) lowers peak combustion temperature and cylinder pressure, helping fight detonation. Where exhaust gas temperatures are too high on turbo motors, tuners may run a little extra fuel or spark timing in the cylinder causing problems—or increase overall compression ratios. Raising compression is preferable to advanced timing. The increased expansion ratio of gases from a smaller combustion chamber results in greater loss of temperature than retarding timing, plus the increased compression ratios improve peak and average cylinder pressures instead of simply peak cylinder pressures.

not 87 octane junk).

However, the NOS ECU does have some nice features; for example, it has the ability to change the granularity of the fueling map in a nonlinear fashion, with rpm-based breakpoints occurring more frequently at some parts of the RPM scale than others. This is a great feature for engines in which a linear interpolation between certain standard breakpoints of loading and rpm do not approximate an ideal fuel curve. You can change the granularity until the linear interpolations *do* approximate the correct fueling, sufficiently. NOS ECUs, as mentioned, can control proportional nitrous, and the ECU can be programmed to control electronic wastegates, and, in fact, it is set up to potentially control at least *fifteen* classes of sensors and actuators!

As discussed earlier, the NOS ECU represents various segments of the fueling map as line graphs, in which pulse width is plotted as a function of rpm and loading. If you change the map, the change first appears as a dotted line, then changes permanently when you download the modification to the ECU.

The HKS electronic valve controller enables the tri-turbo Jaguar to run higher levels of boost than the stock wastegates allow by regulating the manifold pressure as seen at the stock wastegate via an electronically controlled air valve. The engine's NOS fuel injection ECU enables individual cylinder sequential injection, pulsewidth, phasing, and ignition spark timing. Individual cylinder capabilities enable higher levels of power by retarding timing only on critical cylinders, and correction for manifolding design flaws and resonation/pulsing in manifolds.

Chapter 18

Project Vehicle—
The 460 Eddie Bauer Bronco

If you wanted a fuel injected full-sized Bronco in 1986, you had one engine choice: the little 302.

I bought a new 1986 Bronco the last day of 1985, and by early 1993, it was going on 100,000 miles. In that time, only two things had ever gone wrong with it other than routine maintenance: The EEC-IV computer suffered infant mortality at two months old, and an emissions part went out under warranty somewhere around 50,000 miles. At 100,000 miles, it still burned no oil, and it still made 15.5mpg at 75mph.

And it was still dog-slow.

In 1992 I did a story for *Sport Truck Magazine* about a 460 swap kit made by L & L Products to put some serious cubic inches in a full-size Ford pickup or Bronco—a carbureted 1972 460 in

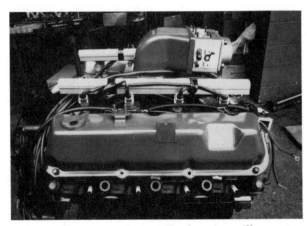

The Emtech-controlled 460ci Ford engine will soon run twin turbochargers. The ultra-strong EFI engine features JE pistons, Accel fuel supply, ARP engine fasteners, and a Competition Cams valvetrain from Turbo Cam. The engine features a GM-type throttle body and a Linkenfelter-Accel adaptor to mount the throttle to the Edelbrock four-barrel manifold. Note the engine coolant hose connections on the throttle body to fight icing in very cold weather. The engine was blueprinted by Joe White Performance Automotive in Austin, Texas.

place of a 1983 carbureted 351M Ford in a F150 Stepside. I became interested in the possibility of doing the swap in the Bronco, but keeping fuel injection, and making the whole thing *legal*— which is why I called the story "going straight."

California laws for engine swaps deal with what are referred to as "Replacement Engines" (basically, either the identical engine, or an engine which matches a configuration offered by the manufacturer for the year, make, and model of vehicle, including all emissions controls). 1986 Broncos did not have a 460 option, although 3/4-ton and one-ton models did have a carbureted 460 engine option. Is a Bronco a pickup? Perhaps this is a gray area. Perhaps not.

California law also deals with "Engine Changes," which refer to the installation of an engine in an exhaust controlled vehicle that is different from the one installed originally and does not qualify as a replacement engine. The new engine should be equipped with breathing and emissions equipment of the same year or newer than the old engine, and should not degrade the effectiveness of the vehicle's emissions controls. A *newer* EFI 460 with the same emissions controls as the 302 should not degrade emissions.

I acquired a carbureted 1986 460 from a one-ton truck which still used the big-port heads, and dropped it off for a rebuild at an engine builder near Houston. Very soon it became clear the engine builders had bigger things in mind than 460 cubic inches—like a bore and stroke to 520ci. I had been considering using a late model 460 EEC-IV computer box to run the motor via a modified version of the existing 302 EFI wiring harness. Unfortunately, the stock injectors and computer injection pulse width calibration would be wrong for the 520 motor, unless the fuel pressure were raised to compensate, or unless you could get injectors proportionally larger (13 percent larger), or some combination. On the other hand, if the 460 ECU calibration is going to be wrong, and you're forced to look for recalibration strategies, why not just use the *stock* 302 EEC-IV computer—along with a set of injectors proportionately larger than the stock *302* injectors (47 percent larger for a 520 engine)? The stock injectors are 18lb/hr flow units. It turned out Accel supplies 30lb/hr injectors within striking range of the ideal (31lb/hr).

The next question is, what about cams? The volumetric efficiency of an engine is heavily dependent on the cam, and the relationship between manifold pressure and engine air flow is incredibly dependent on the cam. This means that for the bigger injectors to fuel correctly for the 520 motor with the 302 ECU firmware, the cam profiles must be selected such that the air flow relationship to manifold pressure at speed is proportionately equivalent to the 302's relationship—or the EEC-IV Speed-Density computer will get the fueling wrong, since it does not actually measure air flow.

Without a black box, I had three tools. In the first place, I could try adapting the engine to the ECU by selecting the right cam or other VE-impacting modifications. I could make adjustments to the fuel pressure and/or injector size. And finally, I could expect the stock ECU's O_2 sensor closed loop mixture control system to strive for a 14.7-1 air-fuel mixture. The EEC-IV is fairly smart; it has an O_2 sensor to feedback how well it's doing on mixture at idle and light cruise, and has the ability to make some "permanent" corrections. Can it do a good enough recalibration job? Figure you might need to modify the fuel curve at part throttle, and figure full throttle might well be wrong—unless you were *really* lucky. I'd have the potential to adjust fuel pressure according to certain formulae in order to change fueling, but this will tend to occur across the board (although manifold pressure referenced regulators will change the way they change fuel pressure in accordance with cam-produced changes in manifold pressure). It might be possible to adjust fuel pressure for perfect mixture under open loop conditions (no O_2 sensor-based dynamic calibration) at maximum torque (most fuel required per injection), and then hope the computer could trim idle and light cruise to stoichiometric mixtures and make the motor run right. But what if this didn't work well enough?

In the meantime, the 520 project ran into a snag, and the engine was no longer available. I put an ad in the paper in Austin, looking for another 460 motor, bought a complete 1973 Lincoln Town Car with running 460 4-barrel, for $50, removed the powertrain, and sold the car to a junkyard for $20. With press time approaching, and months of time wasted on the 520 stroker project, I decided to stick with 460ci. The engine

The rear end of the Ford engine shows the Emtech E6 relays and GM-type connectors.

went to Joe White Performance Automotive in Austin, Texas, for a performance rebuild and blueprinting.

So the new plan became retain stock displacement (+.030 overbore), lower the compression to 8:1, strengthen the motor, and bolt on turbocharger equipment sized for low RPM boost. But with press time approaching on this book, and too many months wasted on the 520 motor that never happened, there was now scant time to experiment with recalibrating the stock ECU.

In the meantime, EFI Technology of Australia (not to be confused with EFI Technology of Torrance, California, builders of sophisticated high-end engine management computer for racing and competition use as on the triple-turbo nitrous Jaguar featured as a project in this book), developers of the original Haltech F3 and F7 programmable EFI computers, introduced the new E6, a state of the art engine management computer, and I got my hands on one for an article in *Turbo Magazine*. Shortly, the modified new plan became this: Let's see if we can get the truck to pass the Federal Test Procedure (FTP) for emissions using the E6 for engine management, with all emissions devices connected, and with twin turbos.

At this point, with the book going to press, I decided to get the vehicle running with *whatever* setup would meet requirements from a *technical* point of view—which included clean emissions—without worrying *yet* about what was legal. Ironically, it would probably be legal to swap a late model carbureted 460 into the Bronco, but the same engine with a precise, clean, efficient aftermarket *EFI* engine management system would not be legal for street use in 50 states without extremely expensive California Air Resources Board (CARB) testing (guilty until proven innocent!). Turbocharging would clearly not be 50-state legal without an exemption order including cold-soak FTP test—but there was no technical reason why it couldn't be *made* legal with the proper testing. A possible plan might be to keep the stock Ford EEC-IV on the engine to control emissions devices and ignition, while providing an aftermarket closed loop Electronic Control Unit (Emtech E-6) that would be programmed to handle fueling and ignition under all conditions.

I began to consult with Competition Cams over selection of a camshaft that could meet emissions requirements that was suitable for turbocharging. The 460 motor could be expected to make lots of low-end torque, turbocharging to make as much high end power as necessary. The ideal turbo cam would have high lift but little overlap (cam lobe separation), perhaps something in the range of 114 degrees lobe separation, which would also be fine for emissions.

Accel supplied a set of 30lb/hr injectors, a huge 1000cfm GM-style two-barrel throttle body, a Linkenfelter horizontal throttle body-to-vertical four-barrel Holley bolt pattern manifold adaptor, and an EFI manifold conversion kit complete with injector bosses, fuel rail, and regulator. Converting a carb manifold is much easier if all intake runners are at the same height, so I obtained an Edelbrock Torker II 429/460 aluminum single-plane manifold. This manifold did not have EGR, but clearly I could adapt it for external EGR when the time came. The Edel-

The engine has Emtech E6 relays, O-ring Accel injectors (top and bottom), and D-section fuel rails. The E6 MAP sensor, coolant sensor, and tachometric adaptor plus injector connects are shown at the front of the engine. The Emtech E6 ECU features Motorola 68HC11 microprocessors that are similar to what's used in some factory ECUs. The difference is that the E6 engine management parameters can be altered dynamically via a laptop PC. The E6 provides ignition control plus closed-loop nitrous injection and fueling control. The E6 has extra features that enhance the capabilities the Australian inventors built into their first effort, the Haltech F3. Outside the US, the E6 is sold as a Haltech product.

brock unit is a large port manifold that is designed to make mid-to-high RPM power, which would tend to hurt low end, and might hurt emissions—with a carb. With port injection, fuel would squirt directly into the intake valve rather than puddling on manifold walls, and should atomize fine in the hot cylinders.

Joe White Performance blueprinted the 460 engine, installing JE custom forged pistons designed for minimal thermal expansion allowing fairly tight piston-cylinder clearances). White installed new crank and cam bearings, and a special turbo 460 cam and valvetrain from Competition Cams, with short cam lobe separation of 114 degrees, but reasonably high lift of 0.500—which is exactly what turbos like. White redid the heads, decked the block, honed the mains, and all other blueprinting operations. American Racing Products (ARP) supplied ultra-strong engine fasteners, including special rod bolts, and main and head stud kits, plus all other engine bolts from top to bottom. In the meantime, Lupton Machine of Austin, Texas, went to work on the Edelbrock Torker manifold, modifying it to accept an Accel port EFI conversion kit, which consists of injectors bosses, O-ring Accel fuel injectors, D-section fuel rail, 1000cfm GM-type horizontal throttle body, and 4-barrel manifold adaptor (see Installation chapter for details on carb manifold EFI conversions). L & L Products of Dallas, Texas, sent down one of its 1986 Bronco 460 engine swap kits, consisting of motor mounts, accessory mounts, headers, remote oil filter kit, rear sump oil pan, new oil pump and rear pickup—everything else I'd need for a swap except a 460 Ford C-6 4WD automatic transmission. (Stock AOD automatic overdrive transmissions for 302 motor does not bolt to 460 without adaptor plate, and will not like the power of a 460, much less a *turbo* 460 motor.) MSD would supply ignition parts compatible with the Emtech E6 ECU ignition driver circuitry. Turbonetics would supply turbocharging equipment.

As of today, the project consists of an ultra-strong, blueprinted 460 motor with homemade port EFI, sitting on an engine stand, with the Emtech ECU sensors installed and the ECU and wiring draped over the engine. As this book goes to press, there are valuable lessons to learn from this project. A number of factors conspired to keep this project unfinished eight months after I acquired the original 1986 carbureted 460 motor. In the first place, the project quickly became very complex. Not just an engine swap, make it an *EFI* engine swap. Not just an EFI engine swap, make it a *custom* EFI engine swap. Not just a stock computer, add a second *auxiliary* computer. Not just a custom EFI engine swap, make it a stroker motor with modified OE fuel injection. Not just a stroker, make it turbocharged. Make it emissions-legal. Make it use an aftermarket engine management system, but also keep the stock computer for emissions control device management.

In short order, the project had escalated from a relatively simple engine swap to a *major* engineering project. As eventually envisioned, this project had escalated to by far the most complex project in this book—a late model multi-computer EFI engine, with heavily modified fuel injection components on a stroked motor with turbocharging, with fully functional emissions controls (also customized), in an engine swap that involved

transmission and linkage changes—which would require complex government testing on a chassis dyno to be legal.

This definitely violated the KISS theory of project management: Keep It Simple, Stupid.

As currently envisioned, the current project backs away—initially—from legality constraints, and backs away from OE engine management control of engine and emissions devices. Given the financial and time resources available, I had bitten off more than I could chew in one bite. And in fact, experience with multiple complex project vehicles indicates that managing a project in

---

Emtech E6—The New Kid in Town

The E6 is currently marketed in the US by Emtech (Engine Management Technology Inc.). The unit combines the philosophy of the Haltech F3 (intuitively easy to use and program) with new, state of the art engine management features that are sorely missing in the Haltech F3. These features include: closed loop feedback air-fuel mixture calibration via the O_2 sensor, ignition timing control, programmable idle speed control, nitrous control, enhanced fueling control via improved internal calibration tables, additional flexibility in engine sensor compatibility, a programmable port for control of nitrous, an emissions device, transmission control, and more.

Several features which were somewhat primitive in the F3 are improved in the Emtech E6: All displays are switchable from metric to US units; real time emulation is improved—there is no loss of an injection event (and consequent stumble) while updating the ECU on line from a PC; acceleration enrichment is improved to include separate low and high speed increase and sustain values, and there is a startup priming feature available that was sorely missing in the original F3. In addition, the E6 includes fully-implemented fuel cut on deceleration. The granularity of fueling is improved with a doubling of the number of speed ranges to include a complete 64 bar loading map for each *500*rpm range. E6 units can be configured to manage on any engine up to eight cylinders, and engine loading estimation can be configured for manifold pressure *or* throttle angle sensing.

Ignition spark advance and closed loop operation are now standard on virtually all engine management computers with the exception of the Haltech F-series; these missing capabilities have been a clear indication of the aging nature of the F3, which had the space onboard for a chip to handle ignition timing control, but had never had this implemented. The E6 unit includes an ignition drive-out wire which can be configured to control most coil-driver units such as the MSD 6 and 7 series, and the Accel Laser II series, as well as direct-fire multi-coil ignition systems such as the Firepower

unit. In order to control ignition timing via magnetic or reluctor trigger, the E6 makes use of tachometric adaptor equipment, customized to interface to various distributors and crank/cam triggers. Optical and Hall effects triggers do not require the adaptor.

Tuners familiar with the Haltech F3 will discover that rather than using manifold pressure and barometric pressure sensors internal to the F3 ECU and connected to the manifold via *rubber hose*, the E6 now uses an external GM-type MAP sensors (one, two, or three Bar). The E6 permits use of various TPS switches via a calibration feature: Close the throttle and hit a key stroke, then open the throttle wide, hit a keystroke—which enables a tuner to arbitrarily define the first sensor voltage at closed throttle as 0 percent throttle opening, and whatever voltage is produced at wide open throttle as 100 percent open. This means any linear potentiometer should work.

The E6 maintains the ease of use of the Haltech F-series equipment, using a graphical interface to program most functions rather than requiring data entry of decimal numbers as is the case in some programmable ECUs. One nice new feature is the Quickmap capability, which automatically builds a series of fuel maps for your specific vehicle based on five or six parameters, including injection time at idle, injection time at peak torque, RPM of peak torque, and the cam-affected difference between fuel use at low RPM and fuel use at peak torque.

The E6 PC software includes hundreds of different ignition timing Maps which a tuner specifies by typing in a two digit number indicating ignition timing at idle, followed by a letter indicating RPM for fuel advance (A=1500rpm, and so on to F=4000rpm in 500rpm increments), followed by a two digit number indicating full load ignition advance, followed by a letter indicating light load advance (A=0, and so on in 3 degree increments to H=21 degrees), followed by a two digit number indicating ignition retard under boost over 3lb (leave blank if normally aspirated engine). Normally, it's easy to check manufacturer's specifications for ignition timing and advance, and so on.

Here's the "Hot Rod Lincoln" 460ci engine just after it came out of a 1973 Town Car. Joe White Performance Automotive blueprinted the engine and it was treated to a port EFI conversion and twin turbos.

small bites is often the sound way to go. How many of us have seen ads for "basket case" vehicles in which someone ripped apart the vehicle or engine in one big bite, and then got lost in the complexity of a project beyond available resources?

The KISS theory. Not a bad concept...

As an example, one might start by swapping a low-mileage, legal, late model 460 into a Bronco with factory EFI and emissions controls as step one. Step two might consist of stroking the motor to 520ci and getting it to work with the stock EFI. Step three could be adding low-pressure turbocharging with fuel enrichment via the stock EFI, perhaps in the form of raising the fuel pressure with special high-rate-of-gain regulators. This step could be followed by increasing turbo boost to higher levels with more sophisticated fuel enrichment—perhaps in the form of an auxiliary black box computer or additional injector controller or even complete add-on ECU with its own port injection system independent of the OE EFI system. The next step might be installing a complete aftermarket engine management system like the E6, and getting it calibrated for best power and fuel economy. The last step might be to make emissions controls work with the aftermarket system, and attempt a California Exemption Order for legal street use in all fifty states. The biggest advantage of the KISS theory is that at each step, you've got an interesting, working vehicle.

The KISS theory... Not a bad concept.

Appendix

Suppliers' Directory

Accel Engine Management Systems (DFI)
(Division of Accel Performance Products)
37732 Hills Tech Drive
Farmington Hills, MI 48024

Accel Performance Products
P.O. Box 142
175 N. Branford Road
Branford, CT 06405

Ace Group
P.O. Box 151
Columbus, KS 66725

Adaptive Technologies
127 N. Ventura Blvd.
Port Hueneme, CA 93041

Aeroquip
300 S. East Avenue
Jackson, MI 49203

Air Flow Performance
P.O. Box 3364
Spartanburg, SC 29304-3364

Arizona Speed and Marine (ASM)
4221 E. Raymond Street, Suite 100
Phoenix, AZ 85040

ARP
250 Quail Ct.
Santa Paula, CA 93060

Automotive Digital Systems (ADS)
P.O. Box 348
Flint, TX 75762

BBK Performance Specialists
2451 Pomona Rincon
Corona, CA 91270

Blower Drive Service (BDS)
12140 E. Washington Blvd.
Whittier, CA 90606

Bosch (Robert Bosch Company)
2800 South 25th Avenue
Broadview, IL 60153

Camden Superchargers
401-M East Braker
Austin, TX 78753

Cartech Performance Systems
11723 Warfield
San Antonio, TX 78216

Cutler Induction
19595 N.E. 10th Avenue, Suite A
North Miami Beach, FL 33179

Digital Fuel Injection [DFI]
(Accel Engine Management Systems,
   Div. of Accel Perf. Products)
37732 Hills Tech Drive
Farmington Hills, MI 48024

Dr. K's Automotive Wiring
11 Lakefront Avenue
Gadsden, AL 35904

Earl's Performance Products
189 W. Victoria Street
Long Beach, CA 90805

Edelbrock Corporation
2700 California Street
Torrance, CA 90509

EFI Technology Inc.
386 Beech Avenue, #4
Torrance, CA 90501

Electromotive Inc.
14004-J Willard Road
Chantilly, VA 22021

Engine Management Technology, Inc.
   (Emtech)
5019 McKinney St.
Dallas, TX 75205

Extrude Hone
8800 Somerset Blvd.
Paramount, CA 90723

Ford Motorsport Performance and
Ford Special Vehicle Operations
   (SVO)
Ford Motor Company
17000 Southfield Road
Allen Park, MI 48101

French Revolution
807–809 Capitol Ct.
Austin, TX 78756

Fuel Injection Specialties
2238 Encino Loop
San Antonio, TX 78259

GM Service Parts Operations
3031 West Grand Blvd.
Detroit, MI 48202

Haltech Inc.
3121 Benton Drive
Garland, TX 75042

Hilborn
25891 Crown Valley Parkway
South Laguna, CA 92677

HKS USA Inc.
20312 Gramercy Place
Torrance, CA 90501

Holley Replacement Parts
11955 E. Nine Mile Road
Warren, MI 48089-2003

Horiba Instrument
17671 Armstrong Avenue
Irvine, CA 92714

Howell
5989 Kensington
Detroit, MI 48224

Hypertech
1910 Thomas Road
Memphis, TN 38134

JE
15681 Computer Lane
Huntington Beach, CA 92649

JTR/Mike Knell
P.O. Box 66
Livermore, CA 94551

Joe White Performance Automotive
4313 Gillis St.
Austin, TX 78745

K&N
P.O. Box 1329
Riverside, CA 92502-9762

Kaufmann Products
12400 Benedict Avenue
Downey, CA 90242

Kinsler Fuel Injection
1834 Thunderbird
Troy, MI 48084

Latham Race Cars
1100 C Regal Row
Austin, TX 78748

Lokar Ltd.
10924 Murdock Drive
Knoxville, TN 37922

Lucas Aftermarket Operations
Lucas Industries Inc.
5600 Crooks Road, P.O. Box 7079
Troy, MI 48007-7079

Lupton Machine
2125 Goodrich Ave.
Austin, TX 78746

Mallory Ignition
550 Mallory Way
Carson City, NV 89701

Marren Motorsports
412 Roosevelt Drive
Derby, CT 06418

MSD (Autotronic Controls Corp.)
1490 Henry Brennan Drive
El Paso, TX 79936

New Age Automotive Electronics
7452 Dogwood Park
Fort Worth, TX 76118

Nitrous Oxide Systems (NOS)
5930 Lakeshore Drive
Cypress, CA 90630

Norwood Autocraft
5020 Tracy
Dallas, TX 75205

Pacific Coast Performance
973 N. Bativia, #A
Orange, CA 92667

Pacific Performance
15631 Graham Street
Huntington Beach, CA 92649

Pantera Specialties
2824 S. Willis
Santa Ana, CA 92705

Power Train Electronics Co.
2063 Maple Avenue
Costa Mesa, CA 92627

Professional Flow Technologies
25740 John R. Road
Madison Heights, MI 48071

Ron Francis' Wire Works
167 Keystone Road
Chester, PA 19013

Russel Performance Products Inc.
2645 Gundry Avenue
Signal Hill, CA 90806

Street and Performance
Rt 5, #1 Hot Rod Lane
Highway 375 S.
Mena, AR 71953

Sutton Engineering
2601 Prospect
Evanston, IL 60201

Top Gun Nitrous Oxide
5111 Troup Highway
Tyler, TX 75707

TPI Specialties
4255 County Road 10 E.
Chaska, MN 55318

Tull Systems
P.O. Box 17912
San Antonio, TX 78217

Turbo and High Tech Performance
   Magazine
P.O. Box 2712
Hamilton Beach, CA 92647

Vortech Engineering
5351 Bonsai Avenue
Moorpark, CA 93021

Wayne's Mail-Order Engine Parts
2200 Business Way
Riverside, CA 9250

Z-Industries
10832 Lemon Drive, #C
Yorba Linda, CA 92686

Zytek
7905 E. Greenway, #203
Scottsdale, AZ 85260

Index

Air density, 66
Air metering sensors, 48-49
Air temperature sensor, 47
Analog-to-digital (A-D) circuitry, 34-37
Arithmetic-logic unit (ALU), 34

Batch injection, 23

Carburetion, 11
Central Processing Unit (CPU), 34
Chevrolet Small-Block V-8, 137-139
Compression ratios, 66-67
Computers, 20, 33-43
Coolant temperature sensor, 46-47
Corporate average fuel economy (CAFE) standards, 7

Digital microprocessor, 33

EFI, programming of, 102-110
Electronic control unit (ECU), 6, 8, 24, 29-43, 98
Electronic fuel injection (EFI) disadvantages, 9
Electronic fuel injection (EFI), advantages, 9, 82-83
Electronic wastegates, 59-60
Engine fans, 59
Environmental Protection Agency (EPA), 5
Exhaust gas oxygen sensor (EGO), 44, 116
Exhaust gas recirculation (EGR) valves, 5, 60

Fuel enrichment, 69-71
Fuel lines, 58-59
Fuel maps, 93-101, 104-110
Fuel metering, 18
Fuel pumps, 58-59
Fuel rails, 90-92

Ignition spark advance, 60
Injectors, 19, 24, 50-58
Intake manifolds, 17, 22, 87-89, 95-97

Knock sensor, 49

Manifold absolute pressure (MAP) sensor, 47-48, 118
Mass airflow (MAF) sensor, 20, 23-24, 40-42, 118
Mechanical fuel injection, 25
Microcomputers, 33
Multi-port injection (MPI), 77, 125-127

Nitrous oxide solenoids, 59
Nitrous oxide, 150-153

Personal computers (PC), 36, 100-101
Programmable Read-Only Memory (PROM) chip, 8, 9, 28-43

Random Access Memory (RAM), 33
Runners, 17

Sensors, 44-49, 99, 115-118
Sequential port injection of fuel (SPIF), 21, 40
Single-point fuel Injection, 25
Spark timing, 61
Speed-density EFI systems, 23-24, 133-134
Startup maps, 104-110

Temperature sensors, 117
Throttle bodies, 92-93
Throttle position sensor (TPS), 47
Throttle-body injection (TBI), 23, 82, 119-122
Titania oxygen sensor, 45-46
Transmission control, 60
Troubleshooting, 111-118
Tuned port injection (TPI), 9, 41, 42, 75-76
Tuned port injection (TPI), GM, 78-86
Turbo boost, 69-70
Turbocharging, 128-132, 134-136, 141-142, 149-150

Valve timing, 62
Volumetric efficiency (VE), 24, 35, 39